STUDENT SUCCESS

HOW TO SUCCEED IN COLLEGE AND
STILL HAVE TIME FOR YOUR FRIENDS

EIGHTH EDITION

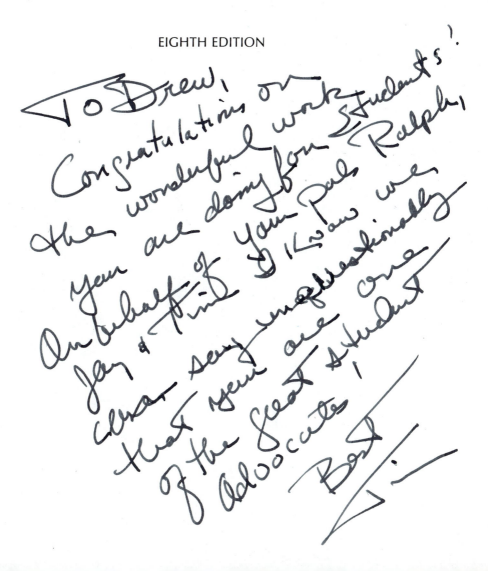

To Drew!
Congratulations on
the wonderful work students'
you are doing for students
On behalf of your pals Ralph,
Jay & Tina I Know we
can say unquestionably
that you are one
of the great student
advocates!
Best
Jim

STUDENT SUCCESS

How to Succeed in College and Still Have Time for Your Friends

EIGHTH EDITION

Timothy L. Walter
Oakland Community College

Al Siebert
Portland State University

Laurence N. Smith
Eastern Michigan University

Harcourt Brace College Publishers

Fort Worth   Philadelphia   San Diego   New York   Orlando   Austin   San Antonio
Toronto   Montreal   London   Sydney   Tokyo

Publisher	Earl McPeek
Acquisitions Editor	Stephen Dalphin
Market Strategist	John Meyers
Developmental Editor	Diane Drexler
Project Editor	Kathryn M. Stewart
Art Director	Sue Hart
Production Manager	Angela Williams Urquhart
Cover Image	©1997 William Schick/The Stock Market

ISBN: 0-15-508278-7

Library of Congress Catalog Card Number: 98-89700

Address for Domestic Orders
Harcourt Brace College Publishers, 6277 Sea Harbor Drive, Orlando, FL 32887-6777
800-782-4479

Address for International Orders
International Customer Service
Harcourt Brace & Company, 6277 Sea Harbor Drive, Orlando, FL 32887-6777
407-345-3800
(fax) 407-345-4060
(e-mail) hbintl@harcourtbrace.com

Address for Editorial Correspondence
Harcourt Brace College Publishers, 301 Commerce Street, Suite 3700, Fort Worth, TX 76102

Web Site Address
http://www.hbcollege.com

Printed in the United States of America

9 0 1 2 3 4 5 6 7 8 039 9 8 7 6 5 4 3 2 1

PREFACE

Student Success has four objectives. They are to:

1. give students a better chance of graduating than students who do not use this book.
2. provide students with study skills for quickly mastering the material in each course-while also having time for friends and important activities.
3. show students how to cope with situations and emotions that prevent many students from graduating.
4. help students develop the skills essential for career success in today's world.

In the eighth edition of *Student Success,* students will discover that by developing effective study skills they can be successful students while spending *less* time studying. They do not have to choose between being either a secluded, bleary-eyed bookworm or living a carefree life filled with parties and play. It is possible to be both a good student and have a good personal life in college. *Student Success* shows your students how.

Earlier editions of *Student Success* have proven to be a valuable resource for thousands of college students. For the eighth edition, Laurence Smith joins the successful author team of Al Siebert and Tim Walter. Laurence Smith's background in student affairs and outstanding record of improving student success brings a wealth of valuable experience to the text.

This revised eighth edition is enriched by the following:

- expanded academic and classroom success strategies linked to student self-management strategies with tools for personal and career success
- updated self-assessments that help students clarify where to work at improving ways to manage themselves as college students
- revised pedagogy that moves beyond the old idea of "getting an education" to "preparing for career success"
- increased number of **Success Group** activities
- examples on how to create a **Portfolio** that documents strengths and accomplishments employers will want to know about
- summary lists of useful **Internet resources** to explore

While making these improvements, we retained features of past editions that made *Student Success* so usable and popular. Take a quick look through the book to get a feeling for what it covers. Ask yourself questions that you, as a new student, might want answered, questions such as:

- What must I do to be successful in college?
- How can studying be easier?
- What are the tips on how to do well on exams?
- How can I write better papers more rapidly?
- Why is there a chapter on study goals?
- How can I enjoy classes taught by instructors I find less interesting?
- Why should I be creating a portfolio of my accomplishments?
- How can I develop critical thinking skills?
- What can I do when I feel too unhappy to study?
- How can I have more friends?
- What does it mean to view life as a school?

Student Success contains the answers to these and many more questions. You will find that *Student Success* is user-friendly. It provides your students with a practical, flexible program for success in college that they can adapt and modify to fit their needs. When students use *Student Success* they are in control of their education and their future!

Timothy L. Walter
Al Siebert
Laurence N. Smith

Acknowledgments

We owe much to many people:

We would like especially to thank Charlotte Hubbard at Eastern Kentucky University and Don Williams at Grand Valley State University for their comments and insights on the new edition.

Beverly, Jeremy, Sarah, and Kate Walter, whose constant smiles and warmth make life such a pleasure.

James V. McConnell, our mentor and friend, whose passing will not diminish the example he set for us as a teacher, writer, and scholar.

Wilbert J. McKeachie, who created a stimulating environment at the University of Michigan for learning how to teach.

Donald E. P. Smith and Glenn Knudsvig, whose interest in and support of our work has been greatly appreciated.

Our parents, who were always proud of their children.

Joanne Smith, for her years of patience, encouragement, and support and for being a best friend and astute critic.

Kristin Pintarich, for her attention to detail and many contributions.

Diane Drexler, for her excellent talents as developmental editor.

CONTENTS IN BRIEF

CONTENTS

Part 1

Time Management and Self-Management

Chapter 1

Succeeding in College Prepares You for Career Success

Professor McConnell peered down at the small group of freshmen sitting in the sunshine on old concrete benches near the library entrance. He shook his head as he thought to himself, "Why did I agree to handle an orientation group? They look so naive. If only they knew what they faced."

McConnell pushed his thick glasses up on the bridge of his nose with one finger. He grinned at the students like he knew a secret and stood waiting.

When the group became quiet, he said: "If you feel anxious or nervous about starting college, you should. The real tests in college are tests of your resiliency and ability to stay focused on what is important. In college you will experience too much freedom and too many demands. At times you will feel like you are in a time warp in which time passes too quickly and too slowly."

McConnell raised his eyebrows and peered over his glasses. "You have entered a world where your mind, emotions, and identity will be criticized, praised, and ignored. Some of you won't survive. During the weeks and months ahead many of your companions will disappear, one by one, never to be seen again."

From the group of students McConnell heard a muffled voice chanting "Woo-woo, woo-woo."

McConnell grinned. He enjoyed making dramatic statements that made students think. "Yes," he said, again pushing up his glasses, "entering college is like walking into the Twilight Zone. You have entered a small universe of unreality where you will be disillusioned and awed by what you learn. It is a world of words without meaning and meaning without words. It is a world where hopes can become fears and fears dissolve into understanding.

"Your life as a college student will be a churning mixture of information overload, too many activities, loneliness, weird friends, unexpected dangers, difficult instructors, parties with drinking and drugs, love and sex, heartbreak, too many tests, uncertainty, overwhelming assignments, and feelings of depression.

"To survive, you will have to develop skills you didn't know were possible and discover abilities you don't know you have. Those of you who do make it through will emerge stronger, better, and more self-confident than you ever imagined possible."

McConnell looked at his watch. "It's time for you to go with Jami, your student orientation leader, to tour the library. I will see you later at the Student Union."

He smiled inwardly as the group walked away. "Yes," he thought, "a good application of the Janis research. Making people worry in advance about the struggles and difficulties they will face increases the probability they will cope well."

SURVIVAL CHALLENGES

At many colleges fewer than 50% of the first-year students make it all the way through to graduate in four years. Many drop out and never complete college. Some "stop out" and return later to finish. Some take 5 or 6 years to earn a degree.

Why do so many students drop out or stop out? Why is college such a struggle for many students?

One reason is that all your life as a student until now has been in a *teaching* environment. How much you learned was strongly determined by the skills of your teachers. They had years of training to become certified. Teachers had to continue taking courses to remain certified. They were evaluated by how well you and your classmates did on various tests.

College, however, is a *learning* environment. Responsibility for what you learn is yours, not the instructors'. You will discover—perhaps to your amazement— that college instructors do not have to have any teaching qualifications to hold a teaching position. Most of your instructors will be very good, but they are not required to take any courses on how to teach effectively. An instructor with excellent teaching skills is a blessing.

As we say to our students, "The name of the game is learning, not teaching!" You are responsible for how well you survive in a learning environment. No one else is responsible. No one will accept the blame if you don't do well.

Even so, you have not been abandoned. Many resources and helpful people are available to assist you in your effort to do well in college. In *Student Success* you will find much useful information about what you can do. *Student Success* will teach you strategies for academic, social, and career success.

After you have rated how you think and act in college in the Self-Assessment, you are in a better position to learn more about the strategies of successful students. If you gave yourself a score of 4 or 5 for almost all the statements, that's terrific! You are an effective learner and highly resilient. Your learning challenge is to become even more efficient at learning and to use your abilities as a basis for deeper learning and advanced assignments.

If you gave yourself a 4 or 5 for the academically related statements, but not the others, you already have good study skills. Your learning challenge is to develop social and emotional intelligence and inner resiliency.

If you gave yourself a 4 or 5 for the more socially related statements but scored lower on the others, you probably will handle the social and emotional tests in college life quite well. Your learning challenge is to develop effective academic skills.

When going though this book, feel free to skim through the chapters covering areas you already handle well. Even if you placed a 5 in front of a statement,

SELF‑ASSESSMENT

Take a minute to fill out this Student Success Profile. The Profile will help you find out how close you are to achieving the level of success you need or want. Each Profile statement will allow you to assess how similar you are to the profile of most successful students. After you have completed your Profile, you can read the chapters that focus on the areas you believe will be most important to your success.

Each statement indicates how much you act or think in ways characteristic of successful students. As you read each statement, place the number in front of the statement that best represents you.

1. = NEVER
2. = Seldom
3. = Sometimes
4. = Most of the Time
5. = All of the Time

_____ I start conversations with students I would like to know and develop new friendships.

_____ I maintain good communications with everyone in my family.

_____ I organize my time well and follow a flexible schedule that gives me time for studying, friends, and other activities.

_____ I study for a planned amount of time every day and then stop.

_____ I read textbooks using a reading strategy that allows me to read quickly and still develop a good understanding of what I read.

_____ I take lecture and reading notes that help me learn important information and prepare for exams.

_____ I feel calm and prepared when I take exams.

_____ I have a predictable and successful strategy for researching and writing papers.

_____ I have a strategy to motivate myself to achieve academic and personal goals.

_____ I accept complete responsibility for being successful without blaming other people for my lack of success.

_____ I appreciate myself for my accomplishments and good qualities.

_____ I actively seek and use college resources available to me.

(continued)

(continued from previous page)

_____ I enjoy spending time with other people talking about what we are doing to get the most out of college.

_____ I recognize when I may be doing things that will hurt my chances for success.

_____ I recognize signs of addiction to alcohol and other drugs.

_____ I would talk with a college counselor if I couldn't stop feeling "blue" or depressed and lacked energy.

_____ I protect myself against realistic dangers.

_____ I take actions to resolve conflicts with people, including instructors, friends, and colleagues.

_____ I feel comfortable with my personality.

_____ I relate well to most people whether they are very similar or quite different from me.

_____ I learn useful lessons from difficult experiences.

_____ I practice thinking positively about my chances for success.

_____ I set realistic goals.

_____ I think about roadblocks to my success and figure ways to work around them.

_____ I study in an environment that is conducive to learning and free of distractions.

_____ I seek assistance from people I live and work with whose behavior affects my academic, social, and career success.

_____ I organize and work well with individuals or groups of students in my courses.

_____ As I read or listen to important information, I think about questions I need to answer.

_____ I gear my studying to learning answers to questions I believe are important.

_____ I ask and answer questions in classes.

_____ I attend class regularly and try never to miss.

_____ I take notes in class and turn them into questions and answers.

(continued)

(continued from previous page)

_____ I prepare for exams by developing and taking practice exams.

_____ I look at successful term papers other students have written to determine the characteristics of successful and well-written papers.

_____ I seek assistance from my instructors and friends to improve my writing skills.

_____ I think about what my instructors expect from me in class and consistently try to meet their expectations.

_____ I discuss with people close to me how and why I need their support and also find out what they expect and need from me.

_____ I try to understand what makes me and people close to me angry and find ways to avoid anger.

however, you will find it valuable to compare the strategies you are using to those we describe in each chapter. By reviewing these strategies, you may see similarities between your strategies and those suggested, or you may see dramatic differences between how you are thinking and behaving and the strategies we offer. Look through these chapters to see if they provide several tips or suggestions that add to what you already know.

Take more time with the chapters covering skills you have not yet acquired. Read them carefully, do the activities, and talk with friends about what you are learning from the chapter. Verbalizing new information helps you "own" it and retain it.

Note that no successful student's actions and ways of thinking include all those we have described. Rather than trying to adopt them all, you need to compare and contrast how you think and act with the profile for success we have developed. You then can choose to adopt the new ways of thinking and acting you feel will be useful for you.

PREPARING FOR CAREER SUCCESS

Students in the past went to college to "get an education." When they graduated they could go to an employer, show their diploma, and be hired. Employers needed compliant workers who would follow their job descriptions. This procedure worked fairly well during an era of large, unchanging organizations with many layers of middle management.

In today's world, however, organizations are leaner, flatter, and constantly changing. Employers need employees who can adapt to change quickly, who make themselves useful without job descriptions, who are self-motivated to constantly learn new skills, who can work well in teams, who exercise emotional intelligence, can cope with setbacks, and hold up under pressure. *Student Success* shows how to acquire and document these personal skills and attributes.

How *Student Success* Will Be Useful to You

Thousands of students using the first seven editions of this book have reported greater success in college and in their careers. In *Student Success* you will not only find valuable information about why students succeed in college but also why they fail. Every chapter covers aspects of student life that if handled well will improve your chances of graduating but that if not handled well will reduce your chances of graduating. It is that simple.

Part 1 covers the psychology of success. Chapter 1 outlines how to use *Student Success* as a resource. At the end of this chapter, you will find suggestions on ways to form a success group right now if you are not enrolled in a course on how to succeed in college.

Chapter 2 describes how to get maximum value from your most important resource of all—you! In Chapter 2 you will learn about important inner factors that influence success in college. (Note: It isn't IQ!)

Chapters 3, 4, and 5 present Larry Smith's highly successful program on how to manage your time and how to study efficiently. In Chapter 3 you will learn how to manage a tight schedule even when you work and have other important activities.

Chapters 4 and 5 provide you with the best, most practical information available on learning how to learn. Chapter 4 shows how to set and achieve study goals. Chapter 5 shows how to organize your efforts so that you can learn more with less time and effort.

Part 2 shows how to develop your critical thinking and learning skills. It describes effective strategies for getting the most from your college courses while achieving high grades. Chapter 6 presents a study method called "SQ4R." It is the most effective, well-proven study method ever used by college students. Chapter 7 emphasizes how to improve your listening, note taking, and critical-thinking skills.

Chapter 8 focuses on how to pass tests with high grades. It includes examples of all kinds of tests—multiple choice, true/false, essay, short answer, and so forth. Chapter 9 provides practical tips on how to use your library and the Internet for writing "Excellent" papers.

Part 3 covers how to handle the human side of college life by developing your emotional intelligence. Poor relationships with instructors, friends, and family can be emotionally draining. Chapter 10 shows you how to overcome false expectations and erroneous beliefs about instructors and difficult people. It helps you handle disillusionments about college life in a healthy way. You learn how to get the most from every course you take.

If you want to improve the instruction you receive, what can you do? Chapter 11 shows how to work effectively with your instructors to obtain positive results.

Concerns about being liked and accepted by friends and family often distract college students from their studies and make them vulnerable to peer pressures. Chapter 12 shows why good friendships are very important, how to develop good friendships, and how to gain support from your family. (Note: If making friends with people is a bit difficult for you, read Chapter 12 right away. Skip around in the book whenever you wish.)

Part 4 digs into some of the most difficult aspects of college life today. Chapter 13 takes a realistic look at serious hazards and dangers you face as a college student. In this chapter Al Siebert describes how life's best survivors thrive in difficult situations instead of becoming victims.

Chapter 14 focuses on developing another aspect of emotional intelligence: how to handle anger. Anger is an emotional state that can undercut all your efforts to succeed in college if not handled well.

Tim Walter has extensive experience helping student athletes succeed academically. During a 5-year period when he was in charge of the student athletes' study center at the University of Michigan, they lost only two athletes for academic reasons. In Chapter 15 he provides student athletes with valuable academic coaching.

More than 40% of students enrolled in college today are age 25 or older. Chapter 16 covers the special needs of students who work and may have family responsibilities.

Action Projects

Success comes not from what you read or hear but from what you do with what you learn. At the end of most chapters you will find one or more Action Projects that suggest ways to apply the information and strategies in the chapter. These activities show how to integrate the methods into your skill base.

Your Portfolio of Accomplishments

At the end of most chapters, you will find suggestions for creating a file of evidence that documents your skills, abilities, and accomplishments. Traditionally, portfolios were used by artists, photographers, and models to show their work. Today portfolios are common in *every* occupation because traditional application forms, résumés, and references do not tell employers everything they want to know.

Employers receive so many applications they need an efficient method for screening the large influx. A one-page summary of your portfolio helps employment officers quickly assess what you can do and shows you are sensitive to their needs.

A carefully compiled collection of materials demonstrating your competencies and skills is evidence of what you know and can do. Your portfolio will document that you can communicate well, problem-solve, work effectively as a team member in a culturally diverse group, lead or follow as needed, think critically, research new ideas, operate computers and programs, reach your goals, and do consistently excellent work.

To impress employers today, you must be able to document your proven abilities. You can find more details about why you should be creating an "Accomplishments Portfolio" in the Appendix.

Create a College Success Group

You can facilitate your learning, develop lasting friendships, and deepen your enjoyment of college life by talking frequently with groups of classmates about your experiences, questions, feelings, and learnings. At the end of each chapter, you will find suggestions for questions and issues to discuss or activities to undertake with success groups.

Many colleges and universities offer a course to help freshmen succeed. In it you will meet regularly with a group of other first-year students to talk about the challenges of college. These courses often are offered for credit. Check your college catalog to see if some kind of "Freshman Seminar" is offered. It will be worth taking. Research conducted at the University of South Carolina, for example, shows that students who take their "University 101" seminar have a significantly better survival rate in college.

Another good idea is to pair up with one or two other students as "college success partners"—a college version of the "buddy system." It is different from having a good roommate or friend on campus. The purpose of college success partners is to interact with others like yourself to facilitate each other's success in college. Frequent interactions with one or two other students who agree to use *Student Success* will help you accomplish your goals in college.

THE BIG PICTURE

As we've emphasized, *Student Success* is a practical, user-friendly book. It covers all aspects of the psychology of succeeding in college. The key to its value, however, is you. *Student Success* is not a formula, recipe, or blueprint for success. Not at all. We wrote the book for individuals who feel responsible for how well their lives work out. In every challenging situation, we talk about how your reaction and your way of interacting with the challenge determines the outcome.

Student Success is for self-motivated individuals who need to do things their own way. It is for students who reject being programmed about what to think, feel, and do. How can it be otherwise? Surviving in an environment that is not always safe requires alertness and your unique solutions to unexpected situations.

You are living in a world much different from what your parents and teachers grew up in. To survive and thrive in a rapidly changing world, you must learn how to orient yourself quickly to new circumstances, how to manage change well, and how to make yourself useful. You will do so many different kinds of work during your lifetime (you could live an active, healthy life of up to 100 years) that you may not even think of it as having several different "careers." National trends predict that soon fewer than 50% of all employees will have full-time salaried jobs with health and retirement benefits.

National boundaries are blurring. The planet is becoming an integrated community. To succeed in your careers, business activities, or profession you must be able to adapt to different cultures, values, beliefs, and lifestyles. Critical-thinking skills and emotional intelligence will be essential for handling constant changes in technology, changing values, conflicting perspectives, and unexpected developments that carry both opportunities and dangers.

Thus we see your time in college as preparing you for an unknown future. By learning how to overcome and handle all the challenges in college, you will prepare yourself for whatever you encounter in your career. You will have self-confidence. You will be a resilient person with good judgment and reliable inner strengths.

Is the effort worth it? Absolutely. Various studies have shown that people with a college degree experience better health, have a longer life span, and enjoy a lifetime income significantly greater than that of adults without a higher education.

Whether you respond to the many challenges in college by getting stronger or by being overwhelmed is up to you. *Student Success* was created to show you how to survive your first year, how to improve your chances of succeeding in your courses, how to enjoy your college years, how to obtain a good education, and how to graduate with your class.

Again, college is more than an academic challenge. It is also an important opportunity to grow, mature, and develop as a person. *Student Success* provides you with guidelines on how to manage your personal growth and development. We show you how to convert stresses, strains, and rough times into strengthening experiences.

Each year thousands of students begin life in college. They are starting a new adventure of self-development to prepare for their future. Chances are you will find out the following in college:

- Difficult challenges force you to develop new strengths.
- Making the transition from home and high school is not without complications.
- The new and exciting adventures and opportunities are filled with risks.
- The campus gives you a chance to identify, try out, and develop your new skills before playing for keeps in your future life roles.
- You will have the chance to build further on the self you've already developed, but new experiences and new self-concepts will bring about the need for change.
- You will have the chance to test your potential and ideas and to clarify your values.

SELF–ASSESSMENT

Why I'm in College

Many students starting college have shared their feelings about this time in their life, the transitions they are facing, and the reactions they had to this extreme change. Here are some of the statements they said about why they came to college and what they felt at the time.

Read each item and check those you feel apply to you. Add any additional items you think should be included:

_____ College is the best chance of getting the life I want in the future and of being successful.

_____ I want to become more comfortable with different kinds of people and different kinds of situations.

_____ I never gave any thought to going to college; it was an expectation I had in my earliest years.

_____ I want to get away from home and prove myself.

_____ I want to test myself and see if I can make it in college-level athletics.

_____ In order for me to develop my potential, I have a lot to learn, and this is the place to do it.

_____ Being in college is a better alternative than having to go out and get a job or going into the military.

_____ Being a good student has been the most successful and interesting life I've experienced, and I want to continue it.

_____ I want a chance to start all over again. That's why I'm glad to be at a college where I'm away from home and old friends.

_____ (other)

_____ (other)

When you are finished, compare your responses with those of other students you know. Did you have the same reasons or different ones? Did you discover other reasons? If you did, add them to your list.

SUCCESS GROUP ACTIVITIES

Plan on taking several hours to go through these activities. If a long session isn't possible, hold several shorter ones.

1.   To get started, meet where you can talk with some privacy. Take turns asking one another about your first reactions, feelings, and impressions of the college.

Make sure each person has the feeling "Others in this group know what I am feeling and experiencing." To accomplish this aim, someone may have to ask encouraging questions of any quiet persons. At other times someone may have to interrupt a long-winded talker who doesn't know how to stop talking. One way is to say, "The main point I hear you making is . . . (summarize what was said). I'd like to hear from Kerra before we stop. Kerra how do you feel about . . ." These are issues your group will have to learn to handle if they come up.

2.   A useful group activity will be to ask one another these questions:

"Do you intend to graduate with our class?"

"Why are you here in college?"

"Why this college rather than another?"

"Was going to college your idea? Your parents'? Whose idea was it?"

"Have you selected a major yet?"

"Do you have specific career goals?"

"What do you think could keep you from getting your degree?"

3.   List and discuss the differences between being a high school student and being a college student. Someone in the group should write down the two lists.

Some freshmen don't survive because they expect college to be some kind of postgraduate high school. It isn't. The two worlds are so different that many students cannot handle the "transition shock." That is why we wrote an entire chapter about problems many students have dealing with their frustrations and anger about their college experience.

Talk with one another about what you expected college to be like and what the reality is. It also helps to write about this on your own.

4.   Before you stop, devote some time to clarifying your expectations and agreements:

How often do you want to meet?

Will everyone make a commitment to show up for every meeting?

Do you want to accept one or two new participants during the first month but no one else after that?

What will be your purposes for getting together? Is it limited to talking and sharing, or might your group also do social activities together?

Where will you meet?

How will you contact each other?

During your first 2 weeks on campus, it will be helpful to meet frequently. Then meet less often as you settle in. Frequency of meetings is up to the group, however. The activity of meeting with supportive friends is more important than the schedule.

Start your meetings with each person speaking briefly about how he or she is feeling today. This "check-in" lets everyone see how present the person will be for the discussion topic.

At the end of each meeting leave several minutes for each person to give a brief comment about how he or she felt about this meeting. This helps everyone stay in touch with how well the group is meeting each person's needs.

Chapter 2

Why Some Students Are More Successful Than Others

"MOST LIKELY TO SUCCEED"

The orientation leaders at your college work very hard to inform you about the many resources available to help you survive and succeed in college. We hope you take advantage of all the resources provided. The key to your success in college, however, lies in how well you also access your inner resources.

David McClelland, a Harvard psychology professor, became internationally famous in the 1960s when he developed a test that could accurately predict which college students would achieve the most career success 20 years after graduation. What was his test? A test of imagination. Years of McClelland's carefully controlled scientific research, conducted on thousands of people in different countries, proved that he could predict a person's future from the pattern of the person's daydreams.

A few years later McClelland stirred up even more interest in his work when he reported the results of a major research project with businessmen in India. He had selected India for his research because, among all English-speaking cultures, people in India are most extreme in believing that external events and their station in life control their lives. In India, McClelland proved that with a few days of instruction, Indian businessmen could learn to use their minds in the same ways high achievers do. Then during the two years that followed, the experimental group, who had learned how to think like high achievers, significantly outperformed a carefully matched control group.

What does McClelland's research mean to you? Many things:

- Your mind can be the best resource you have if you learn to use it well.
- Daydreams serve as a blueprint for your future.
- The mental habit pattern that makes a person more successful can be learned.
- It doesn't take long to learn how to use your mind in ways that make you more successful.

SELF-ASSESSMENT

Think about your decision to attend college. Check off the criteria for successful goal setting that apply to your decision to attend college and pursue a degree.

_____ My decision to attend college was primarily my own; it was self-chosen.

_____ My goal to obtain a college degree feels very challenging but possible.

_____ I enjoy the idea of being a college graduate. I feel motivated to work hard and reach my goal.

_____ I feel nervous about attending college, but it is a pleasant, exciting nervousness.

_____ I believe I *can* reach my goal of graduating from college if I make a solid effort.

_____ I believe I *will* reach my goal of earning a college degree.

MENTAL ACTIVITIES THAT LEAD TO SUCCESS

McClelland's research demonstrated that if you practice thinking about succeeding in certain ways, you are more likely to succeed. Persons exhibiting the following pattern in their imaginative stories are more successful than others. Their daydreams include four elements of goal selection, with the main character in the story . . .

PEANUTS reprinted by permission of United Feature Syndicate, Inc.

1.   Working to achieve a goal, trying to do something better, or striving to accomplish something challenging

2.   Having a strong need and an emotional desire to reach the goal; anticipating the feelings of satisfaction and accomplishment success will bring

3.   Thinking through the details of how to succeed despite obstacles, difficulties, personal limitations, possible problems, or barriers; matching current ability level against the situation to determine that the challenge is neither too easy nor too difficult

4.   Consulting various resources for information about ways to handle obstacles and reach the goal but retaining control over decisions and responsibility for the outcome

Note that the mental activities leading to accomplishment and achievement all occur before the decision is made to work toward the goal.

Recap: To be successful, your goal must incorporate the following qualities:

- Be self-chosen
- Feel moderately challenging
- Have a motivating effect
- Feel slightly risky
- Seem possible to reach with good effort
- Be truly attainable if you apply yourself well

Example: In a visioning session with students in a freshman seminar, Brent went through the four elements of goal selection outlined by McClelland. He decided to reconsider and aim for a 4.0 GPA (grade-point average) his first term. He sized up each of his courses, listed the difficulties he expected with them, and for each one set a realistic grade he truly felt he could earn. He took into account the resources available to him—*Student Success,* the learning center, his own motivation, and so on. He then decided to aim instead for a 3.2 GPA.

For a goal to give you a feeling of achievement when it is reached, it must have a specific, observable, measurable result you can attain by a specified time. Merely saying "I want to get good grades" won't work! Selecting a target grade for each course or a certain GPA for each term has a specific, measurable result that is attainable in a designated time. Then when the date arrives, you definitely know if you achieved your goal or not.

SUCCESS IN COLLEGE IS NOT AN IQ MATTER

Did you know that you do not have an IQ? No one does. What you have in your records are scores obtained from "Intelligence Quotient" tests. And the IQ score you are assigned is not your actual score. It is a number that shows how you compare to the group used to provide the norms for the test. If the normative group is changed, your IQ score changes.

Vocabulary is the most central component in an intelligence test. Most English-language IQ tests are biased toward words the white middle class favors. In 1968 Adrian Dove, a sociologist, showed how important cultural background is when different vocabulary words are used. He published what is called "The Chitling Test." When asked the meaning of terms such as "chitling," (chitterling) "a blood," and "gas head," people familiar with this dialect get higher scores than people who are not familiar with it.

If the issue of IQ is a concern for you, keep in mind, first, that vocabulary is more important than an IQ score. As you will see in Chapter 6, you can increase your intelligence by constantly learning the meaning of new words. Second, the IQ test was invented in France in 1904 to determine which children would not benefit from more schooling. The test was useful. A low IQ score predicted lack of success in school fairly well. A high IQ score, however, did not predict success very well because so many other factors determine success in school, such as your expectations, your ways of setting personal goals, and your self-motivation.

WHAT WORKS: PRACTICAL POSITIVE AND PRACTICAL NEGATIVE THINKING

The story at the beginning of Chapter 1 was a practical application of research findings reported by psychologists. Successful students spend time anticipating difficulties they might encounter when trying to reach their goals. Is it too much negativity to worry about what could go wrong? No, not in the sense of being a negative person.

Mental and emotional flexibility comes from the ability to think and feel in both positive and negative ways about situations. The person who is always positive and seldom negative has difficulty coping well, while the person who is always negative and seldom positive also has difficulty coping well.

A practical person, one with a flexible outlook, combines practical positive thinking with practical negative thinking. Trying to do only one without the other is like trying to drive a car with no reverse gear.

Let's try it out for a moment. You probably have some positive expectations about the many benefits you would gain from doing well in college. But have you considered the case *against* trying to do well? Take a minute right now to answer this question: "If I choose to do really well in college, what are some of the problems and difficulties I might have to cope with?"

When you anticipate the problems and difficulties you may encounter on your way to a desired goal, you are better prepared emotionally to handle them when they occur. Psychologist Irving Janis showed in a research project that some worrying before trying something difficult helps you handle it better. People who don't worry at all and people who worry a lot without practical problem solving don't handle difficulties as well. So keep in mind that a little worrying is useful when it takes place as one part of the entire pattern of problem solving.

BALANCING THE CONSEQUENCES

Looking at some negative consequences of doing well decreases feelings of distress or discouragement if such outcomes occur. More important, however, successful students dream and think about the many payoffs for doing well.

After you the finish the following Self-Assessment, compare the the positive statements you marked with the negative statements you marked in the previous Self-Assessment. As you weigh the consequences (both negative and positive) of

SELF-ASSESSMENT

Successful students are students who do well despite the negative factors they encounter. Place a check mark before the factors you have anticipated or that you believe might happen to you.

_____ Being successful may take more energy.

_____ I may work harder than less committed students.

_____ I will risk failure when aiming high.

_____ I will have less time for friends.

_____ I will have less time to loaf around.

_____ I may get eyestrain, back strain, and neck strain.

_____ Sometimes I will miss some fun because of studying for tests.

_____ People may expect more of me ("If I only get a B, they may have a heart attack!").

_____ I may not be able to go out for sports as often because practice will interfere with studying.

_____ I may be teased and called a bookworm.

_____ My family may get upset because I don't have as much time for them.

_____ If my grades drop a little, people may give me a bad time.

_____ Some people may think I'm weird if I get top grades.

_____ I will have to learn too much too fast.

_____ It may be difficult to study hard and do well in a required course I am not interested in.

being a more successful student, you will feel more comfortable establishing your educational goals. If you are like most students, you can see from assessing the advantages and disadvantages that your gains will far outweigh your losses.

AVOIDING INEFFECTIVE GOAL SETTING

Did You Choose Your Goals?

The goal setting of many students is not self-motivated. They do it because of external pressures to have goals. By now you have become accustomed to teachers, counselors, and advisers asking you to describe your career goals. The people asking you have good intentions. The achievement research, however, shows that

SELF-ASSESSMENT

Place a check mark in front of all the positive results of learning the habits of successful students.

_____ I will become more efficient and effective at learning.

_____ What was hard work in the past will now feel much easier and come more naturally.

_____ I will have time for friends and not feel guilty.

_____ I will spend less time loafing and not feel as though I am wasting my time and life.

_____ Some of the physical ailments, such as eyestrain and neck strain, I once had may fade away with better study habits.

_____ The joy I receive from being more successful on tests will outweigh the feeling of missing out on other activities I would do instead of studying.

_____ My self-esteem will improve.

_____ The perceptions of me by people important to me will improve.

_____ My family will be proud of me and will understand that the time I do have to spend with them is important.

_____ I will become more interesting to myself due to all the new information I learn.

_____ I may develop many new beneficial interests after taking courses I would have been hesitant to take in the past.

_____ I may set even higher goals for myself and establish new career interests.

_____ I may find that as a better student, the career opportunities that open up to me will help ensure a brighter future.

_____ I will find that courses I once thought too difficult are more interesting and rewarding.

how you identify, choose, and emotionally commit yourself to a goal is far more important than inventing one to tell people about.

What some students call goals are really wishes. They would like to have what they see others enjoying, but they don't know how to get it through personal effort. Such students frequently believe external factors and luck determine how well college life turns out.

Be Internally Motivated

One of the most difficult problems for most students entering college is having too much freedom. Until now their lives were organized, controlled, and structured by external forces. For instance, when a high school test was scheduled, the teacher constantly reminded everyone and coached students on what they needed to know. In college, however, an instructor might announce that a test will be given in 5 weeks and then never mention it again. To survive in college you have to keep yourself organized and self-directed.

Before continuing, let's check to find out your attitude about feeling in control of your life. Take several minutes right now to look at the following pairs of statements. Put a check mark by the statement in each pair that, in general, is closest to what you believe is true. Even if you feel both statements are truthful, select the one that is more true than the other.

Gain Control of Your Life

The higher your score on the Self-Assessment attitude survey, the more you feel you have control over your life. Students who know they are personally responsi-

SELF-ASSESSMENT

1. _____ How hard I study determines the grades I get.

_____ I would get better grades if the teaching in this school were better.

2. _____ It is useless to try to change another person's opinions or attitudes.

_____ When I want to, I can usually get others to see things my way.

3. _____ The increasing divorce rate indicates that fewer people are trying to make their marriages last.

_____ Fate determines how long a marriage will last. All you can do is hope your partner will stay with you for life.

4. _____ Finding a well-paying job is a matter of being luckier than the next guy.

_____ In our society a person's income is determined largely by ability.

5. _____ Promotions are earned through hard work and persistence

_____ Promotions usually come from having the right people like you.

6. _____ It is wishful thinking to believe that one can influence what happens in society at large.

_____ People like me can change the course of world events by making ourselves heard.

(continued)

ble for many of the successes and failures that occur in their lives are called "high internals" by Julian Rotter and other social scientists. Such students believe that what controls the important forces and events in their lives is found inside themselves. Students with low scores often believe they are the helpless pawns of fate. They tend to believe that forces influencing their lives are external to themselves. These students are called "high externals."

The point is that both attitudes are correct. Each attitude is self-validating. Students who are high internals believe they can influence much of what happens to them. They take actions to make things happen. The results of their efforts confirm their beliefs. Students who are high externals seldom take action. They believe it won't do any good. Then, sure enough, most of what happens to them is determined by outside forces and other people.

The fact you are reading *Student Success* is an indication you are probably a person who is internally directed. You know that such a book can provide some practical tips on how to be more effective. People who are high externals respond to such books by saying, "It won't do me any good." These people are right. Their habitual way of responding to learning opportunities and chances for personal growth maintains their attitude that it doesn't do any good to try.

(continued from previous page)

7. _____ I am the master of my fate.

_____ When I see an unfortunate person, I sometimes think, "There but for the grace of God go I."

8. _____ Many people are difficult to get along with; it is no use trying to be friendly.

_____ Getting along with people is a skill that can be learned.

9. _____ I am usually a good influence on others.

_____ Running around with bad company leads a person into bad ways.

10. _____ I would be much happier if people weren't so irritating.

_____ Peace of mind comes from learning how to adapt to life's stresses.

To score yourself, count all the check marks in the left-hand column for the odd-numbered items and the check marks in the right-hand column for all even-numbered items. Your score is the total number of checks in these places. (Note: You can count up to 5 check marks on each side, but no more.)

The range of possible scores is 0 to 10. Scores of 8 or higher suggest you are more internally directed than students who get lower scores.

WHAT WORKS: COOPERATIVE NONCONFORMITY

College counselors see extreme differences in students. Some students are so determined to be self-reliant nonconformists that they put energy into proving they can't be influenced by others. At the other extreme, some students passively wait to be told what to do. They drift from one person to another, waiting for advice, guidance, and help. They accept directions from almost anyone, even when they don't need to be helped.

What works best is to balance self-reliance based on inner resources with an ability to accept guidance and direction from external resources. College life can be frustratingly difficult for the student who is always one way and seldom the other.

If you find this information about the relationship of personality factors to success in college useful, that's great! But we aren't done yet. More aspects of personality are strongly related to being more successful or less successful in college. They are your inner "selfs."

HOW YOUR "SELFS" CONTROL YOUR SUCCESS

Your self-esteem, self-confidence, and self-concept control your successes in life. *Self-esteem* is your opinion of yourself. It is the feeling dimension. Without strong, conscious self-esteem, your actions are controlled by worries about what others might think.

Unfortunately for many children, their parents program them to never brag, never appear proud, or never speak well of themselves. These parents have good intentions, of course. But the problem is that these attitudes can lead to low self-esteem, and students with low self-esteem rarely do well in school. When students don't expect to do well, they don't. They can't handle success or praise, so they avoid having to deal with them.

Students with low self-esteem typically put themselves down, constantly repeat how dumb or stupid they are, focus on their mistakes, and engage in a lot of self-criticism. Some try to overcome weak self-esteem with impressive clothing, titles, high income, important friends, the right address, and other material "proofs" of success. They may try to build themselves up by tearing others down.

Other students have inflated self-esteem. They constantly brag. They let everyone know how great they are. The problem is that people with inflated self-esteem can't engage in the kind of healthy self-criticism that leads to self-improvement.

Strong, healthy self-esteem is like a thick skin, and you can develop it. It acts as a buffer to shrug off hurtful criticisms from others. It lets you appreciate compliments. It also determines how much you learn after something goes wrong.

High self-esteem will be necessary in job interviews. Today's employers do not want someone who shows up and says, "Tell me what to do." To compete in today's job market, you must overcome false modesty and speak frankly about your reliable strengths.

Self-confidence controls your prediction of how well you will do in a new activity. It is the *action* dimension. People lacking self-confidence can't rely on themselves. People with strong self-confidence know that they can count on themselves more than anyone else. They expect to handle both adversities and opportunities successfully.

Self-concept involves your ideas about who and what you are. It is the *thinking* dimension. The nouns and adjectives you use to describe yourself during self-talk are like instructions. People with positive self-concepts and people with negative self-concepts act in ways consistent with their beliefs about themselves.

Self-concept determines what you, as a unique individual, strive to achieve, maintain, and avoid in your life circumstances. People with a poor self-concept won't try to change or leave a bad situation at home or work. They may try to be successful by imitating successful people. People with a strong inner identity don't have to prove anything to anyone. They can wear any clothing, be friends with anyone, and live anywhere. They live a unique life that works for them. They have a positive, synergistic effect wherever they are, and they encourage and applaud the successes of others.

SELF-ASSESSMENT

Which of the following are true of you? Check all that apply.

_____ I can accept both praise and criticism.

_____ I can resist manipulation by flattery and shrug off hostile comments.

_____ I don't engage in extreme self-criticism or self-praise.

_____ I usually feel I can count on myself.

_____ I can handle adversity as well as success.

_____ I usually think of myself in positive terms.

_____ When asked, I can describe my abilities and strengths to others.

_____ I can find something good in bad situations.

_____ I have learned how to manage my self-improvement.

_____ I don't try to cover up my weaknesses by trying to impress others.

_____ I don't try to build myself up by tearing others down.

_____ I encourage and applaud the successes of others.

_____ My feelings of success come from my work and my inner feelings of satisfaction.

_____ I believe I have unique qualities and skills.

A positive self-concept is the basis for becoming an excellent professional person. Such people, guided by inner standards and values, are flexible, resilient, durable, and creatively effective. They find a unique way of working. Success to them is measured by excellent results and inner feelings of satisfaction. Prosperity, positions of power, honors, and outstanding success are not their goals. Such rewards are recognition for being responsible, effective, and needed. People without a powerful, positive sense of their unique abilities are destined to be confined to jobs and roles other people create.

It is important that you evaluate yourself honestly to determine what you are like and what you want to be. Building a strong "self" depends on how you want to think about yourself and how you want to behave. Building a strong self is totally under your control.

How to Build a Strong Team of "Selfs"

Increasing Self-Esteem

Self-esteem is the easiest "Self" to develop because it is the most verbal. It is strengthened by positive self-talk. If you have strong self-esteem, it is fairly easy to make a list of everything you like and appreciate about yourself.

Make a list of what you like about yourself. Write down aspects that would be helpful for you to remind yourself of in good times and in bad times.

In tough situations, mentally remind yourself of your strengths. Positive self-talk is a habit you choose to practice. It is not bragging to yourself. It is simply reminding yourself of your strengths and accomplishments.

Part of self-esteem is visual. It influences how you dress, your posture, your grooming, how your room looks, places you choose to visit, where you expect to work after college, and how your course work looks when you hand it in.

Building Self-Confidence

Self-confidence increases as you learn that you can count on yourself. When you commit yourself to something, do it. Develop a reputation with yourself for doing things well. Ask yourself, "What are my reliable strengths?" and "How well do I expect to do in challenging situations?" You will build self-confidence by selecting challenging goals and then reaching them.

Developing a Positive Self-Concept

Develop a positive self-concept by spending time writing out positive "I am . . . " statements. Start by observing your self-talk. Make a list of 10 "I am" phrases and statements you think or say about yourself. Replace negative statements with positive statements.

When all "self" factors are strong, you believe in yourself, you like yourself, you cope well with new challenges, you stay healthy—and the world is a better place for everyone. People want you to be successful.

What Works: Self-Appreciation and Self-Criticism

The ability to successfully reach goals, to learn from failures, and to have good friends usually requires a balance between self-esteem and self-criticism. It takes a blend of self-confidence and self-doubt. It means having a positive self-image that accepts the existence of flaws and weaknesses.

The student who is constantly self-critical without self-appreciation seldom accomplishes much. The person who is constantly self-appreciating without self-criticism seldom admits to mistakes, weaknesses, and errors in a way that could lead to important learning.

Healthy self-esteem, steadfast self-confidence, and a positive self-image provide an inner stability that gives you the characteristics described in the self-assessment list that follows. Which of them is true of you?

SELF-ASSESSMENT

Check off the following attitudes and behaviors that are typical of you. How many do you possess?

_____ I accept praise, recognition, success, and friendships as legitimate.

_____ I examine and learn from mistakes and failures.

_____ I am not pressured into undesirable actions or situations out of fear of being disliked.

_____ I resist and will not be manipulated by insincere flattery.

_____ I reject undeserved criticism as something to ignore.

_____ I admit mistakes and apologize to others for them.

_____ I handle new, unexpected developments knowing I can count on myself.

_____ I value myself as a unique, special human being.

Persistence Through Rough Times

In many ways this chapter can be seen as a way to develop psychological fitness. The main purpose, however, is to cover psychological differences between more successful and less successful college students.

Remember: All students experience anxiety, tension, self-doubt, failure, nervousness, and uncertainty at various times. The key difference is that the more successful students persist. They keep going. The less successful students give up too easily. They quit when they become frustrated, when they don't do well at first, or when they do less well than others. The following Self-Assessment and exercise allow you to examine this issue.

SELF-ASSESSMENT

Students who persist through difficult times have the characteristics found in this list. Check off the characteristics you have.

_____ I can daydream about possible accomplishments with a mixture of practical positive and practical negative thinking.

_____ I handle the freedom, uncertainty, complexity, and difficulties of college life by being both self-reliant and receptive to guidance.

_____ I counteract failure and hurtful criticism with positive self-talk and healthy self-appreciation.

_____ I develop self-confidence and a positive self-image through a balance of self-appreciation and self-criticism.

_____ I accept nervousness, not doing well at first, and fears as normal feelings.

PERSONAL REFLECTIONS

Exercise

Imagine "What If?"

1. If you decide to drop out of school during the next 4 years, what do you think your reasons might be? _____

   _____

   _____

2. What might you begin doing this week to prevent those reasons from developing? _____

   _____

   _____

   _____

Exercise

"Who Am I Now?"

Your growing-up experiences—as a 3-year-old, 7-year-old, 12-year-old, 15-year-old, and 17-year-old—have all been part of preparing you for who you are and what you are doing today, this week, and next semester. Some of these experiences have resulted in important strengths that have prepared you to tackle successfully the new adventures ahead. Other experiences probably have been poor preparation—attitudes and habits that hamper you, what you chose not to learn, and so forth. Who we are now is a mixture of strengths and liabilities from our past experiences with ourselves and others.

For a few minutes, take a trip back into the growing-up years of you and your fellow students. If you were interviewed about succeeding in college, how would you answer these questions?

1. "What do you see as some of your characteristics (attitudes, behaviors, skills, etc.) that would help your success in college?" Some examples of responses are "Positive belief in self"; "Able to organize time and focus on tasks"; "Competitive, wants to be ahead"; "Willing to ask questions and get help"

_____

_____

_____

_____

2. "What do you feel are some of your characteristics that might hamper your success in college and that you would need to work on?" Some examples of responses are: "Tends to put things off"; "Good starter but doesn't follow through"; "Tries to 'do it alone' without asking for help"; "Likes social life a little too much"; "Poor study habits"; "Hasn't learned to manage time very well"

_____

_____

_____

_____

3. As you sit here thinking ahead to your challenges for the first semester, what would you list in these two categories?

   _a)_ Your strengths (assets to use and build on): _____

   _____

   _____

b) Your weaknesses (to work on, overcome): _____

_____

_____

_____

ACTION PROJECT 1

Feedback From the Future

To practice using your imagination in the way that leads to academic achievement, make a chart by following these steps:

1. Get a large sheet of paper.
2. At the top write a heading such as "My 12-Week Success Plan for Fall Term."
3. Fill in four subheadings across the page in the order given here:

    "Feelings I Want to Enjoy at the End of the Term"

    "Resources Available"

    "Obstacles, Difficulties, Potential Problems"

    "Final Exam Week—How I Want It to Be for Me"
4. In the lower right-hand corner, make a space for "Intended GPA."
5. Fill in your chart by asking yourself the following groups of questions:

    *   First, imagine yourself at final exam week. What do you want that week to be like? Do you want to feel well prepared? to have all your term papers and projects finished? to have enough time to study? to be rested and relaxed, with no late-night cramming? to enter finals with a high grade average already established? to look forward to exams with confidence, expecting them to give you a chance to show what you have learned? Under the fourth subhead, write down how you want to experience your final exam week. Be practical. What do you think is possible? What do you expect you have a good chance of accomplishing in the weeks between now and finals?

    *   Second, how much would you like to experience feelings of achievement? of pride? of self-confidence? of self-appreciation? of praise and recognition from your friends? of achieving academic honors? Write down your desired feelings under the first subhead on the left side of your chart.

    *   Next, what obstacles lie in your way? What will make it difficult for you to accomplish your desired goals? Start listing these under the third subhead. Be specific. If your list becomes overwhelming, go back to your hopeful list for finals week and modify it downward. Be practical.

- Finally, what resources are available to you? What information, knowledge, skills, or help do you need? What have you learned about your college resources that might help you succeed more than you first thought? Fill in this information under the second subhead. Should you revise your expectations upward?

Take a few days to fill out these four elements in your success plan for the term. Create a similar plan for each course. Practice imagining yourself as though finals week is now and you feel good about everything you did during the past weeks so that you feel relaxed, self-confident, and well prepared.

As you read Part 2 of *Student Success,* you will find many more practical suggestions on how to succeed in each course and make your plan for the term come true.

ACTION PROJECT 2

Finding Financial Aid

Very few students make it through college without some kind of financial aid. Handle your monetary needs like a successful person. Imagine and feel yourself succeeding well at finding the aid you need. Don't passively wait for your school to find something for you. Don't be discouraged by rumors. When the U.S. government phased out an aid program, applications fell off for many programs. This meant students who applied had a better chance of getting aid than before the phaseout.

Make yourself an expert on financial aid. Visit the financial aid office at your college to learn about the many sources available to students, including the variety of scholarships offered. Track down leads and ask questions.

Places to search on the Internet include the following:

Adventures in Education

http://www.adventuresineducation.org

Financial Aid Information Page

http://www.finaid.org

Financial Aid Search Through the Web (fastWEB)—an excellent free scholarship matching service,

http://www.fastweb.com

Free Scholarship Information Service

http://www.freschinfo.com

US Department of Education, Financial Aid Student Guide

http://www.ed.gov/prog_info/SFA/StudentGuide

YOUR PORTFOLIO

Keep a clean printed record of how you set and reach important goals. Describe what you did and what you learned from each experience that made you more self-confident and more effective the next time.

SUCCESS GROUP ACTIVITY

1.   Show one another your personal Academic Success Plans. Talk with one another about what effect creating the plan has had on each of you.

2.   Discuss the guidelines for developing your inner resources described in this chapter. What is your reaction to learning that it is desirable to be paradoxical? What does self-esteem mean to each of you? self-confidence? a positive self-concept?

3.   Talk with one another about students who seem "most likely to succeed." What are your observations about why some students are more successful than others? Make a list describing successful students you know. Contrast this with a list describing what less successful students do.

Cover the negative side as well. Are some aspects of success in school unattractive to you? What disadvantages do you see to succeeding in college? What drawbacks and problems come with excellence? Discuss why it is normal for all students to feel nervous and anxious, to do poorly at times, and to have doubts about their abilities.

4.   Talk with one another about how you answered the questions in Personal Reflections.

5.   Individually interview one or two third- or fourth-year students who are successful in college in ways you like. Start with questions such as "What do you do to succeed at this college?" or "Can you explain why you are more successful than other students?" Also ask, "What did you wish you had known when you first started here?" Then compare your interview findings with one another.

Chapter 3

How to Manage a Tight Schedule Successfully

SUCCESSFUL STUDENTS ARE MORE ACTIVE

Success in college is closely related to success in activities outside your academic program. One of the main findings of the 1985 study the College Board conducted was that the best predictor of success in college is both scholastic achievement and "follow-through" as indicated by "persistent and successful extracurricular accomplishment."

Students in the study agreed. When they were asked to rate one another on success in college, they picked students who earned good grades and who were also hard-working, well-organized achievers in other areas.

This means your involvement in student government, the marching band, the symphony, the choir, athletics, the college newspaper, media productions, church activities, special interest groups, clubs, special campus events or "drives," and intramural sports can improve your chances of success in college. The same holds true for working students, adult students, and married students. Active students do better in college.

Why is this so? Why doesn't all this extra activity reduce the chances of success? The answer is that when you have to organize your efforts, avoid wasting time, and do well at what really counts, you become better at almost everything you do. When the seniors in the College Board study were asked what contributed to a successful and satisfying career in college, 73% said the "ability to organize tasks and time effectively."

TIME MANAGEMENT IS SELF-MANAGEMENT

To accomplish your purposes for attending college and to succeed in other important activities, you can't be passive. You must actively control what you do with yourself through conscious choices. In other words, you must do well at managing yourself in the time available to you.

The basics of self-management start with the ability to do the following:

- Set priorities
- Not do less important things
- Say no
- Start and stop specific activities at predetermined times

When you have major responsibilities in addition to your classes, your "To Do" list can no longer include everything you want to do. Now your list must identify the most important things to do, and you must postpone or not do the less important things. Olympic athletes succeed in making the team by staying focused on their goal. They concentrate their actions on the future.

Your situation may not have the same magnitude as that of an Olympic athlete, but it has one similarity: You have to manage yourself well or you won't make it.

SELF-MANAGEMENT WITH LISTS, SCHEDULES, AND CALENDARS

If you are going to succeed in life, you have to know what you are doing. That statement may seem extraordinarily simpleminded, but it is worth stating. People who engage too often in nonproductive activities, who don't know which activities can help them reach their goal, who don't finish what they begin—in other words, people who don't know what they are doing—are rarely successful, at least not consistently.

So the fundamental question is this: Do you know what you are doing? Does what you do each day take you closer to your desired educational goals—even while you enjoy time with your friends and fulfill your other commitments? To keep on track, here are some effective ways to organize your self-management plan. We will cover these in greater detail later in this chapter.

Your Daily List

Get into the habit of making a daily list that combines your scheduled activities and the important things you want to do that day. After listing what you want to do, code the most important items, and make sure you give them priority over less important items.

Your Weekly Schedule

To decide what is most important, you need to know your week's schedule. Start each week of the term by making a schedule, using a form such as the one printed in the back of this book. Fill in all your class times, meetings, important events, study times, exams, practice hours, support group meetings, and so forth. We'll discuss this in greater detail in Chapter 4.

Your Term Calendar

You also should keep a long-range calendar. Look ahead—at the start of each term, take the syllabus for each course and fill in your calendar for the term. After the first day of classes, list in your calendar every scheduled exam as well as due dates for term papers, projects, and reports. Fill in all the other important events that will occur during the term. Self-management is simple. You decide in advance what is important for you to do, and then you do it.

WHO HAS TIME?

> *But I'm too busy. I don't have time to fill in calendars, make weekly schedules, and make "To Do" lists every day!*

Our response to that statement is that self-management procedures are essential for the very reason that you don't have enough time for everything. These procedures will help you create the time you need. The student who claims not to have enough time to create the calendar, schedules, and lists is like the man chopping his winter's firewood late in the fall. A couple out walking noticed that he was chopping very hard but not getting much wood cut. When they saw that his ax was dull, they asked, "Why don't you stop and sharpen your ax?" Without pausing in his work, he yelled back, "I can't stop to sharpen my ax. I have too much wood to cut!"

The busier you are, the more essential it is for you to make and use calendars, schedules, and lists. Self-management helps you do what you must do and postpone or say no to the other options. Success in college is not a matter of how much energy you expend or how many hours you spend studying. Success depends on the results of your efforts. With a good self-management plan, you can get better results in fewer hours than students who don't manage themselves well.

MAKING TIME FOR WHAT'S IMPORTANT

Time management is a means for using time to attain what you want from your life and your college experiences. It is more than simple efficiency. It is effectively achieving your goals and thereby getting the results you desire.

Students find time management especially important because their college experience provides an enormous amount of unstructured time for personal, social, and academic activities. Often with a full course load, part-time job, extracurricular activities, and demands from friends and family, the typical student struggles to balance competing interests, course assignments, social interests, and personal activities against rapidly approaching course deadlines. They don't seem to have enough time even to plan ahead. Ironically, some students report they often spend as much time or more time worrying about when to do something than actually doing it.

One interesting aspect of college life is that if you take a full academic load and study an additional 30 hours a week, you will have spent only 25% of your time directly pursuing your major expressed goal—obtaining a college degree.

The following practices will build on your ability to develop an action plan and will provide you with the framework not only for planning but also for accomplishing it all.

Planning Your Time Trip

Regardless of what you set out to do, the mastery of these exercises will help you achieve your goals. Since you already have demonstrated that you can be successful or you would not be in college, you might feel you don't need to know how to manage yourself. It is something you do naturally. It is a practice you have evolved through the experience of trial and error along with the instructions of parents, teachers, and friends.

Once in college, however, many students indicate that much of the structure they had for managing and accomplishing their tasks was imposed on them by their daily routines in high school and at home. They also had frequent—even if casual—reminders from teachers, coaches, employers, and parents of what needed to be done. College, for many students, involves an enormous and somewhat difficult transition from this old learning environment to a new one. Academic and personal expectations are vastly different in the college culture from those previously experienced. One of the most important differences is the personal freedom associated with attending college. It involves many opportunities to make choices. It also requires personal attention to follow through on your choices to see that your intended goals and benefits are achieved.

Overcoming Your Time Blocks

One of the hardest tasks when managing yourself is overcoming the time blocks that keep you from successfully achieving your goals or at least your good intentions. A time block, simply put, is a fixed pattern of behavior—the way you respond to keep from doing what you should be doing. The table lists major time blocks for students. We then show you ways around 15 common time blocks.

Top 15 Student Time Blocks

1. Talking with friends/social events, dating
2. Talking on the telephone/telephone interruptions
3. Daydreaming
4. Watching television
5. Sleeping
6. Listening to music: stereo or radio
7. Drop-in visitors
8. Reading (other than school material)
9. Playing sports or games/hobbies
10. Cleaning my room or apartment, doing laundry, buying groceries, cleaning desk
11. Transportation
12. "Goofing around" or "partying"
13. Eating/snacking
14. Spending too much time in Dining Commons
15. Procrastination/worrying

Common Time Blocks and Ways Around Them

- *Watching television:* Be aware of turning on the television and watching for just a few minutes.
- *Daydreaming (lack of concentration):* Eliminate distractions (visual and auditory). Set a goal. Vary your activities. Don't give in to temptations.
- *Overpreparation for a task:* Recognize that you are avoiding the task. Organize your preparation so that you have everything you need within your reach.
- *Eating:* Nibbling disrupts concentration. Eat only if you're hungry. If necessary, reward yourself with a treat after studying.
- *Telephone interruptions and drop-in visitors:* The problem is the inability to say "no." Tell your friends you are studying and will return the call or visit when you are through. Stick to your original agreement with yourself and develop self-discipline.
- *Procrastination; indecision:* Develop realistic goals and expectations of yourself. Develop a daily list prioritizing activities. Overcome the fear of making a mistake by learning from your mistakes.

- *Worrying about what needs to be done:* This is a way of avoiding something you should be doing when you know you should be doing it. Work on procrastination.

- *Reading (pleasure material):* This belongs in the same category with television. See the first list item.

- *Involvement in too many activities at once:* Set priorities. Concentrate on one thing at a time. Choose your most important activities, and fit them into your study and work schedule. Practice self-discipline.

- *Sleeping:* Do not try to study lying down or while watching television.

- *Lack objectives, priorities, daily plan:* Establish goals, set priorities, and create a schedule.

- *Personal disorganization:* Keep an uncluttered desk, and organize your school and work materials so that you can easily locate them.

- *Lack of self-discipline and inability to say "no":* Recognize that time management is a goal that will take effort and a change of habit, and practice changing those habits. Say "no" firmly but without offending.

- *Leaving tasks unfinished:* Set priorities, and avoid interruptions. Give yourself deadlines and a reward for completion of a task.

Organizing Your Time

Where do you start? What tasks should you think about? In addition to setting up a weekly time schedule, you need to develop a general life plan for organization and success. Consider these five suggestions when you plan your life both on a short-term and long-term basis:

1. Set priorities, main goals, and objectives. You can vary the scope from daily to yearly. Periodically reevaluate your goals and priorities. You may want to have your term paper completed by next Friday or to organize the next four years so that you complete your academic program on time.

2. Limit your course load. Discuss your program requirements with an adviser, and plan your schedule realistically. Do not take on more course work than you can handle well to speed up graduation.

3. Limit your outside activities. A full-time academic program is much like a full-time job. Part-time jobs and recreational activities or clubs should be limited to what you can realistically handle given your academic schedule. A common complaint of students is that they are involved in too many activities. Recognize your limits.

4. Make desired time plans by stating goals/objectives in terms of results.

    a) Purchase a monthly calendar with spaces for you to fill in exam dates and project deadlines. Fill in all the times you plan to go to concerts, special events, and so forth.

    b) On Sunday, plan your goals/objectives for the coming week, and determine the time you need to accomplish each one.

      c) Each evening or early morning, list your daily objectives and the time needed to accomplish each one.

      d) Schedule the objectives along with your daily activities on the daily time log.

5.   Evaluate your progress as appropriate each semester, each week, and each day.

SETTING UP A SEMESTER TIME PLAN

The purpose of the semester plan is to give you an opportunity to record all major deadlines, activities, and events that will occur during the semester. It will give you an overview of the semester and help you recognize your commitments at a glance. You'll know how many actual days are available for you to use, rather than relying on a vague "six weeks 'til midterm." You then can use this structure as a basis for formulating realistic semester goals or objectives. Ultimately, of course, you will be planning your weekly and daily schedules to support the long-term goals you set in the semester plan. Follow these instructions when completing your personal semester plan.

     If you have not purchased a monthly calendar, prepare a form similar to the Semester Monthly Time Plan included here.

Semester Monthly Time Plan

Name ———————————— Month ————————————

Sun.	Mon.	Tues.	Wed.	Thur.	Fri.	Sat.

1.   Fill in your name and the month. Next, fill in the dates of the month in the small box located in the upper right-hand corner of each of the days of the week. Make sure the days and dates match!

2.   Fill in the calendar with the dates of exams and project deadlines. Remember also to mark the calendar with special social events, concerts, or unusual meetings. These items should be considered when scheduling your weekly calendar.

3.   The next step is to define your personal goals for the month or semester. What is important to you? What would you like to accomplish? Use the next section, "How to Set Goals and Objectives," as a guideline for setting effective goals, and list your goals. Set deadlines for yourself for accomplishing your goals, and mark those dates on your monthly calendar.

4.   Remember, break down your goals into specific tasks and activities; stepwise planning will lead to your success.

How to Set Goals and Objectives

A goal is an overall result desired on a long-term basis. "I will get a B in biology" is a long-term semester goal. Long-term goals can be broken into intermediate steps, called objectives. A possible short-term weekly objective supporting the longer term goal of getting a B in biology would be to read a biology chapter and answer the review questions at the end of the chapter. Your weekly objective then could be broken into daily objectives of reading the chapter on Tuesday and answering the review questions on Wednesday and Thursday. Whether you are setting daily and weekly objectives or semester goals, the following specific guidelines will help ensure their achievement.

First, a goal or objective must be possible to achieve within a specific length of time, which can vary from one hour to one semester, and you must commit to that amount of time. You must believe you can achieve your goals in the periods you have committed to them. They must be realistic; for instance, it is unrealistic to think you can condense a whole term's course into three nights of study.

The goal must be specific. You must be able to put it into words. Hazy or vague commitments to "write a paper" are not defined in terms of behavior required to achieve the goal. However, "I will have my history paper ready for submission to my professor by December 1" is a long-term specific goal that can be broken down into smaller weekly and daily tasks or objectives. Three weeks can be devoted to research, two to writing the first draft, one week for each additional draft, and one week for typing. On a daily basis, specific hours should be set aside for accomplishing these tasks.

When you commit yourself to a goal or objective, you must present it without alternatives. It is not acceptable to say you will either study history or practice the piano. You must make a specific commitment: "I will read one chapter of history," or "I will practice the piano for two hours."

The goal must be measurable. "I will become proficient at the piano" is not measurable. What determines proficiency? However, "I will be able to play Chopin's

Polonaise in A-flat without error by the end of spring term" is measurable, specific, and committed to a time frame.

Goals and objectives must be demanding enough to provide a sense of accomplishment and to measure specific progress but flexible enough to adjust to unforeseen or unusual circumstances.

For a goal to be achieved, it must be something you want to do, as opposed to something forced on you. A goal cannot be set by someone else for you. What do you want for yourself? How can you get what you want? What is important to you?

SETTING UP WEEKLY OBJECTIVES

Looking at the week ahead is an integral part of maintaining control of your time. Before we move to daily planning, weekly objectives need to be thought out and incorporated into a plan that will guide you through the week. Done regularly each week (Sunday nights are ideal times), this practice becomes an indispensable planning tool. Follow these steps:

1.   Copy or prepare a form similar to the Weekly Objectives form shown next.

2.   Refer to the monthly calendar and determine which tasks need to be done during the coming week.

3.   List these on the Weekly Objectives sheet according to category, along with any other objectives you may have for this week.

4.   Remember the criteria for goals and objectives: They must be stated in clear and concise terms and must be time bound, realistic, and measurable.

5.   Estimate the amount of time you will need to accomplish each objective. Add this to the chart.

SETTING UP A WEEKLY TIME MANAGEMENT PLAN

With 168 hours in a week, it would seem you have plenty of time to do everything. Failing to review and plan those hours in advance makes it easier to waste them. Suggestions for weekly planning follow:

1.   If you do not have a weekly calendar, prepare a form similar to the Weekly Time Management Plan I included here.

2.   Enter your activities—already committed periods—on the grid. Use the key, adapting it as necessary. For example, it may help you to identify each of your courses by name, instead of just listing "class" time.

3.   Plan remaining, uncommitted time by scheduling your weekly objectives. Use the estimates of "Time Needed to Do" on the Weekly Objectives form to accomplish projects during the week and in concentrated blocks of time.

Weekly Objectives

Objectives for the week of _____

Be specific! State objective in terms of results desired.

Objective	Time Needed to Do
1.	
2.	
3.	
4.	
5.	
6.	
7.	
8.	
9.	
10.	
11.	
12.	
13.	
14.	
15.	
16.	
17.	
18.	
Time Needed	

4. Be sure to budget time for social and leisure activities.

5. Eliminate "dead" hours by using time between classes and during meals to take care of some tasks.

6. Always leave some extra time to complete a project. A good rule of thumb is to leave 20% extra time.

Weekly Time Management Plan I

How I Plan to Spend My Time

	Mon.	Tues.	Wed.	Thur.	Fri.	Sat.	Sun.
6:00 A.M.							
7:00							
8:00							
9:00							
10:00							
11:00							
12:00 P.M.							
1:00							
2:00							
3:00							
4:00							
5:00							
6:00 P.M.							
7:00							
8:00							
9:00							
10:00							
11:00							
12:00 A.M.							
1:00							
2:00							
3:00							
4:00							
5:00							

Key: C = Class W = Work Sa = Student Activity S = Study

  L = Lab Sl = Sleep M = Miscellaneous

SETTING UP DAILY PRIORITIES

You should ask yourself a number of questions about each item on your daily "To Do" list when setting up daily priorities.

- Is it necessary to do today?
- Is it my responsibility, or can this item be given to someone else to do?
- How does it help me meet my semester goals and weekly objectives?
- Is this something I have been postponing?

If so, why? Will I be postponing it again today?

It may help to think of each priority item as something "I should do today for maximum effectiveness." Be sure to distinguish between urgent and important needs. Urgent items have to be dealt with immediately, whether or not they are important to you. (You can keep most items from becoming urgent by planning ahead.) Plan to do the least desirable priorities first. If you get the unpleasant or difficult tasks out of the way at the start, the rest of the day will be easy. Since we always find time for what we want to do, you should save those favorite tasks until later as a "reward." Take the following steps to set up your daily priorities plan.

1. Copy or prepare a form similar to the Daily Action Plan shown next.
2. Enter the date on your daily priorities sheet.
3. Refer to your Weekly Objectives and Weekly Time Management Plan I to see which objectives you already have planned to accomplish today.
4. Enter these in the "Things to Do" or "Assignments" column, and add everything else you have to do: all the reading, writing, shopping, and calls you must make.
5. Assign a priority to each. Write down these numbers next to the priorities. It may help to set a deadline for the top priorities.
6. Then enter the activities in the schedule. Plan each day this way, either in the morning or the night before.

By relying on the plans you already have made on your Weekly Plan and Weekly Objectives charts, you can develop a detailed schedule for the Daily Action Plan that will enable you to accomplish as many of the day's priorities as possible. Put to use time that normally would be wasted (time between classes or waiting for an appointment), but allow some extra time for projects that may take longer than expected. And remember that along with setting priorities, evaluating your accomplishments each day is essential for managing your time. Filling out the Weekly Time Management Plan II provided next is an excellent way to evaluate and then integrate your priorities into future Daily Action Plans. At the end of each day, record on such a form how you actually spent your time. This will help

Daily Action Plan

Date _____

Schedule	Assignments	Things to do
7 A.M.		
8 A.M.		
9 A.M.		
10 A.M.		
11 A.M.		
12 P.M.		
1 P.M.		
2 P.M.		
3 P.M.		
4 P.M.		Review for Tomorrow
5 P.M.		
6 P.M.		
7 P.M.		
8 P.M.		
9 P.M.		

you determine your time management patterns and to identify areas where you need to exercise greater effort.

ANALYZING YOUR DAILY ACTION PLAN

First ask yourself the following questions as you think about your use of time each day.

Weekly Time Management Plan II

How I *Actually* Spent My Time

	Mon.	Tues.	Wed.	Thur.	Fri.	Sat.	Sun.
6:00 A.M.							
7:00							
8:00							
9:00							
10:00							
11:00							
12:00 P.M.							
1:00							
2:00							
3:00							
4:00							
5:00							
6:00 P.M.							
7:00							
8:00							
9:00							
10:00							
11:00							
12:00 A.M.							
1:00							
2:00							
3:00							
4:00							
5:00							

Key: C = Class   W = Work   Sa = Student Activity   S = Study

          L = Lab   Sl = Sleep   M = Miscellaneous

PEANUTS reprinted by permission of United Feature Syndicate, Inc.

1. Was my plan a realistic one?

2. Were my expectations for the day too high or too low?

3. Did I allow enough time to accomplish (or at least move ahead) on my priorities?

4. How did my actual use of time today correspond to the use I had planned on my weekly schedule?

5. Which items could I have deferred or asked someone else to do?

6. What distracted me from my plan?

7. How have I avoided the distraction?

8. Did I recover immediately and return to my plan?

After you've answered these questions, record how you actually used your time today on the Weekly Time Management Plan II. At the end of the week, compare the Weekly Time Management Plan I to how you actually used your time (Plan II). Use the following form, the Weekly Time Management Plan Analysis, to do so.

What is your analysis? What will be your plan for next week in light of this analysis? Were you surprised by your results? Or are you satisfied? Do you feel you are managing yourself well and on the way to achieving your goals?

ACTION PROJECT

Go to the bookstore and look through the various calendars and weekly and daily schedules for sale. Also look at the personal organizer systems. Most people find them very useful. If you don't see anything you like, consider creating your own forms and duplicating them at the copy center.

YOUR PORTFOLIO

Keep a record of how you developed an effective time management plan for yourself. Describe the difference between how you used to spend your time and what you now can accomplish.

SUCCESS GROUP ACTIVITIES

1.   Tell one another about your experiences using lists, schedules, and calendars. Have you ever made a list of everything you had to do and then separated the most important from the least important items? What practical tips can you give one another about how to use lists and schedules?

2.   Tell one another how you feel about making something you enjoy a low-priority item. Also tell one another how you feel about saying no when someone asks you to do something.

3.   Now that you've completed a chapter on self- and time management, can you handle the idea that time is an illusion? Time does not exist in the universe. It is only in your mind. As Einstein said, time is an experience of relative motion, of something happening in relation to the earth spinning around the sun at a fixed rate. Does this perspective help you understand why we emphasize self-management throughout this chapter?

4.   Celebrate your accomplishments: Go to a movie, have a party for yourselves, or do something that's for fun you as a group.

Weekly Time Management Plan Analysis

Symbol	ITEM	I No. of hours	%	II No. of hours	%
C	Class				
L	Lab				
S	Study				
W	Work				
Sa	Student Activity				
Sl	Sleep				
M	Miscellaneous				
	TOTAL				

Analysis

_____

_____

_____

_____

_____

_____

Plan

_____

_____

_____

_____

_____

Chapter 4

Setting and Achieving Your Study Goals

SELF-ASSESSMENT

Place a check mark by the statements that are true for you.

_____ I set specific study goals each time I study.

_____ My study goals are based on questions I ask.

_____ I learn faster when I list the specific tasks necessary to reach my goals.

_____ Using a studying checklist motivates me to study and is constantly rewarding.

_____ Checklists help reduce my anxiety and forgetfulness.

_____ I know that rewarding myself for completing study goals is important.

_____ Checklists keep me on schedule to complete my work and then stop studying.

HOW TO SET COURSE AND STUDY GOALS

You need goals to know where you're going in the process of educating yourself. When you know what you want to achieve, you can set your mind to it, achieve it, and stop worrying about whether or not you'll do well in your courses. Setting goals is one of the strongest ways to motivate yourself to study efficiently and effectively.

Students who don't set specific study goals are usually uncertain about when they are going to do what is necessary to do well in their courses. If you can determine what you should study to pass a course and set up a schedule to achieve those goals, you'll be in good shape. Now let's make sure you know how to set study goals and to design a schedule to achieve them. We're going to develop a detailed plan for succeeding in each of your courses.

How do I figure out what my study goals should be?

First, you have to ask, "Who or what can tell me what I have to do to learn what I want to learn and to earn my desired grade in the course?" The best sources of information are listed here. Put a check mark by those you know you could use more often:

___ MY INSTRUCTORS

___ OTHER STUDENTS

___ ASSIGNED COURSE MATERIALS

___ CLASS DISCUSSIONS

___ COURSE OUTLINES

___ STUDENT MANUALS AND STUDY PROGRAMS

___ COURSE SCHEDULES

From these sources you usually can tell what important tasks you have to accomplish to achieve your desired grade and become a more intelligent person.

What types of tasks are usually required of students who wish to learn a lot and earn good grades?

Good grades don't come without effort. To succeed academically you must complete course requirements and optional projects, including the following:

- Attending class
- Passing tests
- Passing quizzes
- Writing term papers
- Participating in class discussions and presentations
- Completing projects

What should I consider when scheduling my study activities?

In addition to knowing the types of tasks you must accomplish, you should know how, when, and where they should be accomplished. As you set up your study schedule, ask yourself the following questions. Put a check mark by the ones you typically ask.

___ WHEN MUST EACH STUDY GOAL BE COMPLETED?

___ HOW MUCH TIME DO I HAVE TO COMPLETE THE SPECIFIC STUDY GOALS?

___ HOW MUCH CAN I REASONABLY EXPECT TO ACCOMPLISH BETWEEN NOW AND THE TIME THE ASSIGNMENTS ARE DUE?

___ ARE SPECIFIC REQUIREMENTS—SUCH AS FORMAT FOR TERM PAPERS, NUMBER OF PAGES, OR STYLE USED FOR REFERENCES—NEEDED TO COMPLETE THE ASSIGNMENTS?

___ HOW CAN I DIVIDE MY STUDYING SO THAT I DON'T PUT EVERYTHING OFF UNTIL THE END?

___ HOW MUCH SHOULD I DO EACH DAY IF I WANT TO ACCOMPLISH MY SPECIFIC GOALS ON SCHEDULE?

___ HOW WILL I BE REQUIRED TO DEMONSTRATE THAT I HAVE ACCOMPLISHED THE GOALS?

After answering these questions, you'll be better equipped to design an effective schedule for completing the study tasks that lead to your course assignments and goals. You will know where you are going, how you will get there, and how to recognize when you've arrived.

UNDOING THE BLOCKAGES TO SELF-MANAGEMENT

One thing that surprises many faculty, students, and professional staff members is the number of students who need help but have difficulty seeking it. Likewise, forces just as powerful often keep people from giving help to others.

Most of our difficulties seeking and giving help arise more from our internal feelings than from cues we receive about the situation itself.

A lecturer saying, "Raise your hands if you have any questions" strikes fear in many students. "If you need help, stop by my office" and "See me after class" are instructors' invitations not taken advantage of by students who could benefit from extra help.

Just as important are feelings that block our helpfulness when we see students or others who could use our assistance. "I'll be seen as trying to get a good grade rather than as just wanting to help" or "What if I'm told to mind my own business?" are just two examples of our self-talk in a situation where we could be helpful.

Stop for a few minutes and think about how you feel in situations where you could seek or give help. Do these occasions make you feel ambivalent about taking action? Do they make you feel stressful? Do they arouse concerns about time demands?

What internal dialogue occurs, the "voices" you hear within yourself that support or urge caution about your seeking or giving help? Write these voices down on the following Internal Dialogue Sheet, the first of several exercises to help you undo any blockages to self-management.

Exercise

Your Inner "Voices": Internal Dialogue Sheet

1. On acting to seek or give help:

_____

_____

_____

_____

2. Voices of support/enthusiasm:

_____

_____

_____

_____

3. Voices of caution/self-protection:

_____

_____

_____

_____

4. What are the external supports (persons or groups) for these voices you hear?

_____

_____

_____

_____

Share some of these voices and supports with your friends. In what ways are you feeling similar or different? How can you help each other?

Exercise

Why People Don't Seek Help

Listed next are reasons many students have given for why they don't seek help. Put a check mark by all the reasons that best describe you. After reviewing this list, add any others you can think of.

_____ THEY FEEL SET UP TO FAIL, THAT IT'S IMPOSSIBLE TO SUCCEED IN THE CURRENT STRUCTURE.

___ IT'S RISKY (THEY DON'T WANT TO SEEM INADEQUATE).

___ THEY FEEL THEY CAN SOLVE THEIR PROBLEMS THEMSELVES.

___ THEY HAVE A TOO LIMITED PERSPECTIVE.

___ IT'S ADMITTING WEAKNESS.

___ THEY THINK THEY ALREADY ARE DOING THE RIGHT THING.

___ THEY FEEL IT CAN'T BE SOLVED—THEY TRIED TO SOLVE IT ONCE BEFORE.

___ THEY'RE UNABLE TO GAUGE THE SEVERITY OF THE PROBLEM.

___ THEY FEAR PUBLIC EXPOSURE.

___ GETTING HELP MAY OR DOES EXPOSE OTHER PROBLEMS THEY DON'T WANT YOU TO KNOW ABOUT.

___ THEY FEEL THE PROBLEM WILL GO AWAY.

___ IT'S NOT ANYONE ELSE'S BUSINESS.

___ THEY FEAR IT WILL RESTRICT FUTURE GROWTH.

___ THEY DON'T SEE THE NEED.

___ THEY DON'T KNOW HOW TO ASK.

___ THEY'RE AFRAID HELP WILL INVOLVE FUTURE INDEBTEDNESS.

___ THEY'RE TOO PROUD.

___ THEY FEAR THEY'RE UNABLE TO HANDLE THE SITUATION.

Exercise

Why People Don't Give Help

Listed here are reasons many students have given for why they don't give help. Check off all the reasons that best describe you. After reviewing this list, add any others you can think of.

___ THEY'RE TOO CONCERNED WITH THEIR OWN PROBLEMS.

___ THEY'D HAVE TO CHANGE THEIR PRIORITIES AND GIVE UP THEIR OWN WORK.

___ THEY FEEL THE PERSON IS BEYOND HELP.

___ THEY THINK THE PERSON WILL PULL THEM UNDER WITH HIM OR HER.

___ THEY BELIEVE THE PERSON DOES NOT WANT HELP OR SEE THE NEED FOR HELP.

___ THEY PERCEIVE THE PERSON AS WANTING MORE THAN HELP, AS HAVING ULTERIOR MOTIVES.

___ THEY FEEL NO PERSONAL OR INSTITUTIONAL REWARDS ARE GIVEN FOR HELPING.

___ THEY DON'T WANT TO GET ENTANGLED.

___ THEY FEEL THEY WOULDN'T BE APPRECIATED.

___ THEY DON'T WANT TO IMPOSE A DIFFERENT VALUE SYSTEM.

___ NO SUPPORT IS OFFERED FOR GIVING PEOPLE HELP.

___ THEY MAY HAVE HAD A BAD EXPERIENCE WITH AN INDIVIDUAL NEEDING HELP.

___ THEY THINK HELPING CREATES A PATHWAY, THAT THEY'LL END UP ALWAYS HELPING.

___ THEY FEEL THEY WILL BENEFIT FROM OTHERS' FAILURES.

___ THEY THINK IT'S TOO LATE TO DO ANYTHING.

Exercise

What's in It for You?

List in the following spaces all the benefits you gain from seeking help and all the benefits you receive from giving help as you try to manage your time and life more successfully:

1. Benefits:

_____

_____

_____

_____

2. Benefits gained from giving help:

_____

_____

_____

_____

3. Benefits gained from seeking help:

_____

_____

_____

Discuss with your friends how asking for and giving help has influenced your life. Think of your earlier school experiences and your current situation. Think of yourself in high school, planning for college or work, and your first experiences at college. Can you think of examples when you found it difficult to ask for help or to give help and examples of the payoffs when you asked for help?

HELPING YOURSELF TAKE ACTION NOW

WHAT'S THIS ALL ABOUT?

Most of us really want to do many things, including those we are committed to do, but we find ourselves avoiding, "forgetting," postponing, getting sidetracked, or, in other words, procrastinating. Each of us has internal voices that continually carry on conversations. We all need practice listening to those internal conversations to know ourselves better, to resolve some of the inner conflicts, and to become wiser for making decisions and taking action.

Some of those inner conversations are between "take action now" voices and "do it later" or "avoid it" voices. Do some of the voices in the next exercise sound familiar to you?

Exercise

Listening to Your Inner Voices

Look at these two lists and check off the voices you have heard recently.

"Take Action Now" Voices

___ LET'S GET IT OVER WITH.

___ IT'S ALREADY LATE.

___ YOU KNOW IT, SO JUST DO IT.

___ THEY'LL BE PLEASED WITH WHAT I'VE DONE.

___ IT'S A CHALLENGE.

___ IT'LL BE FUN WHEN I GET INTO IT.

___ ONCE I GET STARTED IT'LL GO QUICKLY.

___ IF I DON'T DO IT NOW, I'LL HAVE TO DO IT LATER.

"Do It Later" Voices

___ I DON'T FEEL LIKE IT NOW.

___ I STILL HAVE TIME.

___ I'LL DO IT LATER.

___ THIS OTHER THING IS MORE IMPORTANT.

___ I'LL BE BETTER PREPARED LATER.

___ IT MAY SOLVE ITSELF IF I WAIT.

___ IF I WAIT, SOMEONE ELSE MAY DO IT.

___ I NEED MORE INFORMATION.

Both kinds of voices are important to listen to and consider. We need to hear the "postponement" voices and understand that they lure us to reactive reasons for delaying or finding easier paths, and we need to hear the "proactive" voices and understand that they help us achieve significant goals. A first step in mastering your path toward success as a student and as a person is to learn to recognize and cope with the "postponement" voices as well as the "take action now" voices.

The greatest support for learning this step will be the sharing and analysis of your self-talk with friends. Are the "take action now" voices and the "do it later" voices similar among your friends? different? Which ones are the most troublesome? The following exercise and Self-Assessment will help you develop your Action Plan for following your proactive voices. Then you will fill in the plan using the sample provided.

Exercise

What Does Your Action Plan Require?

Review your answers to the following, and observe yourself for clues about your behavior style and your desire for change. Circle the multiple-choice answers.

1. I find myself postponing what I want/need to get done.

    a) Very frequently

    b) Quite often

    c) Sometimes

    d) Hardly ever

2. Compared to the other people I know best, when I have things to do

    a) I put things off more than most people.

    b) I'm the same as most people about doing them.

    c) I'm better than most people about doing them.

3. How much do I want to improve my ability to get myself to do what I should or want to do at the right time?

    a) I want very much to improve.

    b) I'm quite interested in improving.

    c) I'm somewhat interested in improving.

    d) I don't feel any special need to improve.

SELF-ASSESSMENT

Here are some strategies others have used to help themselves actually do what they want to do. Which of these do you use? How often? How successfully?
Rate the following in one of these four ways:

1 = QUITE OFTEN

2 = OCCASIONALLY

3 = NEVER

4 = WANT TO TRY

1. ____ I make a list of things to do and check off when I do them.

2. ____ I write deadlines for myself.

3. ____ I tell someone else so I'm more likely to do it.

4. ____ I promise myself a reward or celebration when I finish.

5. ____ I do it with somebody else.

6. ____ I do a little bit to get started.

7. ____ I get some sleep and tackle it first thing in the morning.

8. ____ I research more facts to prepare better.

9. ____ I decide on the best timing.

10. ____ I do the difficult part first.

11. ____ I break it into small parts or steps to get started.

What are some other strategies you or your friends use to get into a "take action now" mode? Which of these strategies do you want to use actively in the next two weeks?

4. How well do I maintain a balance of my four development challenges: my personal self, my social self, my academic self, and my career self?

5. Do I tend to avoid putting energy and attention into one or two of these selves as an escape from more difficult or less interesting activities?

Share and discuss your answers with your friends. Do you feel it is worthwhile to add more "do it now" behavior into your lives?

CREATING AN ACTION PLAN

You now should realize the importance of a proactive—instead of reactive—lifestyle for success as a student. You also have begun to work on using others as a source of support to help you do what you want to do.

An Action Plan will assist you in these efforts. Review your list of strategies from the previous Self-Assessment. Select two or three you want to develop as proactive initiatives for yourself in the next two weeks. Then use the Action Plan that follows to make sure your good intentions will really happen. Such Action Plans give you practice meeting your goals.

Date _____

Action plan for (Name): _____

The Strategies I want to try to use:

I have shared my intention to act with

1.

2.

The payoffs I hope for from this initiative:

When will I review to assess progress?

With whom?

How might I celebrate my progress?

STRATEGY FOR DEVELOPING A CHECKLIST

Now that you have learned how to take action, you are ready for the next step: creating and following checklists. Successful students create checklists to schedule the specific tasks they need to do to achieve their study goals. Such progress reports help you to keep on track, reduce anxiety, and allow you to reward yourself.

What things should I include in my checklist?

When you make up your checklist of things to do, follow these guidelines to decide what to include:

1.   Specify each of the tasks you must accomplish to achieve your overall goal.

2.   Arrange the tasks in order of importance and according to when each is most easily accomplished, and then list them in the first column of your checklist.

3.   Indicate in the next column when you expect to achieve each task.

4.   In the third column you will record the actual date each task is completed.

5.   Next, record the reward you will give yourself for having accomplished each task.

6.   Record whether or not you have rewarded yourself for accomplishing the task on time.

7.   Record whether or not you have rewarded yourself for having accomplished the overall goal.

What would a checklist look like for the student whose goal is passing her next test?

The student in our example made a preliminary list of things to consider before developing her checklist:

- *Name:* Alexa Shaughnessy
- *Course:* Introductory Psychology
- *Goal:* To receive a grade of at least 90% on first test of the semester
- *Exam date:* September 29
- *Today's date:* September 1
- *Responsibilities:* Read Chapters 1–5 in the textbook.

After thinking about what had to be accomplished, Alexa then prepared her checklist.

A copy of Alexa's checklist before she completed her work is on the next page. Take a minute to look it over before reading on.

In the past, Alexa put everything off until the last minute and became panic stricken when she realized how much she had to do. Now, she decided to reward herself each time she completed one of her tasks on time. She set due dates and then recorded when each task was completed and whether or not she had received her reward. It was important for her to list her rewards so that she had something

Alexa's Beginning Checklist

Study Behavior	Due Date	Date Completed	Reward	Yes/No
1. Read Chapter 1, and generate questions, answers, and summary	Sept. 2			
2. Read Chapter 2 (same as 1)	Sept. 5			
3. Read Chapter 3 (same as 1)	Sept. 9			
4. Read Chapter 4 (same as 1)	Sept. 16			
5. Read Chapter 5 (same as 1)	Sept. 23			
6. Generate questions from today's lecture and take practice quiz	Sept. 1			
7. Same as 6	Sept. 3			
8. Same as 6	Sept. 5			
9. Same as 6	Sept. 8			
10. Same as 6	Sept. 10			
11. Same as 6	Sept. 12			
12. Same as 6	Sept. 15			
13. Same as 6	Sept. 17			
14. Same as 6	Sept. 19			
15. Same as 6	Sept. 22			
16. Same as 6	Sept. 24			
17. Same as 6	Sept. 26			
18. Generate questions from old test	Sept. 10			
19. Make up and take practice test for Chapters 1, 2	Sept. 7			
20. Make up and take practice test for Chapters 3, 4	Sept. 17			
21. Make up and take practice test for Chapter 5	Sept. 24			
22. Make up and take practice test from all sources of questions	Sept. 27 & 28			
23. Meet with study group to make up practice test	arrange			
24. Take exam	Sept. 29			
25. Achieve goal: Pass Exam				

to motivate her to complete her tasks on time. Whenever she completed a task on time and gave herself the reward, she wrote "Yes" on the chart.

Alexa listed several rewards to choose from whenever she completed a task on time. She was free to choose rewards from outside the list, but we encouraged her to develop a list that would motivate her to keep up with her studies.

Alexa's Reward List

Listen to music	Read favorite magazine
Eat snack	Jog
Watch television	Play video game
Watch music video	Call boyfriend
Ride bike	Go to movie
Make lunch date	Reward for passing test: Party!
Take nap	

Alexa's list of rewards will be different from yours. Perhaps your list would include a back massage or playing cards. Remember, everyone works for rewards they value. We encourage you to reward yourself for studying effectively, just as most people reward themselves for going to work by collecting paychecks.

Isn't it rather time consuming to make checklists? Couldn't the time be better spent by studying?

The checklist took Alexa 10 minutes to write. Once it was completed, she knew what she had to do and when she had to complete each task. Afterward, she spent less time worrying about whether or not she was doing the right things and whether she was ahead of or behind schedule. The checklist was an excellent time investment in learning to study efficiently and effectively. You may use any type of checklist you wish. This one is simply a model our students have used with much success.

BENEFITS OF A CHECKLIST

What can you guarantee the checklist will do?

A checklist of specific activities is very helpful. If you have everything written out in an organized fashion, it is easy to refer to. You can see what needs to be done more easily. You won't be overwhelmed by the amount of information you need to learn. Also, you are much less likely to be surprised by an important test or paper.

If Alexa follows her checklist, she will have ten advantages. First, have a good set of questions, answers, and summaries for each chapter. Second, she will not be faced with the problem of having put off reading the chapters until just before the exam. She will study the chapters periodically over a month and will finish them at least a week before the test. Third, she will make up questions and answers immediately following her lectures and will practice quizzing herself to prove she really comprehends the lectures.

Fourth, Alexa will take a practice test for each chapter before she takes a final practice test. Before the exam she will be well prepared and will have spent less time in final review. Students who make this change from poor study habits feel a tremendous positive effect on their digestive tracts and fingernails. Stomachs and fingers often take a beating when students wait until the last minute to figure out what will be asked on the exam.

Fifth, Alexa will find out from other students in the course what they think will most likely be covered in the exam. Sixth, she also will obtain a fair idea of what will be asked on this year's exam by looking at a copy of last year's exam. Seventh, she constantly will be reminded whether she is ahead of, keeping up with, or behind her study schedule. Eighth, she may get encouragement and recognition from her success group partners. Ninth, she will reward herself for completing each of the tasks leading to her goal of passing the exam.

Finally, Alexa will increase her motivation to study. In fact, when talking to us about this schedule, she became so enthusiastic that she wanted to do the first two chapters immediately to get a head start. We suggested to her, however: "Don't let yourself jump ahead; only allow yourself to study for a certain amount of time. When you've finished, reward yourself, and go on to something else."

It is interesting to compare Alexa's proposed checklist from the beginning of the month with the same checklist after she had attempted to follow her schedule of tasks and to reward herself for completing the tasks on time. This completed checklist is found on the next page. As you see, she chose most of her rewards from her original list. Periodically she satisfied a whim or spur-of-the-moment desire she hadn't included on her original list of rewards. It is important to notice that she did not have to spend much money to reward herself. By choosing activities she enjoyed but seldom found time for, she could encourage and reward her good study behavior while keeping herself out of debt.

Many students ask, "But what can I reward myself with? Everything costs so much." Yet students often complain that they never have time to do what they enjoy—playing cards, watching television, riding their bikes, or going out with their friends to enjoy life. Scheduling rewards for completing tasks encourages students to partake of their favorite activities. They have no reason to feel guilty, as so many students do when they take time away from their studies. The rule of thumb is when you earn a reward for studying, take it, and never, never cheat yourself.

Notice that Alexa failed on a few occasions to complete her tasks on time. Therefore, she did not reward herself. It was important that she receive the reward only when the task had been completed on time because procrastination had been a big problem for her in the past. She decided she needed her chart to serve as a means of encouraging her not only to complete her work but also to complete work on time.

For other students, punctuality may not be a problem. It would not be necessary to reward themselves only if their tasks were finished on time. But we usually find that if a person begins skipping tasks or finishing them later than

Alexa's Completed Checklist

Study Behavior	Due Date	Date Completed	Reward	Yes/No
1. Read Chapter 1, and generate questions, answers, and summary	Sept. 2	Sept. 2	Hour T.V.	yes
2. Read Chapter 2 (same as 1)	Sept. 5	Sept. 5	Hour T.V.	yes
3. Read Chapter 3 (same as 1)	Sept. 9	Sept. 9	Read Mags.	yes
4. Read Chapter 4 (same as 1)	Sept. 16	Sept. 16	Sundae	yes
5. Read Chapter 5 (same as 1)	Sept. 23	Sept. 23	Hour T.V.	yes
6. Generate questions from today's lecture and take practice quiz	Sept. 1	Sept. 1	Hour Nap	yes
7. Same as 6 *(late)*	Sept. 3	Sept. 4	none	no
8. Same as 6	Sept. 5	Sept. 5	Cards	yes
9. Same as 6	Sept. 8	Sept. 8	Rode bike	yes
10. Same as 6 *(late)*	Sept. 10	Sept. 11	none	no
11. Same as 6	Sept. 12	Sept. 12	Ice cream	yes
12. Same as 6 *(late)*	Sept. 15	Sept. 16	none	no
13. Same as 6	Sept. 17	Sept. 17	Tennis	yes
14. Same as 6	Sept. 19	Sept. 19	Walk	yes
15. Same as 6	Sept. 22	Sept. 22	Cards	yes
16. Same as 6	Sept. 24	Sept. 24	Call Friend	yes
17. Same as 6	Sept. 26	Sept. 26	Hour T.V.	yes
18. Generate questions from old test	Sept. 10	Sept. 10	Sundae	yes
19. Make up and take practice test for Chapters 1, 2	Sept. 7	Sept. 7	Show	yes
20. Make up and take practice test for Chapters 3, 4	Sept. 17	Sept. 17	Show	yes
21. Make up and take practice test for Chapter 5	Sept. 24	Sept. 24	Show	yes
22. Make up and take practice test from all sources of questions	Sept. 27 & 28	Sept. 27, 28	3 hours T.V.	yes
23. Meet with study group to make up practice test	arrange	Sept. 27	Nap	yes
24. Take exam	Sept. 29	Sept. 29	Date	yes
25. Achieve goal: Pass Exam	Exam Grade	92%	Concert	yes

planned, he or she tends to return to less effective study techniques, like cramming before exams.

IMPORTANCE OF REWARDS

Why is rewarding myself so important?

It is human to try to escape from or avoid adverse situations. Students often want to take the pressure off themselves, finish reading the stupid book, get the test over with, and keep from flunking out or doing poorly. In our estimation, this attitude is tragic. Students can enjoy going to school.

Student Success shows you many study strategies that will make your studying more enjoyable. We want to increase your enjoyment of studying and doing well in school by encouraging you to reward yourself for accomplishing tasks and achieving goals.

Students often say, "Well, isn't rewarding myself bribery? Why should I reward myself for something I have to do?" The answer is simple: You're more likely to do what's good for you when you encourage yourself to do it. We suggest rewarding yourself with free time—for television, reading magazines, or whatever you enjoy. Again, the rewards need not cost anything. Rewards may simply be opportunities to participate in activities you enjoy. Go ahead and give yourself periodic rewards for accomplishing tasks.

HOW TO USE PROGRESS RECORDS, CHECKLISTS, AND REWARDS

Okay. I'll give these strategies a try. Do you have any special rules I should follow when using them?

Yes. We suggest, first, that you always post your schedules, checklists, and progress records in a highly visible location. When constantly visible, they will serve as steady reminders of what you should be doing and how well you are doing it.

Second, ask yourself what you really can do in the amount of time you have to accomplish your goal. Schedule your work, as we suggested earlier, so that all the tasks for a particular course aren't crammed into a short period. Spread your work out. Give yourself time to relax before the test or the date your term paper is due.

Third, list the rewards you will receive for accomplishing your goals. Always reward yourself as you accomplish your goals. We can't say it enough: Never cheat yourself!

Fourth, show your success team partners how well you are doing. The response from our students throughout the years to checklists, schedules, and progress records has been exceedingly favorable. Students have enjoyed the benefits of having more predictable study schedules. Needless to say, students also enjoy their rewards. Equally important, students have seen improvements in how much they have learned and in their grades. If you'd like the same results, we encourage you to give these tactics a try.

WHERE WE ARE

Scheduling your tasks and recording and rewarding your progress will be important to your success. You now have specific guidelines about practical strategies to organize your time and energies for successful learning. Next, in Chapter 5 we will focus on all the psychological factors that affect your success managing your time and work. Once you have completed Chapter 5, you'll be ready to develop a sound plan for scheduling your course work and managing your time.

ACTION PROJECT 1

Develop a Checklist for One Course

Take a few minutes to develop a checklist schedule for accomplishing a goal in one course. Try following the important steps we list for developing a checklist. It will be helpful to review the model checklist presented in this chapter to develop a sense of what you might include in your own list.

It is important that you start small. By starting out with a checklist for one major task in one course, you will become comfortable with using checklists. When you have finished Chapter 5 on time management, you will be ready to develop a complete time management and scheduling system for all of your course work.

ACTION REVIEW

Checklist for Success in Setting and Achieving Your Study Goals

For the following statements, place a check mark by those that are true of you, and place an *X* by those you will try to develop.

_____ I SET GRADE GOALS FOR EACH COURSE.

_____ I SET SPECIFIC STUDY GOALS FOR EACH COURSE.

_____ I CREATE A SCHEDULE TO ACHIEVE STUDY GOALS.

_____ I RECORD MY PROGRESS AT ACHIEVING STUDY GOALS.

_____ WHEN I ACHIEVE STUDY GOALS, I REWARD MYSELF.

ACTION PROJECT 2

Form a Test-Passing Group

Ask several students in one of your courses to form a study group. Ask them to develop a study-goal checklist schedule similar to Alexa's in this chapter. Arrange to get together to exchange practice questions and to quiz one another as you manage the course.

SUCCESS GROUP ACTIVITIES

1.   Have some fun comparing and developing your personal lists of rewards for reaching study goals. You may want to include rewards you can obtain from one another, such as trading compact discs or videotapes.

2.   Compare your ideas for developing study-goal checklists. Discuss each person's plan for using the checklist during a course.

Chapter 5

Learning More With Less Time and Effort

SELF-ASSESSMENT

Place a check mark by the statements that are true of you.

_____ I know how to overcome the factors that interfere with learning and remembering.

_____ I can set up a reasonable and effective study plan when I want to.

_____ With practice, I can increase my concentration span.

_____ I have reduced visual, auditory, and territorial distractions that can interfere with studying.

_____ My approach to studying works well for me.

_____ I reward myself with appropriate breaks as I study.

LEARNING ABOUT LEARNING AND MEMORY

Have you ever felt frustrated during an exam because you can't quite remember something you know you studied? This chapter will show you strategies that will help you do much better. First, let's look at some problems you may face as you try to learn and remember important material.

Years of research by psychologists have established that the following factors interfere with learning and remembering:

- Information can't be remembered when it isn't learned well.
- Recognizing information you have read is not the same as learning information you can recall. Recognition is the easiest learning; recall is the most difficult.

- You don't learn or retain information well if you are distracted. Noise, television, music, and people talking all divert part of your brain's attention from what you are studying. Preoccupation or worry also can distract you from learning and remembering.

- Information does not transfer from short-term memory to long-term memory without effort, repetition, and practice.

- Your memory of information lasts longer when learning is spread out over time.

- Your ability to remember information drops very sharply following the learning. Although the main points of a morning lecture may be recalled while you are talking to a friend at lunch, much of what you learned will be forgotten 2 weeks later. Only a small percentage of information is retained if you do not use it or practice relearning it.

- Trying to learn too much information too fast interferes with accurate recall. Your nervous system needs time to assimilate new learning before taking in more.

- Retaining recently learned information will be hampered by similar information learned soon after. This is a process called retroactive inhibition, whereby you have difficulty recalling new information too similar to other new information.

- When you have an emotional dislike for the learning material, you will have difficulty recalling it objectively and accurately.

- Your learning and remembering are less efficient when you lack interest in the material or lack motivation to learn.

Knowledge about the factors that may interfere with learning and remembering can help you develop strategies to learn more in less time and with less effort. Chapter 5 will focus on the factors that enhance and hinder your learning and management of time.

Study Regularly

Many first-year students act as though a successful student is different from succeeding as a musician with the Chicago Symphony Orchestra, a running back with the Detroit Lions, or a New York stockbroker. Yet few people would question that to be a successful musician, athlete, or businessperson, you need to practice your profession regularly.

One of the most helpful insights for many students is that succeeding means treating college like a job. These students accept the reality that their success in college requires studying almost every day and studying more than they did in high school.

This line of thought only makes sense. Can you imagine the conductor of an orchestra saying to its members, "Our next concert is 3 weeks away. Let's get together the night before the concert, and we'll practice for 7 hours." Or how about a football coach saying to his team, "Guys, to prepare for next Saturday's game, we'll practice 14 hours on Friday. Until then, have fun and get ready for a real workout!"?

To do well at anything, you've got to practice frequently for reasonable periods. Too much practice too late will make you a physical and psychological wreck.

Like any professional, you need a regular training schedule. As a professional student, you need a study schedule that allows you time to learn everything you need to know at a pace that helps your learning settle in and stick with you for years to come.

Some students really believe they can learn just as much by cramming all their studying into a few intense study periods before an exam. If you believe this, ask yourself, "Can I bake a cake faster by turning the oven up to 500°? Can I make a garden grow faster by constantly flooding it with water and surrounding it with heat lamps?" No.

The same holds true for your learning. That's why your courses are scheduled over several months rather than crammed into a single intensive week of study. Studying for brief periods on a regular basis will lead to better learning than if you try to cram all your studying into a couple of longer periods before an exam.

Most of your courses will require constant preparation and review. As we have noted, some students seem to think that because they may have only a few tests in each course, most of their studying can be done within a week before the test. Last-minute cramming tends to have fatal consequences.

Adopting the habit of keeping up in each course may be difficult for you, especially if you have a couple of courses that are more demanding than the others. You'll be tempted to spend most of your time on the difficult courses and to let the so-called easy courses slide. This is another fatal error.

For years college instructors have been telling students they need to spend 2 hours studying outside of class for each hour they spend in class. The truth is that you'll need to spend more time for some classes and less time for other classes.

What it all boils down to is that you need to do the reading and assignments for each class on a regular basis. You want to keep up with each class. You don't want to have that lingering fear, accompanied by nightmares, that you may be committing academic suicide by letting one class slide until the last minute. Let's look at how you can set up a reasonable schedule.

SET UP YOUR SCHEDULE

As we've said before, one of your greatest aids will be to use and follow a time schedule. Obtain a month-by-month calendar with spaces you can fill in with

SELF-ASSESSMENT

The most successful academic time management plans are built on the following steps for effective scheduling. Check off those you believe are most important to you.

_____ Establish a well-defined and reasonable schedule, one I can live with.

_____ Budget my time to prepare for each class and all my examinations.

_____ Budget my time to manage all my other personal responsibilities.

_____ Study my course notes as soon as possible after each class period, rather than waiting until the last few days before my exams.

_____ Give my difficult subjects preferred times with the fewest possible interruptions and disturbances.

_____ Reserve time for leisure activities and make sure I do not study during these periods!

_____ Stick to my schedule and reward myself for having achieved my study goals in the allotted time.

important dates and obligations, such as when examinations will occur and when term papers and projects are due. Next, fill in all the times you plan to go to concerts, shows, family gatherings, or meetings; fill in your plans for trips or other events; and so on.

After developing a picture of your major commitments for the months ahead, you are now ready to create a weekly schedule of your classes, study hours, and other obligations. A weekly schedule gives you a clear picture of what you are doing with your time; it helps you spot an extra hour or two during the day that you can use for studying or other responsibilities. This way you can plan more free evenings to do what you want.

A SCHEDULE THAT WILL WORK FOR YOU

A good schedule will motivate you. Knowing that you have an hour on Thursday morning reserved for studying mentally prepares you to spend that hour doing the studying.

Warning: Do not allow yourself to study too much! Schedule time for your other activities, and stick to your schedule. Many students become so involved in their studying when they first start using *Student Success* strategies that they keep right on studying through their scheduled breaks. Don't let yourself do this.

When you reach the scheduled time to stop, go get some exercise, or do whatever you want to do. Learn how to make yourself stop studying.

For many students, the problem is not studying too little; the problem is they study so much that they are inefficient in their studying habits.

How Much Time Do You Really Need?

One of Parkinson's laws is that work expands to fill available time. You may have experienced this phenomenon with projects such as washing and waxing your car. Let's say you have 3 hours available on Saturday morning. Then you probably will take 3 hours to finish the job. But let's also say that before you complete the job, you receive a telephone call informing you that some very special people want you to drive over and pick them up. You probably, in that circumstance, would be able to wash and wax your car to your satisfaction in less than an hour. The approach we suggest in this book is that you decide what has to be done, do it, and then stop, not filling all your available time doing it.

DEVELOPING YOUR LEARNING SCHEDULE

A weekly study schedule will show you that you have many more hours during the day than you might have realized. You will find a blank copy of a weekly schedule at the back of the book. Feel free to tear it out and use it as you wish. After finishing Part 1 on time management (Chapters 1 through 5), you can develop your own weekly schedule. First, let's look over several weekly schedules of other students to give you an idea of what you might want to include in your own schedule.

On the next few pages, you will find a schedule for Mark, a college freshman who has no work or athletic obligations, as well as schedules for a student athlete and a student who has a part-time job. These weekly schedules will show you the types of activities a student can plan for on a weekly basis.

Assessment: What Do You Observe?

Before reading further, take a minute to review the schedule of Mark, a nonworking student. As you review the schedule, ask yourself, "What scheduling strategies does Mark use that will improve his learning and memory?" List them here.

1. _____

_____

2. _____

_____

3. _____

Example: Mark's Schedule (a Nonworking Student)

HOUR	Sunday	Monday	Tuesday	Wednesday	Thursday	Friday	Saturday
7–8		Read					
8–9	Sun. list	Bio & English	Library Read	Read Bio, English	Library Read &	Read Bio English	Sat. list
9–10		Biology	Study Art	Biology	Study Art	Biology	Basketball
10–11	Church	English	Art	English	Art	English	
11–12		Review Notes	Review Notes	Review Notes	Review Notes	Review Notes	
12–1			Lunch with Friends				
1–2		Psych		Psych		Psych	
2–3		Library	P.E.	Review Notes	P.E.	Review Notes	
3–4	Work out		Bio. Lab	Workout	Run	Work out	
4–5					Success Group		
5–6		Run					
6–7	Success Group		Library	Library	Library		
7–8		Mon. night Football	Eng.	Psych. Study Group	Bio. Study Group	Movie or	Party or
8–9	Laundry		Bio.	Eng.	Psych.	Date	Date
9–10			Psych	Bio.	Eng.		
10–11	Schedule week Mon. list	Tue. list	Wed. list	Th. list	Fri. list		
11–12							

4. _____

5. _____

Mark's Scheduling Strategies

Notice how Mark prepares for each class by reading ahead in his textbooks. During his reading sessions, he writes out questions he would like to have answered in class. Some of these tasks are scheduled on his checklist, discussed in Chapter 4.

After class he reviews his lecture notes and writes exam questions. The first few minutes after class is the best and easiest time to complete the day's lecture notes. Waiting even a few hours makes it more difficult to remember what certain terms meant.

What doesn't show are the many brief periods during the week when Mark can sit down for 5 or 10 minutes and review notes, write questions, or update his "To Do" list.

At lunch, he usually meets with his success group partner or partners. There they talk about what is happening and show each other what they are doing.

His evening study schedule is now a planned mix of all his subjects. In his first attempt at a study schedule, he reserved one evening for each subject. That proved to be inefficient and didn't get good results. Now, by alternating subjects every hour or so, he learns the material more quickly and more accurately.

Mark's schedule reflects his personal aims. He wants to have most of Saturday and Sunday free, he wants to watch "Monday Night Football," he wants time for working out and running, and he wants Friday and Saturday evenings free for parties, dates, and movies.

Other Scheduling Strategies

The point is that Mark's schedule suits Mark. Your own schedule may be much different. This is merely a demonstration to show how you can control your week. First, fill in your monthly calendars to lay out the term. Your calendar helps you create your weekly schedule. Then your weekly schedule provides the basis for your daily "To Do" list.

As an example of how different these schedules can be for different students, we have included two other weekly schedules. The first is a schedule of a student athlete. The second is the schedule of a working student.

Example: Student-Athlete Schedule

HOUR	Sunday	Monday	Tuesday	Wednesday	Thursday	Friday	Saturday
7–8		← Breakfast →					↑
8–9	Sleep	English 125		English 125		English 125	Game
9–10	Breakfast	Speech 100	P.E. 100	Speech 100	P.E. 100	Speech 100	
10–11	Church	P.E. 110	Library	P.E. 110	Library		
11–12		Psych 171	Library	Psych 171	Library	Psych 171	
12–1	← Lunch →						
1–2	← Movies, Taping, and Treatment →						Day
2–3							
3–4	Relax	Practice					
4–5	Dinner						Dinner
5–6	Relax						
6–7	Dinner						
7–8	Library / or					Relax	
8–9	Study Table						
9–10							
10–11	Sleep						relax
11–12							

Example: Working Student Schedule

HOUR	Sunday	Monday	Tuesday	Wednesday	Thursday	Friday	Saturday
7–8		Work —		Dorm			
8–9				Cafeteria			
9–10		Math 105	Library	Math 105	Library	Math 105	Errands
10–11		German 201	German 201	German 201	German 201		Errands
11–12		Psych 444		Psych 444	Library	Psych 444	Errands
12–1	Work —		Dorm				Band
1–2	Cafeteria						Band
2–3		History 191	Laundry	History 191	Library	History 191	Band
3–4	History*	Library	Laundry		Library		Band
4–5	History*	Marching Band					Relax
5–6		Practice					Relax
6–7		Dinner					Relax
7–8	Math*	History	Math*	History	Math	Relax	
8–9	German*	German*	German*	German*	History*	Relax	
9–10	Psych*	German*	Psych*	German*	Psych*	Relax	
10–11							
11–12	Sleep						

* Library study

CONCENTRATE WHILE YOU STUDY

You've set up your schedule—but how can you make the most of your study time? The key to concentrating effectively is to set a goal for yourself. People who concentrate well focus on achieving a goal they have set. If you decide to study for an hour, ask yourself, "What is my goal for the hour? What will I focus on learning and accomplishing during the hour? Am I going to read a chapter and answer eight questions about it? Am I going to solve eight calculus problems? Am I going to write an outline for my paper and start the introduction?" Good concentration requires that you set a specific goal, focus on the goal, and work to achieve the goal.

ELIMINATE DISTRACTIONS

More than likely, your family, roommates, or friends have habits and attitudes that interfere with good studying. These people may have no idea that their behavior bothers you. In contrast, some people will bother you just to get your attention—especially young children.

Let's think of the situations that typically distract students. While you're studying, someone turns on the TV in the next room. You say, "Please don't turn on the TV; it bothers me." The person says, "I'll keep it low." Someone else walks in and wants to talk or needs to be driven to a friend's house. A never-ending barrage of interruptions competes for your attention.

So how do you create a peaceful study atmosphere? If you are like many people, you start out by pleasantly asking people not to bother you. If that doesn't work, you may act angry. Often that doesn't work either. You may even try to enforce some rules regarding your study time. You may designate the area where you are studying as off limits or a quiet area. Then you try to enforce the rules of "Be quiet and leave me alone!" We would suggest another approach. Here's why.

"Quiet hours" in residence halls and in people's homes are often a failure. The minute you make rules requiring people to keep noise down or leave you alone, some people seem to go out of their way to demonstrate that the rules can be broken. If you shout, scream, or demand that people keep the noise down, you probably won't get the desired results. Even calm rule enforcement can lead to ruffled feathers and headaches. Rule enforcement requires time, which you simply don't need to waste. If you try to enforce rules and people break them, then, instead of studying, you're uptight and furious at what is occurring.

We suggest a better approach to changing the behavior and attitudes of people around you: Ask your friends or family for what you want! Think about what is reasonable and possible, and then ask for it. Be clear and specific, and explain in detail exactly what you would like to have from them. For example, you might ask someone to watch TV later or to record the program, with a full explanation of why you need to concentrate. You may be surprised at how understanding and supporting people can be.

Remember, you may be asking the people around you to behave quite differently from what they're used to. Their behavior isn't likely to change dramatically overnight. Be patient. Track positives: Notice and appreciate any slight improvement in the direction you are encouraging. It's up to you to then express your appreciation whenever people abide by your wishes. Be sure also to let the people share in your progress.

If you have a friend or family member who still is not cooperative, develop a plan for yourself so that you can study and do your course work. This may involve rearranging your schedule or finding a quieter place, such as a library. Avoid feeling victimized. Instead, create a plan that will let you continue getting the education you want. Use strict rule enforcement only as a last resort. Remember, your aim is to minimize the amount of time and energy taken away from your real interest, that of studying and learning.

Visual Distractions

Benita is like most students. She has created a comfy nest for herself in her study area at home. As she closes the door to the den, the wonderful family pictures covering one wall draw her attention. Benita takes several minutes to gaze nostalgically at the photos of herself and Bill at the ocean. The next thing she knows, she's ready to pull out the slides and not bother with studying. Walking to her desk, she spots a pile of magazines she hasn't had a chance to read. Benita considers the TV in the corner. Why not turn it on and catch the last half of the special she wanted to watch? "I can read and watch TV at the same time," she thinks to herself. Everything in the room has a pull for Benita. She feels as though magnetic forces are drawing her to every item in the room.

And that's the trouble. Before she knows it, 20 minutes have slipped away. She glances at the clock and suddenly thinks, "Why have I wasted so much time? Okay. I'll get to work. That's the last time I'll get distracted." That's what *she* thinks.

As Benita returns to her studies, her mind is distracted from her notes. The family photo on the desk keeps catching her eye. The phone reminds her of several calls she has to make. She starts worrying, "If I don't make those calls tonight, I'll have real problems next week." Before she knows it, she has blown another 15 minutes rehearsing her phone calls. Pictures, telephones, magazines, and television programs constantly distract her from studying.

Minimizing Visual Distractions
If you study at your desk, try to keep it as free of distractions as possible. Once it is cleared off, you won't miss what is gone. Don't go berserk and carry the principle too far. We're not suggesting you create a monastic cell with nothing but bare walls and a small light at your desk. We simply suggest you sit in a comfortable chair at a desk that is free of articles that carry memories, free of articles that cry out, "Pick me up, play with me, use me, gaze at me."

Try placing your desk so that you face a wall void of your family history and photos. A blank wall in front of you prevents your eyes from leaving the pages of your notes or text. Place your chair so that you are not looking out a window at the passing scene. Your chair can easily face an area that will not distract you.

To reduce eyestrain, your room should be well lit, with the main light source off to one side. A light directly behind or in front of you will be reflected from the glossy pages of your textbooks. A constant glare tires your eyes more quickly than indirect lighting. If you can't shift the lamp, shift your desk. Place the desk so that no portion of the bulb shines directly into your eyes. A strong light source pulls your eyes toward it. The constant strain of trying to avoid looking at the light causes eye fatigue.

Spend a few minutes arranging your study environment. It does not help to feel uncomfortable. The few minutes you spend will save you hours of distracted study and constant mumbling and grumbling—"I just can't get a thing done. I just can't keep my eyes on the pages. I keep thinking of a thousand other things. And my eyes are killing me!" All of these distractions needn't get in your way if you design your study area to encourage comfortable studying and not daydreaming. You need to have the best study area possible.

Auditory Distractions

As we noted, "quiet hours" rarely work as well as the rule makers hope. Distracting sounds still interrupt studying. Doors slam, phones ring, horns honk, and people move around. In fact, the quieter the study areas, the more distracting these sounds become.

Steady background sounds can mask distracting noises. Play your radio or stereo softly while you study to create a steady background of "noise" to mask occasional sounds. Experiment with stations or records until you find what works best for you. FM radio stations playing instrumental music are usually best. Talk shows and fast-talking disc jockeys are usually worse for concentration than nothing at all. Some people say that turning on their hair dryers helps them to study. One student reported that he turns his radio to a place where no program is playing. The static keeps him from being distracted.

Don't try to study with the television on. If you want to watch a program, watch it. But don't try to avoid feeling guilty by having your book open to read during commercials. Studying with your television on is academic suicide. Use television time as a reward. After you have completed a successful study period, say to yourself, "I've earned a reward. I'll watch television."

Territorial Distractions

If you need to escape from distractions, go to your favorite library! Libraries have been designed to help you succeed. People can't yell at you. Your friends can't ask you for attention. Your girlfriend can't bother you with her phone conversation. Your boyfriend won't have "Monday Night Football" blaring. Your roommate can't drag you into a conversation. Only you can prevent yourself from studying once you are in the library. The obvious exception is the nitwit who sits across from you talking to his girlfriend or tapping his pencil. You then can move to a quieter spot if any are available. With minor exceptions, most places in a library are good for studying.

When you first go into a library to find a good spot to study, allow yourself a little warm-up time. Whenever you enter a new territory, your senses are drawn to the environment. You automatically scan new surroundings. You check the walls, floor, and ceiling. You look at the lights, decorations, and furnishings. You look at the people, wonder about certain sounds, and spend time adjusting to the feeling of a new chair. Every time you go to a new place to study, you check out the surroundings before you settle down to work. To improve your efficiency, pick one spot and always try to study there. Studying in the same spot will shorten your warm-up time and will allow you to concentrate better.

If your library is a campus social center, try to find a spot with the least amount of people traffic. Find a remote table or desk where you won't be tempted to watch all the action.

ACCEPT YOUR HUMANNESS

Brent is a sophomore engineering major. During the summer he decided that when he came back to college, he would study 3 hours every night without interruption. He put a sign on his door:

Is he studying more? Yes and no. He can make his body sit at his desk for several hours at a time, but he has a problem he hardly knows exists. While his eyes look at his book, his mind takes breaks. He sometimes reads several pages and then realizes he has no idea what he has read. He has been daydreaming while reading.

Does Brent need more willpower? No. He needs to accept the idea that he is a human being. He needs to accept the idea that humans have limitations on what their mind can be expected to do.

Concentration Span

The way to make studying easier is to start with what you can do now and build on that. On the average, how long can you study before your mind slips off to something else? Twenty-five minutes? Ten minutes? Most students can concentrate on a textbook 10 to 15 minutes before they start to daydream.

The next time you study, keep a notepad on your desk and notice approximately how long you can read your textbooks or notes before you start to daydream. Don't set any particular goals for yourself yet. First, find out what is the typical amount of time you can read textbook material before your mind starts to wander. Let's say you find your average concentration span is about 12 minutes. Now the question is, what would you like it to be—30 minutes or, perhaps, 45 minutes?

Whatever goal you set for yourself, make certain you allow for your humanness. Be realistic. Set a goal you can reach with reasonable effort, and give yourself enough time to reach it. As a rough guideline, you might aim for a time span of 15 minutes by the end of your freshman year, 25 minutes in your sophomore year, 35 minutes in your junior year, and 45 minutes in your senior year. Graduate students should be able to study for about an hour without losing their concentration.

Mandatory Breaks

Once you determine your concentration span, set up your study schedule so that you take a brief break after each study segment and a long break about once an hour. If you do, you will find that you can start and return to your studies much more easily than before.

In fact, you will find the end of a study segment coming so quickly that you will be tempted to continue. Don't do it. Keep your agreement with yourself. When you promise to take a quick break after 12 minutes, do so. Do not allow yourself to study more than the allotted time.

Personal reports of most students emphasize why it is necessary to take these breaks even when they don't want to. With segmented study hours, studying is easier than expected, but after a while the old ways of studying creep back in.

What happens? The critical point comes when you reach the end of a study segment and find yourself so interested in the material that you decide to keep on. If you do, your mind seems to say, "I can't trust you. You promised me a break after each 14 minutes, but after I fulfilled my part, you kept me working."

When you promise your mind a break after 12 or 14 minutes, keep your word! No matter how much you want to continue, make yourself take a short break. Get up and stretch. Get a drink of water or a breath of fresh air before starting the next study segment.

SELF-ASSESSMENT

Checklist for Learning More With Less Effort

Use this list to review how well you are managing your learning effort. Some students place this list on their wall or in a conspicuous place to remind themselves how to manage their daily learning.

_____ Have I outlined a weekly study schedule for myself?

_____ Do I write out and follow daily time schedules?

_____ Have I asked people to be considerate of my need to study?

_____ Is my study area free of distractions?

_____ Do I mask distracting sounds with soft music or some other steady background noise?

_____ Have I arranged good lighting?

_____ Do I study in the same place each time?

_____ Do I avoid studying one subject too long?

_____ Have I determined my concentration span and planned study segments geared to my present ability?

_____ Do I take short breaks after study segments and a long break each hour?

_____ Have my grades improved from using these scheduling and management strategies?

ACTION PROJECT 1

Learning About Learning and Memory

See how much you can learn about how the human mind works by completing the following activities:

1. Read the sections on memory and forgetting in several different introductory psychology textbooks.
2. Make a list of all the principles and factors that help or hinder learning and memory.
3. Look through *Student Success* to see how it is organized using the knowledge of these facts and principles.
4. List several techniques you could use on a regular basis to improve your memory.
5. Get together with some other students who are motivated to do well in college, and talk about what you have learned from this information about learning and memory.

ACTION PROJECT 2

Managing a Learning Schedule

At the back of this book you will find a schedule that can be removed. Tear it out and use the suggestions in Chapters 3, 4, and 5 to create a weekly schedule to manage your time.

Post your schedule where you can see it. As you complete the activities during the week, cross off each square that represents that activity.

By keeping track of the activities you complete, you are likely to find that you are motivated to stay on schedule. Notice that we are not trying to encourage you to schedule your entire life. Just schedule the activities you have to complete for your academic and personal satisfaction.

Make sure you leave time for just doing what you please and for all those spontaneous activities that make life so rewarding. At the end of the week, review your schedule to determine the percentage of activities you have completed. If you feel you have done well keeping to your schedule, give yourself a little reward.

ACTION PROJECT 3

Quiet Roommates

One of the most important supports any college student can have is his or her roommate. However, too often roommates inadvertently create distractions for each other. Rather than wait to complain when your roommate creates auditory and visual distractions that drive you up the wall, take a few minutes to have a frank discussion first. Ask him or her what conditions the two of you can create so that you can both accomplish your studying.

It will help to be as honest as possible. If you can't stand hearing rock music, even playing softly, when you are trying to read, say so. Even if you regularly study in the library, you'll periodically work in your room. Agree with your roommate what will and will not occur during studying time.

Don't forget to be human. Both you and your roommate will break the rules now and then. Laugh it off. Make a joke about the distraction. Everyone tests rules. Once you and your roommate adjust to each other's study needs, you'll have reduced one of the greatest sources of conflict that typically develop between roommates.

SUCCESS GROUP ACTIVITIES

1.   Compare your weekly schedules. Support one another in creating a personally suitable schedule. Does one person prefer to get up early and start studying at 6:00 A.M.? Does another prefer to sleep late and study until midnight or 1:00 A.M.?

2.   Compare samples of your daily "To Do" lists. Talk with one another about how well it is working to set priorities and to do only the most important things each day.

3.   Talk about the ten principles affecting learning and remembering listed at the beginning of the chapter. What effects have this chapter and Action Project 1 on learning about learning had on you?

Part 2

Critical-Thinking and Learning Strategies: Keys to Classroom Success

Critical Thinking and Effective Reading

INTELLIGENCE AND CRITICAL THINKING

Do you believe that "critical thinking" means to be critical of others? We hope not. Critical thinking is the ability to evaluate facts and information from different perspectives using reasoning and good judgment. It is an ability that reflects a level of intellectual and emotional development far beyond that of memorizing facts and information.

Anyone with an excellent memory can score high on an IQ test. It takes critical-thinking skills, however, to add common sense and wise thinking to inborn brightness. You probably know several very bright students who are not very "life competent" and several others who are bright and have "good heads."

Students with critical-thinking skills have broad vocabularies and solve problems more easily than others. By combining intelligence with critical thinking, you can earn high scores on tests of facts and answer questions that require evaluative thinking. If one of your goals in life is to be an intelligent person with common sense and good judgment, it is important to understand what you should know and be able to do.

Most college students believe they are intelligent people. A favorite pastime of many students and instructors in psychology and education is to discuss topics such as these: What is intelligence? Is intelligence inborn? Can it be increased? Is an intelligent person creative? What is the difference between being intelligent and street smart? Why do highly intelligent people often lack common sense? Does more than one kind of intelligence exist? If so, what are the different kinds? What is critical thinking?

We encourage you to search for your own answers to these questions. For the time being, here are some answers that work for us.

ASKING QUESTIONS: THE KEY TO EFFICIENT LEARNING, CRITICAL THINKING, AND SUCCESS IN CLASSES

If you want to enhance your intelligence and critical thinking, then practice the behaviors associated with intelligence and critical thinking. Most psychologists agree that an intelligent person is an eager learner. He or she learns and remembers more than other people. But what behavior leads to this trait? The answer is asking and answering questions. An intelligent person who thinks critically asks important questions and searches for the answers.

Educators and psychologists believe that vocabulary is one of the best single indicators of intelligence. How do people acquire a good vocabulary? They wonder, "What does that word mean?" and then find the answer.

One way to find answers to vocabulary questions is to obtain a thorough, inexpensive dictionary and use it. Equally useful is asking what people mean when they use certain terms. Searching for the best words to describe something will improve your vocabulary and enhance your intelligence. Searching for information and for answers to questions is the key to improving your intelligence, enhancing your critical-thinking skills, and helping you become more successful in school.

If you talk with your friends or members of your success group about what a student must do to succeed, it will be clear to you that you must ask and answer good questions. You must do so when writing papers, reading your textbooks and notes, talking in discussion groups, attending classes, and taking tests.

Think of one of your textbooks. It consists of answers to many questions. Your instructors spend a fair amount of their time developing questions to ask you in class and on tests. Think of the notes you take. Are notes anything more than answers to questions? Your instructors have carefully analyzed important books, lectures, films, and other resources to generate a body of information they present to you in class. The final task for you is to answer important questions about this information.

USING EFFICIENT LEARNING STRATEGIES

Let's look at some very simple, highly effective learning techniques developed from many years of working with college students. Students using these techniques report that once they learn to ask and answer intelligent questions, they become highly successful in school. They save hundreds of hours of time spent studying and preparing for courses. As a result, they can spend more time going to movies, watching television, playing sports, visiting with friends, taking weekend trips, attending concerts, and leading the "good life."

If these activities interest you, let's spend a little more time discussing how you can learn the correct strategies. One reward we promise is that you will achieve your academic goals with a great deal more pleasure and far less pain than you have known in the past. But we sound one caution: Learning these new strategies may require you to change some of your old habits. Such changes are sometimes difficult or painful.

Why? Well, when you are used to a routine set of study habits and thinking strategies, you often become comfortable with them and resist change. Even when you try the new study strategies and they seem to work, you'll have a tendency to return to your old study habits. After all, these old habits have helped you accomplish your goals in the past. You have learned to live with them even though they may be time consuming and not as effective as you would like.

Once you become accustomed to the new study and thinking strategies, many of your old self-defeating habits and attitudes related to studying and becoming educated will fade away. You will begin to receive positive feedback from professors, friends, and yourself that indicate the new strategies save time. You will achieve your goals and have time for activities you never had time for in the past.

THREE PRINCIPLES OF CRITICAL THINKING

PRINCIPLE I: READ AND STUDY TO PASS TESTS

Whenever you are reading from curiosity, allow your mind to travel any direction it wishes. But, when you study, study as if you were practicing to take a test. As you read, practice asking and answering questions! If you don't, you are wasting valuable time! After all, it's your time, so why waste it?

Doesn't studying as if you were practicing to take a test go against the idea of simply learning for the sake of learning?

When you focus your reading and studying by looking for answers to questions, you make the material meaningful and learn significantly more. Whether or not you will take a test on the material you are reading is secondary. Your main aim is to develop the habit of getting the most out of your reading by asking and looking for answers to questions.

PRINCIPLE II: ASK INTELLIGENT QUESTIONS

What is an intelligent question?

First, an intelligent question is one you would like answered. Second, it is framed so that by seeking the answer you will learn new and useful information. Third, it might be close to a question your instructor asks on a test. Fourth, it can be a way to demonstrate what you already know.

How do you learn to ask intelligent questions?

Practice is the key to asking intelligent questions. Practicing anything you want to improve is a useful personal habit to acquire. At first it takes some work to consciously ask questions, but later questions arise without much effort.

What will good questions help you do?

Are you and your instructor interested in the same aspect of a subject? You'll only know by asking questions. You may wish to study information that is of no interest to your instructor. That's fine. But regardless of your own interests, you want to make sure you do well in your course by knowing the information your instructor defines as important.

If you ask good questions, you can focus on the important points of your lectures and readings. Effective questions help you determine what your lecturers and the authors of your texts believe you should remember.

A major function of your questioning process should be to prepare yourself for exams. By practicing answering the questions you develop, you'll find out just how ready you really are to do well. After all, have you ever taken an exam that wasn't composed of questions your instructor wanted you to answer? That's why we cannot overemphasize the value of proving your brilliance by answering your questions!

Another point not to be overlooked is that you will please your instructors no end if you ask and answer good questions in class. The hundreds of hours you'll save in preparation to do well in your classes and on exams is clearly one of the hidden bonuses of the question-and-answer regime we recommend.

How can I recognize good questions to prepare for exams?

An intelligent study question usually starts with a phrase such as one of the following:

- Give several examples of . . .
- Which of these is an example of . . .
- Describe the function of . . .
- What is significant about . . .

- List the important . . .
- Compare and contrast . . .
- Interpret the following . . .
- What is the structure of . . .
- Identify the following . . .
- Why does . . .
- Discuss the relationship between . . .

What does a completed good study question look like?

Here are some examples of worthwhile questions you could ask yourself or that your instructor might ask on a test:

- Why do both your hunger pangs and your stomach contractions tend to decrease after lunchtime even if you didn't eat anything?
- How would you test your auditory threshold?
- Compare the major psychological differences between chimpanzees and humans.
- Give several examples of imperialism in South Africa during the early 1900s.
- What functions are associated with the two hemispheres of the brain?

PRINCIPLE III: ANTICIPATE YOUR INSTRUCTORS' QUESTIONS

How can I predict what an instructor will think are important questions?

Pretend you are the instructor, and develop questions from your texts, lecture notes, and old exams. Think of questions before you go to class, and then listen to find out whether other students ask the same questions or whether the instructor supplies answers to those questions.

Write out questions for a lecture or an assignment. Then ask your instructor whether or not he or she thinks these questions are important and what other questions you should attempt to answer.

Do not be afraid to ask your instructor what he or she thinks are the important questions. Most instructors are happy to tell you what they think is important. Give them a chance.

Ask your professor what goals he or she has for the students in the class. If you want a clear answer, you must learn to ask questions that help the professor clarify the questions he or she wants the class members to answer. You might ask questions such as these:

What should we be able to do, and what important questions should we be able to answer after completing this chapter (unit, training, program)?

What important questions do you think we should examine in this unit (chapter, assignment)?

Can you suggest particular articles or books that highlight the issues we will be discussing in this unit?

What important things should we be looking for in this particular reading (film, case study)?

When you ask questions, ask them in a positive manner. Students have a tendency to put instructors on the defensive. Think of it as your job to ask an instructor in what direction the course is headed and to reward him or her for telling you. A comment such as "Thanks, that really clarifies things for me" is a response most instructors appreciate.

Now that I know what intelligent study questions are, what is the best way to get into the habit of developing questions and answers?

To help you become proficient at developing study questions and answers, let's start by focusing on your critical-thinking and reading strategies. You can learn quickly how to get much more out of your reading by turning it into a question-answering process. In the following chapters, we will focus on critical-thinking strategies you can use for note taking, test preparation, and test taking. But because basic critical-thinking and reading strategies are the most important, that's where we'll begin.

READING EQUALS QUESTION ANSWERING

READ TO FIND QUESTIONS AND ANSWERS

Studying your texts is not the same as reading your Sunday newspaper or other casual reading. Most textbooks are not written to entertain you. You can't get away with reading only the parts that interest you. When it comes to studying, you want to choose reading strategies that motivate you to reach out mentally and emotionally and grasp important information.

Studying can be fun, but sometimes studying is very hard work, as hard as any physical labor. Your reading shouldn't seem like labor. But reading often seems like drudgery when you passively read your textbooks and lecture notes over and over without any focus. You need an active reading strategy that keeps you focused—so that as you read, the answers to your questions seem to bounce off the page at you.

The reading strategy we suggest will keep you awake, focused, and constantly aware of how much you are learning. When you use this strategy, you will consistently find answers to important questions. Finding answers will excite you.

Finding answers builds confidence that you're learning what you want to learn and that you'll do well on your tests.

If you are not reading and studying textbooks and notes as if you are preparing to take a test, you are not using your time wisely.

INCREASE YOUR READING SPEED AND COMPREHENSION

One of the fastest ways to spend less time reading assignments is to learn how to figure out where the important information is located in your reading. You want to find the important questions and answers as quickly as possible.

It will help you to know that a large percentage (perhaps as many as 80%) of the words you read are not critical to your understanding of the important concepts. Most words simply link ideas. The ideas are the answers to the questions you wish to answer. So, the strategy we will teach you will show you how to determine where the important questions and answers are located. We don't want you wasting a lot of time focusing on information that isn't essential to grasping the important concepts.

Then, once you have found the important information, you need a strategy that helps you turn it into something meaningful that can be remembered easily. The strategy we will teach you also focuses on turning information into answers. Why? Because when you restructure important information into answers, you will remember it better. Thus, the key to improving your comprehension and memory is restructuring information into meaningful answers. Go ahead and try this strategy to see how it improves your speed at reading and understanding the material.

THE SQ4R STRATEGY

Survey-Question-Read-Recite-Write-Review: These are the components of the SQ4R strategy.

Your comprehension of what you read will improve as you practice answering questions from your reading assignments. The strategy of reading to answer questions is considered the most efficient and effective means for getting the most out of your reading material in the least amount of time by many experts on study skills and reading improvement.

READING TEXTBOOKS

To help you learn the SQ4R strategy, we recommend that you practice each step of the strategy with one of your textbooks. Pick out a text for an introductory course such as psychology, biology, sociology, or anthropology. As you read through the following description of the SQ4R strategy, each time you come to an exercise follow the directions to see how you can apply the SQ4R strategy to your text.

Step 1: Survey and Question

The goal of surveying a chapter is to determine two essential pieces of information: What important questions are answered in the chapter? Where are the answers to the important questions located?

First, go to the beginning and end of the chapter to see whether or not it has chapter objectives, a list of questions, or a chapter summary. If so, read them right away! This is where you will find the important points that authors stress and the questions students should be able to answer after completing the chapter.

If you can answer the questions and already know what is in the summary, you probably won't have to read the chapter as thoroughly. But don't decide yet. If it has a set of questions, a list of objectives, or a chapter summary, you're ahead of the game; if not, you soon will be.

How do you survey? Surveying involves quickly skimming the chapter to determine what important questions it answers and where the answers are located. Look for headings, subheads, illustrations, pictures, charts, lead sentences in paragraphs, and questions that will give you a basic idea of what the chapter is about.

While you are surveying, it is easy to turn headings, subheads, and lead sentences into questions. Writing questions as you survey keeps you alert to the important points in the chapter. Reading becomes an active, goal-oriented process. As you survey, you formulate and write out questions that, when answered, give you a good summary of the chapter. The result of your survey will be a list of questions and an idea of where the answers are located in the chapter.

To prove your brilliance, you may wish to try to answer the questions you developed while surveying before you even read the chapter. This self-quiz tells you how much you already know about the chapter before spending an exorbitant amount of time reading. Many students are amazed at their ability to answer a large percentage of the questions they have formulated in their survey.

Another helpful strategy is to quickly summarize what you have learned about the chapter from your survey. Talking to yourself about the chapter helps you focus on the important questions you should be able to answer after having read it.

Exercise for Step 1.   Try surveying your own chapter. Your goal will be to develop 10 basic questions. These questions, when answered, should make you feel you have a good understanding of the basic concepts in the chapter. In addition to developing several important questions, your survey will give you a general feeling for where the answers to your questions are located.

As you survey your chapter, write down 10 questions you believe cover the basic concepts presented in the chapter. Use the spaces provided here.

Questions and Answers for Steps 1–3 of the SQ4R Strategy

1. _____

   _____

2. _____

3. _____

4. _____

5. _____

6. _____

7. _____

8. _____

9. _____

10. _____

_____

_____

_____

Step 2: Read to Answer Questions

It is now time to read your chapter. Read as quickly as you can. Read to find the answers to the questions you developed while surveying the chapter and to find new questions and answers you didn't predict while surveying.

Remember, in many instances your questions and answers will be found in the headings, subheads, or first few sentences of a paragraph. Occasionally, you will read well beyond the headings for more important details, but not with the regularity that caused you to waste a lot of time in the past reading over less important information.

When reading to answer questions, you read selectively. You read to find sources of information that answer your questions. When you come to a section of information that answers a question, slow down and pay careful attention to the most important points that answer your question.

Reading this information is different from understanding it. To understand the information, you must pause to work it around in your mind, putting it into your own words until you have an answer to your question that makes sense to you.

You then leave that information, start reading more rapidly, and look for the answer to your next question. When you find your next answer, you slow down and start the process over again.

You can see that you are never reading at a constant rate. You read rapidly to find important information. When you come to the information, you spend time understanding it by turning it into the answer to a question and then move on.

When you come to information that answers a question you hadn't predicted, you slow down, formulate the question, and make sure you know the answer. When you come to material you are very familiar with, you don't spend much time on it—you just look it over quickly to see that it includes nothing new. Then, you keep on reading to find out what you don't know.

Reading to answer questions sounds reasonable. But how can I be sure I will remember the answer once I have read over the information?

When reading to answer questions, good readers follow an important process. When you find information that answers a question, you need to restructure that information into an answer that makes sense to you. You need to make the information meaningful and easy to remember.

For example, when you see that a paragraph contains the answer to one of your questions, you don't try to memorize the paragraph. You read over the information in the paragraph and think through a meaningful answer.

As you read, you are always restructuring information so that it makes sense to you. Information is easiest to remember when it is restructured into answers. That is why as you watch good readers, you will see them looking over several paragraphs as they think and talk out an answer to a question.

Exercise for Step 2.   Read through your chapter, looking for answers to the 10 questions you developed in the exercise for Step 1. As you find your answers, stop and write them in the spaces provided there.

Step 3: Recite and Write Answers and Summaries

Now go back and read through your questions and answers: You have accomplished the first three steps of SQ4R. You developed some questions, read to answer your questions, and wrote out meaningful answers to your questions.

Reciting and writing the answers to your questions is the key to remembering the important information from your chapter. By restructuring the information into questions and answers, you'll improve your recall of it. You then can use your questions and answers to help prepare for your exams.

After you have recited and written your answers, you may want to try another strategy that will improve your recall of the chapter. Take a minute to summarize the chapter aloud. By talking to yourself about your answers and relating them to one another in a summary, you'll help improve your understanding of how all the concepts fit together.

Don't hesitate to talk to yourself (even if people think you're a little crazy) about the answers to your questions. Students often rush on to a new chapter before thoroughly proving to themselves that they are familiar with the information in the chapter they just read. They say to themselves, "I read it. I know what it's about." Don't make that mistake! Prove to yourself by answering your questions and summarizing your chapter that you really do comprehend the important information in your chapter.

Step 4: Review

If you have followed the steps so far, you are ready to review your chapter at any time. You will have a set of questions and answers representing the important information in the chapter. When preparing for your exam, you can quiz yourself over your questions until you know you can give accurate answers if the questions appear on your exam.

If you have practiced summarizing the chapter to yourself, you can compare your summary with the author's summary of the chapter. Taken together, these activities will let you know you've mastered the material. When you know you can answer questions correctly and make accurate summaries, you will be more confident that you understand the chapter and will do well on the exam.

The Result

You now have completed the following tasks, using the SQ4R strategy:

1. Surveyed your chapter
2. Developed questions
3. Read selectively to answer your questions
4. Found questions and answers that you hadn't predicted
5. Recited and written meaningful answers to your questions
6. Summarized the chapter silently or aloud
7. Reviewed the chapter by answering your questions and summarizing the chapter

If you followed these steps, you have a basic understanding of the chapter.

This Book Is an Example

For another example of how to use SQ4R, look at how this book is organized. The Preface explained the main objectives and purposes of *Student Success*. We listed questions students typically ask and then urged you to skim through the book rapidly to ask questions about it. Now, you are reading the book in greater detail and talking about the new information you are learning (reciting) with yourself, your success group, or your study partners.

At the end of most chapters is an Action Review. The review questions help you specifically determine whether or not you are putting into practice what you are learning.

We wrote this book in a way that helps you put into practice what we know works for students!

ADVANTAGES AND DIFFICULTIES OF SQ4R

Why should I believe this approach works?

Evidence collected at the reading and learning skills centers and other learning centers at many colleges has shown that most good students use these strategies. When average or weak students learn SQ4R, they raise their grades, reduce study time significantly, increase reading speed, and improve comprehension of textbooks.

SQ4R is designed to help you focus on learning what is important to you. You don't waste time reading and looking for information you already know. With SQ4R you spend less time memorizing facts you will soon forget. You focus on learning efficiently and effectively the important concepts in your texts and readings.

Your preparation for tests is a continual process. You learn to organize and structure your studying. You state your goals as questions, seek answers, achieve your goals, and move on. You focus on grasping the key concepts. Details are much easier to remember once you have grasped the big picture.

You learn to take an expert's point of view and to think things out for yourself. By the time you take the test, you will find that you have answered most of the essential questions and feel confident that you have learned what is important to you.

However, you may at first encounter difficulty using SQ4R. After all, it is difficult to change old study habits. You may be accustomed to reading every word, always afraid that you're going to miss something. A new strategy such as SQ4R may appear reckless because you focus on learning what is important and not on trying to memorize everything you read.

It would be easy to stick with your old habits. It takes more energy to ask questions and develop summaries than it does to let your eyes passively read printed pages. It is easier just to open a book and start reading. With SQ4R, you study frequently for shorter periods, instead of waiting until the end of the course and cramming.

So how can you reconcile SQ4R's advantages and difficulties? Everything has advantages and disadvantages! This is true for both successful and unsuccessful students. If no difficulties were involved, if it were easy, then everyone would be more successful. Succeeding has costs, but, once you know SQ4R, the gains are worthwhile.

Imagine yourself agreeing to run in a 10-kilometer race several months from now. You will be running with friends, and it is important for all of you to do well. To be at your best, would you loaf around until the last few days and then prepare by running day and night until the time of the race? No. You'd start now with a weekly schedule of jogging and running. A little bit of practice on a regular basis is the best preparation. The same approach is true for effective studying and remembering.

Try the SQ4R study strategies and look for results such as the following:

- The quality of your questions and answers will improve with practice.
- The amount of time it takes you to develop questions, answers, and summaries will decrease.
- The amount of time it takes to verify and improve your answers will decrease with practice.
- You will be able to cover large amounts of material in far less time.
- You will find that you produce the same questions as your instructors, textbooks, and friends.
- With practice, you will find that the summaries you develop come closer to those by the author.

These techniques are based on several well-established principles of learning. When you learn information under conditions that are similar to those you will be tested under, you have a greater likelihood of remembering it. People learn information faster when it is meaningful and of some interest than when the information appears unrelated or confusing. Learning new material (answers) is easier when you associate it with familiar material (questions).

The SQ4R strategy sounds helpful, but could I start by just using parts of the strategy or using the whole strategy on small sections of my work?

Our students report best results when they begin practicing the entire strategy at once. But some people will adjust best to the SQ4R strategy by practicing on a small section of work in one course to see immediate results. They gradually increase their use of this method as they become more comfortable with it.

READING JOURNALS AND TRADITIONAL BOOKS

How do I read and predict exam questions form sources other than my textbooks?

Once you accept the value of always studying as if you were practicing to take a test, you'll be on the right track for studying all sources. It is important to gear your study behavior to collecting questions and answers you expect to find on your exams. By using the reading strategies we have suggested, you will have a good start. Your reading always will be geared to asking and answering important questions.

In addition to this style of reading, several other strategies will help you collect a good set of exam questions and answers. Taking notes, asking friends and instructors, collecting old exams, holding discussion groups, and using textbook and study guide questions are several we'll discuss in the next few chapters. But first we need to help you learn to read for important questions and answers in sources other than textbooks.

The three sources that students tell us typically present the most difficulty are journal articles and fiction and nonfiction books.

JOURNAL ARTICLES

Journal articles present college freshmen with some of their greatest reading problems. This shouldn't surprise you when you think about why the articles were written. Journal articles are written by professionals for professionals. No psychologist in the world writes a complex analysis of his or her research with the freshman student in mind.

Journal articles are written to convey important scientific discoveries, philosophical positions, analyses of problems, and other significant ideas. They are typically written for a professional community of high-level scholars. That is why you don't see them sold at newsstands or commonly advertised in popular magazines.

Independent of who the intended audiences of journals may be, it is common for college instructors to assign journal articles to first-year students. The problem the students often face is that they are overwhelmed or intimidated by the articles. If you talk to most of your college professors, they will tell you that they felt the same way when they were freshmen. Most people, whether they are college students or professional businesspeople, don't know how to make heads or tails of complex journal articles.

We often find that not only are college students overwhelmed and intimidated by the articles, but also students often don't read them or else read them inefficiently or ineffectively. It is not uncommon for the typical first-year student to tell you that he or she would assume that to read and comprehend an average journal article, they might spend an hour or more.

When you ask freshmen how they would read the article, they tell you: "I would start at the beginning and read through the article, trying to remember the most important points." "I would try to memorize as much as possible." "I would read it slowly, trying to figure out how it related to the textbook and lectures." The common element of most students' comments is that they would read slowly, hoping to memorize it. From our perspective, this is academic suicide. The reason for saying this should make sense when you consider the following discussion.

When you ask students why instructors want them to read a journal article, they typically say, "To understand an important concept or idea." If that is the case, then why not read the article rapidly, looking for the most important concept or idea? Reading slowly to memorize the article defeats your purpose of quickly getting the big picture of what the article has to say. Reading slowly for detail is exactly opposite of the strategy you should use if your instructor wants you to understand only the major concepts from an article.

Think about the test your instructor will give you. If it will include a question about the article, what does your instructor expect you to understand? Does he or she expect you to have a detailed knowledge of each of the sections in the article? to answer a number of very detailed questions about the article? Or, should you simply have the big picture of the article so that you can answer a short essay or objective question that focuses on a few major concepts?

If you think critically, you will ask yourself, "What do I need to know from this article?" and "What reading strategy will help me efficiently and effectively learn what I need to learn?" Let's think critically about the goal of reading a journal article and the reading strategy that will help you learn the most.

To do so, we must look at what most articles look like and how you attack them. We have placed a sample journal article in this chapter (pp. 110–120) to help you see that our critical-thinking strategy makes sense. The article is coauthored by Tim Walter and is titled "Predicting the Academic Success of College Athletes." For the following exercises on reading journal articles, refer to the sample article as you complete each step of the reading strategy. As you follow these steps, you will see that we are suggesting a very realistic approach to learning what you need to learn rapidly.

What do journal articles look like?

Let's take a look at the traditional sections in a journal article: the abstract and the conclusion. As you read the article, let the abstract and conclusion guide your reading and learning.

The Abstract

A traditional scientific article usually starts out with an abstract, which is a summary of the article's main points. The abstract is usually at the top of the first page before the article begins. You want to read the abstract first. After reading the abstract, you typically will know two important things: What questions did the authors try to answer? What conclusions did the authors reach? In some cases this may be enough, but you will want to consider reading other sections of the article to see if they give you additional important information.

The Conclusion or Summary

Just as when you read a textbook chapter using the SQ4R technique, you want to read the conclusion or summary before you read a journal article. The conclusion will give you answers to the big-picture questions. Once you have read both the abstract and conclusion, you will have a good idea as to the important questions the authors tried to answer and what they concluded.

Exercise

Take a minute to read the abstract of the article we have included (p. 110). Then read the conclusions (p. 119). What were two of the major questions the authors were trying to answer? Did you find the answers? If so, what were they? Write the two questions and answers in the following spaces.

1. _____

   _____

   _____

   _____

2. _____

   _____

   _____

   _____

Further Reading

With the information you gather from the abstract and conclusion, you already may know a good deal of what your instructor expects you to know. You probably can give an adequate summary of the article. But, you need to quickly look at the rest of the article to see what questions and answers you might have missed.

Think critically about what we are asking you to do differently. Are we asking you to start at the beginning of the article and read it slowly? No! We are suggesting you read the abstract and then go to the end of the article and read the summary or conclusion. These two steps may give you most of the information you need.

However, as we said, you will want to look at the rest of the article as well. What you will find in the other sections, as well as what you probably will be expected to know from these sections, is discussed next.

The Introduction. A journal article typically begins with an introduction telling you why the research was done. Here is where, for the second time, you may find out what important questions the author is attempting to answer. The introduction may summarize what research has been done to date to answer these questions.

The questions you want to ask yourself as you read the introduction are "Will my instructor expect me to have a detailed knowledge of the introduction information or simply to be able to summarize the main points?" "What will I need from the introduction if I want to be able to answer a short essay question about the material in this article?" "What did I learn from the introduction that I didn't already know from the abstract and conclusion?"

Exercise

Read the first part of "Predicting" that begins after the abstract. Notice that in this particular article, the title "Introduction" isn't used—but the first part is obviously the introduction. As you read the introduction, did you find two main questions the authors were trying to answer? Does the introduction give you a better grasp of the important questions than you got from reading only the abstract and the conclusion? After reading the introduction, abstract, and conclusion, do you have a solid grasp of the important questions and answers? You may want to ask yourself, "How much more do I really need to read to feel I have comprehended the main points of this article?" In the following space, write in any further questions and answers you found in the introduction that you believe an instructor might ask on a test.

1. _____

_____

_____

_____

2. _____

_____

_____

_____

The Methods Section. The introduction is typically followed by a methods section. Here is where you find out who the study subjects were, how the scientists measured change, and the statistical procedures and research design.

Exercise

Survey the method section of "Predicting" (pp. 112–113), and then answer the following questions:

1. Would my instructor expect me to have a detailed knowledge of the information in this section? _____ YES _____ NO

2. Would an instructor really expect a freshman or sophomore student to understand the detail in a methods section? _____ YES _____ NO

The Results Section. The next section is often the real killer! It is the results section, which is a complex presentation of all the data gathered. The scientists show the reader how they analyzed the data. This information is often presented in graphs, tables, and charts.

Exercise

Think critically. Does it make sense to think about what is really expected of you when reading the methods and results sections? These are very complex sections that often confuse students. How do you make sure you don't get lost in the forest? Survey the results section of "Predicting" (pp. 113–117), and answer the following questions:

1. Would my instructor expect me to have a complete understanding of this data analysis? _____ YES _____ NO

2. Would my instructor expect me to be able to describe several basic conclusions the authors want me to draw from their presentation of the data in the results section? _____ YES _____ NO

3. Has reading the conclusion section first helped me understand the results section? _____ YES _____ NO

4. Does reading the abstract, the conclusion, and then the introduction help me avoid getting lost in the details of the methods and results sections? _____ YES _____ NO

The Discussion and Implications Sections. The results section is typically followed by a discussion section. Here the authors discuss which questions may have been answered by their research as well as which questions haven't been answered. The results section may be followed by an implications section if the authors wish to put themselves on the line. Authors typically want to discuss the direction of future research to solve the mysteries or the questions left unanswered by their research.

Exercise

Read the discussion and implications sections of "Predicting" (pp. 117–119). As you read, answer the following questions:

1. Would my instructor want me to be able to discuss the questions the authors believe their study may have answered? _____ YES _____ NO

2. Do the discussion and implications sections tell me anything more I really need to know about the research? _____ YES _____ NO

3. Do these sections for the most part confirm what I have already learned from reading the abstract, conclusion, and introduction? _____ YES _____ NO

What Have You Learned?

What does this analysis of journal articles suggest about reading them efficiently and effectively? As you answered the questions in the five Exercises, we hope you got the message that you are not going to be responsible for studying and memorizing a complex scientific article—not if you are an undergraduate student in an introductory psychology, sociology, or biology course. The expectations for a freshman or sophomore are very different from those for a senior majoring in one of these areas or for a graduate student seeking a Ph.D. in an area.

You need to quickly figure out what information is "nice to know" as you read the articles versus what information you "need to know." Nice to know and need to know are very different for different audiences. If you have all kinds of time, you can read everything. But if you are like most students, you have to think critically about what you need to know and often skip what might be nice to know.

Since you are an undergraduate student in your first year or two of college or possibly still in high school, your reading strategy will be based on different expectations than for more advanced students. But the strategy we'll suggest for reading is the same. The difference is only in what and how much you have to know or comprehend.

Applying the SQ4R Strategy to Journal Articles

To apply the SQ4R model to journal articles, recall the components of the strategy presented earlier in this chapter: Survey-Question-Read-Recite-Write-Review.

Survey and Question. Survey the journal article by first reading the summary. Remember that journal articles have two summaries: the conclusion at the end of the article and the abstract at the beginning. If you read the abstract and the conclusion, will you have a good survey and summary of the article? Will you have a good idea of the questions addressed in the article and the basic answers to those questions?

We want you to see that you can make a useful survey of the article and form good questions and answers by first reading the conclusion and the abstract.

Read. Now you'll want to quickly read through the introduction to see what other important questions the authors may be addressing that you didn't pick up as you read the abstract and conclusion. Then ask yourself, "Do the methods or results sections include anything that will help me answer the questions addressed and answered in the abstract, conclusion, and introduction?" If not, just rapidly skim them and move right on to the discussion section. In the discussion section, read to see if any information answers important questions you haven't already answered in your reading of the abstract, conclusion, and introduction.

Recite, Write, and Review. If you have followed this procedure, you now can talk and write out answers to the key questions answered in the article. When it is time to review the journal article for a test, you don't need to reread the article, which is what most students tell you they try to do. You just review the questions and answers you found in the article.

What are the payoffs of this strategy?

The main benefits that stand out for this strategy are that you can gain an understanding of much complex information very efficiently and effectively. You will learn the "need to know" information and won't confuse yourself with the "nice to know" or "don't need to know" data. In addition, you will have spent much less time trying to understand the article. When you finish, you will have answers to questions. You won't be saying to yourself, "Do I need to reread this article?"

TRADITIONAL BOOKS OF FICTION AND NONFICTION

Many students look at books of several hundred pages and wonder, "How am I going to have time to read this, let alone understand it?" These books don't have the typical study aids—no chapter summaries, lists of questions, or chapter objectives. But by now, you should have a good idea as to the strategy you can use to read and comprehend this type of book. Just think of the strategies you would use to read a textbook or journal article, and apply the SQ4R model.

Surveying and Questioning

You can survey the book by reading the front and back covers. You can read the introduction and skim through the table of contents and chapter titles to get a sense of what questions are answered in the book.

Surveying is what you do every time you go to the bookstore and look at books you are considering purchasing for leisure reading. When you remove the book from the bookstore shelf, you ask yourself, "Is this book worth the money?" Even inexpensive paperbacks cost $6 to $10. So you browse the cover and the introduction and skim through the book. Does this book look like it would be fun to read? Does it discuss interesting topics? any important ideas? If your survey tells you the book answers enough interesting questions, you may decide to buy it.

What might be good questions for this type of book?

The list of questions is endless. The critical concern is that your survey provide you with a set of questions to focus on. Your questions will wake you up. They will direct your reading and help you spot when new topics are raised that you hadn't predicted. Whether you are reading a biography of Ernest Hemingway or Hermann Hesse's classic tale of Siddhartha, your questions will help you see that you are benefiting from your reading. Some examples of good questions are these:

Who are the main characters in the story?

What is the relationship of the characters to one another?

Who is the narrator of the story?

What is the plot?

What are the subplots?

Is this work characteristic of the author's other works?

Reading

After surveying the book and creating questions, you'll read each chapter. As you finish the first chapter, ask yourself, "Is this book asking and answering the same questions I thought it would?" As you read each chapter, look to see if you are getting answers to the questions you need answered. You may find that new questions are raised that you hadn't predicted. Your reading should not be aimless; you'll need to read rapidly looking for answers to questions.

The problem you and all readers face when trying to read a work of fiction or nonfiction is the concern that you should try to read and remember everything. No human being after reading a book can tell you word for word what was on any page.

When you close the book, you remember the major ideas presented. You remember answers to questions. You can sit and summarize the book to yourself, your friends, or your instructor. So don't worry about reading slowly to remember everything. Be realistic. Read each chapter so that when you finish you can give a decent summary of the important ideas and concepts the author was trying to express.

Reciting, Writing, and Reviewing

As with textbook chapters, you want to answer questions as you read each chapter. This means you want to talk to yourself as you are reading. You don't want to wait until you have finished a chapter in a biography of Ernest Hemingway, for example, before you summarize what you have just read. As you read, stop and think and talk out answers to questions. Carry on a dialogue with yourself.

Once you finish each chapter, summarize for yourself what you have just read before you move on to the next chapter. Don't have any fears about memorizing each chapter. Just try to remember the main points. After reading each chapter, if you can talk to yourself or other people about the main points or write a good summary, then you will have accomplished a lot. The ability to answer questions or summarize a chapter will result in remembering what you need to for a long time.

What Next?

Now that you have practiced reading strategies that will help you in the questioning and answering process, we need to look at two other important strategies. Listening and note-taking strategies are the other critical-thinking skills that will have the greatest effect on your success at learning and remembering important information.

Action Review

Checklist for Successful Reading

Here is a list of guidelines that will help you improve your success at reading texts, journals, and traditional fiction and nonfiction books. Before you read any of your assignments, put yourself in a positive mental framework. Read through this list to remind yourself of what you want to do. You may choose to place this list on your wall as a constant reminder of your new strategy for reading and learning.

- I am going to focus my reading by first finding the most important questions that need to be answered.
- I am going to try to read a summary of the chapter or article before I start reading.
- As I read, I will practice talking to myself about the questions I need to answer.
- When I finish reading a section, I will summarize for myself what I have just read.
- I will remind myself to talk out and write out answers to questions while I am reading and after I have finished reading.
- I will avoid returning to my old style of reading when I tried to memorize everything.

- I will reduce my test-taking anxiety by proving to myself that I can answer questions that may be on the test.

ACTION PROJECT

Explore the following Internet resources for study skills tips:

Middle Tennessee State University Study Skills Help Page
http://www.mtsu.edu/~studskl/

Virginia Tech Counseling Center Study Skills Self-Help
http://www.ucc.vt.edu/stdysk/stdyhlp.html

Dartmouth College Academic Skills Center
http://www.dartmouth.edu/admin/acskills/#study

Georgia State University—Resources for Academic Success
http://www.gsu.edu/~esljmm/studyskills/Studyweb.htm

Learning Skills Program—University of Victoria
http://www.coun.uvic.ca/learn/hndouts.html

University of Toronto—Getting There
http://www.campuslife.utoronto.ca/handbook/02-GettingGoodGrades.html

Self-Help Counseling Center, University at Buffalo, State University of New York
http://ub-counseling.buffalo.edu

YOUR PORTFOLIO

Keep clean copies of any papers you write that demonstrate excellent critical-thinking skills.

SUCCESS GROUP ACTIVITIES

1. Ask one another for examples of how you read to answer questions, and discuss how that affects how fast you comprehend the material.

2. Discuss the strategy of writing papers to answer questions. Have you ever tried this approach before?

PREDICTING THE ACADEMIC SUCCESS OF COLLEGE ATHLETES

Timothy L. Walter, Donald E. P. Smith, George Hoey and Rowena Wilhelm
University of Michigan

Samuel D. Miller
University of North Carolina

Our purpose was to assess the impact of NCAA Bylaw 5-1-(j), pre-facto, on admission and graduation rates of student athletes at the University of Michigan by answering two questions: (a) Does the SAT predict equally well for blacks and nonblacks? and (b) Does limiting admissions have an effect on grade point average (GPA) and on graduation rates? Subjects comprised all grant-in-aid football players entering the program from 1974–1983; the measures were SAT verbal and math scores (SATSUM), high school grade point average (HSGPA), and first semester college grade point average (CGPA). SAT scores were unrelated to CGPA for black athletes and were weakly related for nonblacks; HSGPA alone predicts CGPA. SATSUM of 700 would have resulted in nonadmission of 60% of blacks (of whom 86% actually succeeded). Graduation rates would have been affected similarly. Limiting admission had no positive effect on GPAs or graduation but a severe negative effect due to nonadmission of blacks.

Key words: student-athletes, aptitude tests, blacks, NCAA, college admission and graduation.

Because academic institutions are the primary gatekeepers of careers in professional sports, gifted high school athletes are drawn to colleges with strong sports programs. College sports programs, in turn, recruit such athletes to generate both income and alumni support. Therefore, college sports programs and college athletes engage in a mutually exploitive relationship. Despite the numerous advantages of this arrangement, one disadvantage, the potential victimization of student-athletes, has long been of concern to both the National Collegiate Athletic Association (NCAA) and numerous critics (Underwood, 1980; Perkins, 1983; Edwards, 1984). Since 1906, the NCAA has modified its rules in a number of ways to insure student-athletes a sound education (Toner, 1984). Its most recent attempt, Bylaw 5-1-(j), was adopted in 1984 and has been a subject of some debate.

Briefly, Bylaw 5-1-(j) states that eligibility for freshman participation in sports in the 278 schools of the NCAA's Division I shall be contingent upon a high school grade point average (HSGPA) of 2.00 in defined courses in addition to a Scholastic Aptitude Test (SAT)—combined verbal (v) and mathematics (m)—score (SATSUM) of 700 or better or a score of 15 on the American College Testing Program

(ACT). A league rule, maintenance of a college GPA (CGPA) of 1.6 determining eligibility to participate, would remain in effect.

Pre-facto estimates of the impact of Bylaw 5-1-(j) on admissions and graduation rates of athletes, both blacks and nonblacks, have been determined by Klitgaard (1983, 1984) and by Advanced Technology (1984) under contract to the NCAA. Both authors agree that Bylaw 5-1-(j), if it had been in effect in 1976, would have disqualified nearly 60% of previous, college-admissible black athletes compared with about 15% of non-black athletes, primarily due to the SAT cutting score. Furthermore, among those who would have been disqualified had the requirement been in effect in 1976, some two thirds of blacks actually graduated from college while one third of "disqualified" nonblacks actually graduated. Overall, then, *pre-facto* studies indicate that, in its present form, Bylaw 5-1-(j) would be grossly inequitable to black athletes because it overpredicts failure.

A number of alternative plans based upon HSGPA, and SAT (or ACT) scores have been evaluated by these authors, and all appear likely to founder on the inequity problem—including Klitgaard's "PRED 200" proposal, 1984, an index combining HSGPA and SAT-SUM. (See also Advanced Technology, 1984, p. 17–20).

The NCAA Governing Board is in a quandary: A policy is required which will protect potential student-athletes without excluding worthy candidates from the grants-in-aid which make a college education possible. (It is commonly, though perhaps incorrectly, assumed that coaches will not recommend grant-in-aid for athletes who would be ineligible to practice or to play in the freshman year.)

A solution to the policy problem may turn on tests of two common but questionable assumptions.

1. Academic aptitude tests are equally valid predictors of academic success for athletes and nonathletes, for black athletes and nonblack athletes, and for black athletes and nonblack, nonathletes.

Numerous writers (e.g., Edwards, 1984) apparently assume that "separate standards" for blacks mean "lower standards." It may well be that SAT scores seriously underpredict the academic success of athletes, both blacks and nonblacks, and are, therefore, of questionable validity as predictors and, therefore, as barriers to admission. A recently reported cooperative study by the American Association of Collegiate Registrars and Admissions Officers and The American Council on Education showed that athletes consistently had higher academic success rates than nonathletes matched on several measures available at college entrance (AACRAO, 1984). Similar findings have been reported by others (e.g., Kirchner, 1962; Parsons, 1969). At the least, then, the assumption of equal validity of predictors for various subpopulations of entering freshmen should be evaluated.

2. The best policy for improving the quality of outputs is to limit inputs, in this case, the best policy for improving GPA and graduation rates is to raise admission standards.

There is at least one alternative assumption, that academic achievement can be influenced by improving the education process in colleges. It is understandable that administrators would prefer to manipulate inputs: It is far simpler to change admissions standards than it is to monitor the educative process.

One strategy stemming from the alternative assumption, the provision of academic support programs for entering students, allows administrators to influence student success. Such programs have a long and reasonably successful history of raising student learning skills to ameliorate deficits in instruction (see, e.g., Kirschenbaum & Perri, 1982). Another strategy, also based on the assumption that achievement can be influenced by improving the educative process, is to focus on graduation rates. If the number of allowable grants-in-aid were based on the institution's success in graduating students, the graduation rate would very likely increase. Rather than pressuring the student alone, such a strategy would distribute the pressure for achievement between the student and the institution. Whether or not one agrees with the value of support programs or the usefulness of focusing on graduation rates, the assumption of limiting inputs to improve outputs should be evaluated.

This report provides a limited test of the first assumption—that academic aptitude tests, specifically the SAT, along with HSGPA, are valid predictors of academic success for black and nonblack athletes equally—and it provides data relevant to the second assumption. The test is limited by the nature of the population, several classes of football players at a single institution, The University of Michigan. This university is widely thought to require the same high academic standards for both athletes and nonathletes while accepting students of widely differing academic backgrounds. Therefore, the population provides an opportunity for a stringent test

of the foregoing assumptions. The study differs from those of Klitgaard (1983, 1984), who studied NCAA institutions in the lowest decile of SAT scores.

The following major question were considered:

1. Do aptitude tests, specifically the SAT, predict equally well for blacks and nonblacks?

2. Would raising admission standards, specifically by using an SAT cutoff score of 700, provide a practicable way of improving GPAs and graduation rates?

METHOD

Subjects

The study group for predicting GPAs comprised all grant-in-aid recruits entering the football program in the years 1977 to 1983. The seven classes of recruits varied in number from 25 to 27 with a median of 26 and a total of 183. Blacks totaled 77 (42%), nonblacks 106 (58%), with proportions equally distributed across years. The study group for predicting graduation rates comprised all grant-in-aid recruits from 1974 through 1979 (N = 162).

Measures

High school grade point averages (HSGPA)—not necessarily in core courses only—and rank in the student's high school graduating class (HSR) were obtained from admissions data along with the SAT combined verbal plus mathematics scores (SATSUM). Although not commonly included in studies of this kind, high school rank was added as a potential predictor. First-semester college grade point average (CGPA) and graduation rates were listed by the registrar's office. Race was determined by interviewing the coaching staff.

Table 1

ENTRANCE DATA AND CGPAs OF BLACK AND NONBLACK TENDERED ATHLETES AT THE UNIVERSITY OF MICHIGAN—1977–1983

Group		Measures[a]			
		HSGPA	HSR	SATSUM	CGPA
Black	M[b]	2.46	56.1	708.8	2.12
(n = 77)	SD	.51	23.6	188.7	.58
Nonblack	M	2.79	65.2	882.9	2.44
(n = 106)	SD	.54	20.6	197.5	.60
Both	M	2.65	61.4	810.5	2.30
(n = 183)	SD	.55	22.3	211.6	.61

[a]*HSGPA: High school grade point average, 4-point scale; HSR: High school rank; SATSUM: Scholastic Aptitude Test, vocabulary plus math; CGPA: College grade point average, first semester, 4-point scale.*

[b]*Means used for missing data.*

Procedure

The seven classes of recruits were compared by analysis of variance (ANOVA) using entrance data and first-semester CGPA to evaluate equivalence of groups. Other data procedures consisted of correlation and regression analyses with HSGPA, HSR and SATSUM as predictors of CGPA and graduation rates as dependent variables.

RESULTS

Predicting GPA

Descriptive Data. High school measures, scholastic aptitude scores, and first-semester GPA were used to evaluate the equivalence of recruiting classes over the 7-year period, 1977–1983. Mean HSGPA varied from 2.58 to 2.82 ($F(6, 171) = .87, p>.05$). Mean HSR varied from 56.0 to 71.2 ($F(6, 170) = 1.38$, $p > .05$). Mean SAT total scores varied from 749 to 885 ($F(6,164) = 1.17$, $p>.05$). Because differences across group means were not significant, the group data were combined.

Means and standard deviations for independent variables and for CGPA are shown in Table 1 for the total group and separately by race.

There are differences between blacks and nonblacks at the mean on all variables. The SATSUM differential (708.8 for blacks and 882.9 for nonblacks) should be educationally significant ($F(1,164) = 32.48, p < .0001$). Note also that the mean score for blacks is near the cutting score specified by Bylaw 5-1-(j).

Regression Analysis. Table 2 shows the relationships among the several performance variables separately by race. High school measures for both groups are substantially related to each other (r = .78 to .86), moderately related to SATSUM (r = .49 to .71), and less so but still significantly related to CGPA (r = .35 to .45). Note, however, that the relationship between SATSUM and CGPA varies from .16 ($p > .05$) for blacks to .29 ($p < .01$) for nonblacks.

Table 2

RELATIONSHIPS (r) AMONG SAT SCORES, HIGH SCHOOL AND COLLEGE PERFORMANCE OF BLACK AND NONBLACK TENDERED ATHLETES AT THE UNIVERSITY OF MICHIGAN—1977–1983

Group		HSGPA	HSR	SATSUM	CGPA
Black	HSGPA	—	.78**	.50**	.45**
n = 77)	HSR	.78**	—	.49**	.35*
	SATSUM	.50**	.49**	—	.16
	CGPA	.45*	.35*	.16	—
Nonblack	HSGPA	—	.86**	.71**	.39**
(n = 106)	HSR	.86**	—	.61**	.36**
	SATSUM	.71**	.61**	—	.29
	CGPA	.39**	.36**	.29*	—

*p < .01

**p < .001

The dependent variable, CGPA, was regressed on the following predictors: HSGPA, HSR, and SATSUM. Since mean differences were significant in the subpopulations, blacks and nonblacks, on each of the three predictors, a separate regression analysis was performed for each group.

To find which combination of variables would account for the greatest variance (R^2), CGPA was regressed on all possible combinations of predictors with the condition that any predictor which did not further explain a significant proportion of the variance ($p >$ .05) would be dropped from the equation. After these analyses, a forward selection procedure was used (criterion level for inclusion = .10; maximum level of steps = 6).

Of the possible combinations for blacks, only tow equations were significant, HSGPA (F (1,70) = 18.180, $p <$ .001) and HSR (F(1,70) = 9.68, $p <$ .01). Due to the high relationships among

the three predictors (Table 2), no significant additive relationships were found. For blacks, HSGPA has the strongest predictive power with CGPA (R^2 = .206) with a regression equation of:

$$CGPA = .82243 \pm .52789 \text{ (HSGPA)}$$

Note that SATSUM does not contribute to the power of this prediction. As expected, the regression analysis using the forward selection procedure confirmed these results. For nonblacks, three predictors were significant, HSGPA ($F(1,97) = 17.61, p <$ .001), HSR ($F(1,96)$ = 9.08, $p <$ .002) and SATSUM ($F(1,91)$ = 8.35, $p<$ .01). As with the prior analysis, no additive relationships were found. For nonblacks, then, HSGPA is also the strongest predictor of CGPA (R^2 = .154) with a regression equation of:

$$CGPA = 1.2255 + .43261 \text{ (HSGPA)}$$

Once more, the forward selection procedure confirmed these results. In sum, then, of the possible combinations

Table 3

COMPARATIVE ACCURACY (%) OF THE SAT, PRED 200 AND HSGPA FOR PREDICTING CGPA

		Predictive Accuracy[a]					
		Correct[b]			Wrong		
Group	**Measure**	**+,+**	**–,–**	**Total**	**+,–**	**–,+**	**Total**
Black	SAT	30	10	40	6	54	60
(n = 68)[c]	PRED	49	9	58	7	35	42
	GSGPA	84	0	84	16	0	16
Nonblack	SAT	78	5	83	5	13	18
(n = 93)	PRED	88	3	91	6	3	9
	HSGPA	91	0	91	9	0	9
Both	SAT	57	7	64	5	31	36
(n = 161)	PRED	72	5	77	6	17	23
	HSGPA	88	0	88	1	0	12

[a] *%given based on probation GPA of 1.6*

[b] *+,+ success predicted, was successful; –,– failure (probation) predicted, failed; +,– success predicted, failed; –,+ failure predicted, succeeded.*

[c] *Means differ from Tables 1 and 2 due to missing data.*

of predictors, HSGPA alone is most useful. It is apparent, furthermore, that even this predictor doesn't explain about 80% of the variance in CGPA for blacks, while the unexplained variance for nonblacks is about 85%.

The comparative predictive accuracy of HSGPA and the SAT, based on a cutting score of 1.6 and the SAT total score, can be derived. Klitgaard (1983, 1984) has combined the two into a formula, PRED 200, which allows the student to compensate for either a low high school average or a low SAT score. We have included accuracy data for all three predictors, SAT, HSGPA, and PRED 200, in Table 3. Note that *N* differs between Tables 1 and 2: Any subject with one missing datum was dropped. Four indices, (test prediction, subject achievement), must be evaluated, correct predictions—(+,+; –,–)—and incorrect predictions—(+,–; –,+).

For blacks, the SAT correctly predicts success (+,+) for 30% with PRED 200 correctly predicting success for 49% and HSGPA correct for 84%. The measures correctly predict failure (–,–) for 10% (SAT), 9% (PRED 200), and 0% (HSGPA). Of the incorrect predictions, predicting success for those who fail (+,–) shows HSGPA to be less effective than the SAT predictors, 16% compared with 6% (SAT) and 7% (PRED 200). But note the SAT overpredicts failure (–,+) by 54% and PRED 200 by 35%, while HSGPA does not overpredict failure at all (0%). In other words, to reduce the chance of admitting unsuccessful students from 16% (HSGPA) to 6% (SAT), 54% of potentially successful blacks must be rejected.

Table 4

GRADUATION OF ATHLETES (CUMULATIVE %)—1974–1979

Group	n	Years 4.0	4.5	5.0	6.0	Nongraduates
Black	55	30.0	40.0	50.9	52.7	47.3
Nonblack	86	39.5	51.1	74.4	74.4	25.6
Both	141	36.2	48.8	65.2	65.9	34.1

Table 5

RELATIONSHIP OF PREDICTORS TO COLLEGE GRADUATION OF ATHLETES—1974–1979

Group	n	HSGPA	n	SATSUM
Black	55	.421**	44	.210*
Nonblack	86	.193*	66	.129*
Total	141	.315***	110	.225*

*$p > .05$

**$p < .01$

***$p < .001$

Predictive accuracy for nonblacks was similar for the three indices with a slight edge for the HSGPA (91%) and PRED 200 (91%) over the SAT (83%). For blacks and nonblacks taken together, HSGPA maintains its superiority (88%) over the others (77% and 64%). In sum, then, HSGPA predicts most accurately by avoiding predicting failure for those who actually succeeded and, at the same time, by overpredicting success with only a small error margin.

Predicting Graduation

Descriptive Data. Graduation rates are based upon six recruiting classes, those beginning college in 1974 through 1979, less 21 who transferred or withdrew (13%). By the present date [1986], none of these subjects is still in school. The 13% transfer and withdrawal rate

for athletes compares to 29.9% for the university-wide entering class of 1977 (Nordby, 1983). Of the remaining 141 recruits, 39% were blacks and 61% were nonblacks. Table 4 shows cumulative graduation rates over 4 to 6 years for blacks and nonblacks and for both groups together.

Degree recipients comprise 65.9% of the total. Of the subjects, 34.1% failed to receive a degree within 6 years. Table 4 shows that 52.7% of blacks received degrees while 74.4% of nonblacks finished.

Prediction estimates are shown in Table 5. Briefly, HSGPA predicts graduation rate ($r = .421, p < .01$) about as well as it predicts GPA for blacks. For nonblacks, HSGPA does not predict graduation rate ($r = .193, p > .05$). SATSUM coefficients are .210 ($p > .05$) for blacks and .129 ($p > .05$) for nonblacks.

"Turning professional" was also investigated. Of those attending from 1974 to 1979, 28% became professional athletes, 35.2% of blacks and 23.3% of nonblacks. Among blacks, 42.1% of those turning professional have their degrees; if not professional, 57.1% have degrees. Among nonblacks, analogous data are 75% and 74%.

DISCUSSION

Two primary question relevant to predicting academic success were raised:

1. Do aptitude tests, specifically the SAT, predict equally well for black and nonblack athletes?

2. Would limiting admission standards, specifically, by using an SAT cutoff score of 700, provide a practicable way of improving GPAs and graduation rates?

We have assumed that SAT must account for variance in CGPA beyond that accounted for by HSGPA. We have defined athletes as football recruits because the NCAA's Bylaw 5-1-(j) seems aimed primarily at this group. Finally, we have carried out a *pre-facto* analysis on appropriate data for only one institution, The University of Michigan. From this analysis, we hope to be able to provide information relevant to the policy question, "Can exploitation of student athletes be reduced by implementing Bylaw 5-1-(j)?"

The data analysis shows that blacks and nonblacks differ substantially in HSGPA (2.46 vs. 2.79), in SATSUM scores (709 vs. 883), and in CGPA (2.12 vs. 2.44). It also shows that the SAT is unrelated to CGPA for the blacks in this population ($r = .29, p = .01$). Furthermore, regression analyses demonstrate that the SAT adds nothing to prediction equations for either group; that is, it

accounts for no variance beyond that accounted for by high school grades. In fact, although HSGPA is predictive of CGPA, it accounts for only some 20% of variance in CGPA for blacks and 15% for nonblacks.

The attempt to improve academic achievement by limiting admission to students with an SATSUM of 700 would have resulted in rejection of 60% of blacks and 18% of nonblacks. Analogous data reported by Klitgaard for the lowest decile of schools (1984, p. 4) are 56% and 14%. More serious, of 43 blacks predicted to fail, 37 (86%) actually succeeded. Among nonblacks, of 17 predicted to fail, 12 (70%) succeeded.

While PRED 200 is somewhat more effective than the SAT alone, it remains inferior to HSGPA alone.

In answer to our first question as to whether the SAT predicts equally well for blacks and nonblacks, it must be concluded that it fails to predict academic success for blacks and would manage to bar a substantial proportion of potentially successful blacks from college. But because it would bar almost an equal proportion of potentially successfully nonblacks (70% for blacks vs. 86% for nonblacks), we must conclude that the SAT does predict equally well, that is, poorly, for both groups. It should also be noted that for the SAT, membership in the subgroup "athlete" appears to be more relevant than membership in either ethnic group.

The graduation rate for blacks is predicted about as well by high school GPA as is college GPA ($r = .421, p < .01$) but HSGPA does not predict graduation rate for nonblacks ($r = .193, p > .05$). For the total group, the SAT correlates to a small extent with graduation rate ($r = .225, p > .05$), accounting for about 5% of the variance.

It is of some interest that graduation for nonblacks (74.4%) is superior to that of blacks (52.7%) and that blacks who become professional athletes have a lesser tendency to complete the degree (42.1%) than those who remain amateurs (57.1%). These data may be compared with university-wide data reported by Nordby (1983). Of all nonblacks matriculating during the years 1975–1977, the 5-year graduation rate was 67.7%; for blacks, it was 43.4%. This 8–10% superiority in the graduation rates of both black and nonblack athletes is congruent with the findings of the AACRAD report (1984) and contradicts the stereotype of "the black dumb jock" (Edwards, 1984).

The answer to our second question as to whether raising admission standards is the best way to improve academic performance appears to be that limiting admission to applicants with SAT scores above 700 would have no noticeable positive effect on either GPAs or graduation rates. It would deny entrance to many blacks. Although that group does have a lower completion rate than nonblacks, there is no guarantee that the excluded blacks would be those who fail; first, 86% of those who would have been denied entrance actually succeeded in terms of GPA, and, second, the SAT correlates with graduation rate to the extent of only $r = .210$ ($p > .05$). We conclude that efforts to influence academic success in terms of GPA and degree completion should be made through variables other than admission standards.

We can only speculate what those variables might be. They might include instructional effectiveness, the provision of a strong academic support program, attitudinal variables (such as the apparent absence of need for a degree among those who expect to become professional athletes), and what might be called "maturity," the ability to withstand the many distractions of college life. These variables are subject to modification after the student reaches campus.

IMPLICATIONS

For the University of Michigan and similar NCAA Division I schools with high academic standards, less than 20% of the variance in academic success is attributable to admissions criteria. That amount can be achieved by accepting only those recruits with HS-GPAs of 2.0 or above. The causes of the remaining 80% of the variance in academic success is yet to be identified. Certainly the most obvious place to begin the search is among those variables intrinsic to college life. Perhaps for athletes as well as for politicians, "the office makes the man."

Our sociology peers must raise an eyebrow at these predicted effects of Bylaw 5-1-(j). Since its implementation would apparently deny admission to a large proportion of black athletes who could succeed in college if given a chance, the question must be asked if the proposition's intent is to exclude black athletes from college. Perhaps more important, one might hope that this kind of data, if replicated, would still the clamor of those writers and media commentators who insist that we do no service to black athletes by admitting them to college.

Finally, our findings raise further questions about the assumptions with which we introduced this study. First, while aptitude measures may be valid for total groups (such as all those who apply for college admission), it should not be assumed that they are equally valid for all subgroups. Second, the common administrative strategy of attempting to improve outputs by limiting inputs appears to be inappropriate when applied to college admissions. More than that, it wastes talent. The focus for improving outputs may well turn out to be the educational process as it occurs on the college campus.

CONCLUSIONS

Within the limitations of the single institution studied and the focus on football recruits only, the following conclusions appear justified:

1. Bylaw 5-1-(j) would fail to correct the problem of student exploitation and would have serious negative consequences for black athletes.

2. For athletes, high school grade point average is the single best predictor of college success among predictors commonly used and is not improved by adding an aptitude measure.

3. Contrary to the common stereotype of "dumb jocks," student-athletes graduate from the University of Michigan at a rate nearly 10% higher than that of their peers.

4. Attempts to improve the academic success of college athletes should focus on variables of campus life.

REFERENCES

Advanced Technology (1984). *Study of freshman eligibility standards: Public Report*. Retson, VA: Advanced Technology, Inc.

American Association of Collegiate Registrars and Admissions Officers (1984). *Athletes and academics in the freshman year: A study of the academic effects of freshman participation in varsity athletics*. Washington, D.C.: U.S. Government Printing Office.

Edwards, H. (1984). The black "dumb jock": An American sports tragedy. *The College Board Review, 131* 8–13.

Kirchner, R.J. (1962). *Participation in athletics and its effects on academic success at Central Michigan University*. Unpublished doctoral dissertation, Michigan State University, East Lansing.

Kirschenbaum, D., & Perri, M. (1982). Improving academic performance in adults: A review of recent research. *Journal of Counseling Psychology, 29* (1), 76–94.

Klitgaard, R.E. (1983). Strengthening academic standards in college athletics. Unpublished manuscript, Harvard University, John F. Kennedy School of Government, Cambridge.

Klitgaard, R.E. (1984). Possible improvements on Proposition 48. Unpublished manuscript, Harvard University, John F. Kennedy School of Government, Cambridge.

Nordby, V.B. (1983). *Minority students at the University of Michigan, 1982–1983*. East Lansing: University of Michigan, Office of Affirmative Action Programs (Report to the Regents).

Parsons, T.W. (1969). *A descriptive analysis of the achievement level realized by grant-in-aid athletes as compared to nonathletes at The Ohio State University*. Unpublished doctoral dissertation, The Ohio State University, Columbus.

Perkins, H.D. (1983). Higher academic standards for athletes do not discriminate against blacks. *Chronicle of Higher Education, 27,* 88.

Toner, J.L. (1984). A statement of NCAA policy and intentions regarding Proposal 48. *The College Board Review, 131,* 13–15.

Underwood, J. (1980, May 19). Writing on the wall. *Sports Illustrated,* 36–72.

Submitted: September 26, 1986
Accepted: November 13, 1986

Chapter 7

Listening, Note-Taking, and Critical-Thinking Strategies

SELF–ASSESSMENT

Place a check mark by the statements that are true of you.

_____ I believe most lectures can be viewed as a series of questions and answers.

_____ I can use lecture notes for exam preparation.

_____ As I sit in a lecture, I think about what questions the instructor is trying to answer.

_____ As I listen to instructors lecture and talk, I think about whether I disagree or agree with what they are saying.

_____ I try to take lecture notes that are well organized and make sense.

_____ As I review my lecture, I pretend I am the instructor and try to develop a few good questions that could be asked about the lecture.

_____ When I see instructors lecturing from notes or books, I recognize that this is essentially information that will be turned into questions and answers.

_____ I recognize that trying to memorize notes is an inefficient strategy of learning.

_____ I like to share my notes with other students to see if I am on the right track.

_____ I regularly turn my notes into questions and answers, which I use to prepare for tests.

_____ I would consider showing my notes to my instructor to see whether he or she thinks I am grasping the important information.

ACTIONS THAT LEAD TO EFFECTIVE LEARNING

If you are to think critically about information, you have to have information to think about. This rather obvious statement presents a big problem many new college students face.

If you ask the college freshmen of the '90s if they took good notes in their high school classes, a typical answer is, "I hardly ever took notes in high school!" In contrast, if you ask college instructors what they expect students to do in their courses, most will tell you, "Students need to participate in class and take good notes!" Do you see why so many college freshmen have a hard time adjusting to their college classes?

College instructors are amazed that such a great percentage of new students aren't used to listening critically and taking notes. What bothers instructors even more is that some freshman students have poor class attendance. We have found that many students who aren't used to taking notes or who don't have good listening skills can quickly learn a set of listening and note-taking strategies that make their classes more enjoyable and meaningful. The result is that they are less likely to miss class.

In this chapter we want to reemphasize that successful critical-thinking, listening, and note-taking strategies all revolve around developing good questions and answers. Whether you are attending a business meeting, a student organization meeting, or a class, if you are not focusing on getting answers to questions, then you are likely to report problems. Put a check mark next to the following problems that apply to you.

_____I OFTEN ASK MYSELF, "WHAT AM I GETTING OUT OF THIS MEETING?"

_____I CAN'T SEEM TO CONCENTRATE ON WHAT IS GOING ON.

_____I FEEL TIRED OR SLEEPY, EVEN THOUGH I AM WELL RESTED.

_____I FIND THAT WHILE OTHER PEOPLE ARE WRITING THINGS DOWN, I AM NOT WRITING MUCH.

_____MY NOTES DON'T MAKE MUCH SENSE IN COMPARISON TO THOSE OF OTHER STUDENTS.

_____I KEEP WONDERING WHEN THE NEXT CLASS OR MEETING WILL BE OVER.

_____I FIND MYSELF SKIPPING CLASSES OR MEETINGS, THINKING THAT I WON'T BE MISSING MUCH.

_____WHEN OTHERS ARE LISTENING ATTENTIVELY, I WONDER WHAT IS KEEPING THEIR INTEREST.

Many students tell us that these thoughts are typical of those that pass through their minds before, during, and after classes. Since these are common problems, let's focus on some useful thinking, listening, and note-taking strategies that will make your life a bit more pleasant and give you answers to the important questions you need to ask. All of these require one significant behavior on your part: attending class regularly. When you attend class, you engage in active learning.

ATTEND CLASS

Attending class is such an obviously useful thing to do that we're almost embarrassed to have to mention it. Yet, a research study reported by H. C. Lindgren found that an important relationship exists between attending class and the grades received. A comparison of grade point averages and class attendance showed the following percentages:

CLASS ATTENDANCE

	STUDENTS WITH B AVERAGE OR HIGHER	STUDENTS WITH C– AVERAGE OR LOWER
Always or almost always present	85%	48%
Sometimes absent	8	7
Often absent	7	45

The percentages in the table suggest that attending class always or almost always helps maximize your chances of success. The percentages also indicate that the student who is often absent probably will receive low grades.

SCOPE OUT WHAT YOUR INSTRUCTOR WANTS

Use the First Lecture

Successful students actively determine the requirements for each course. During the first class sessions, they typically find out answers to key questions. Place a check mark in front of the following questions that you typically ask during the first few days of class.

_____ WHICH CHAPTERS IN THE TEXTBOOK WILL BE COVERED?

_____ WHAT OTHER WORK WILL BE REQUIRED?

_____ WHEN WILL THE EXAMS BE GIVEN?

_____ WHAT MATERIAL WILL EACH EXAM COVER?

_____ WHAT TYPES OF QUESTIONS WILL BE ON THE EXAMS—ESSAY, MULTIPLE CHOICE, TRUE/FALSE?

_____ WHEN WILL WORK BE DUE?

_____ HOW WILL THE WORK BE EVALUATED?

_____ HOW WILL GRADING IN THE COURSE BE DETERMINED?

_____ DOES THE INSTRUCTOR HAVE AN OUTLINE OF THE MOST IMPORTANT TERMS AND CONCEPTS TO BE COVERED?

_____ WHAT DOES THE INSTRUCTOR WANT EACH STUDENT TO KNOW BY THE END OF THE COURSE?

_____ SHOULD TEXTBOOK CHAPTERS BE READ BEFORE LECTURES?

These questions are a starting point. Others will occur as you take the course.

Remember, be cautious about making instructors feel you are cross-examining them. Be assertive but *tactful*. If an instructor is not prepared to answer all these questions, back off. Try to find out when the information may be available. In general, you will find that instructors enjoy answering questions about what they believe is most valuable in their courses. A few instructors may be poorly prepared, however, and could become defensive if pressed too hard.

Some instructors will have the answers to most of these questions on written handouts, so read these first before asking questions. If you don't receive a handout, be sure to write everything down in your notebook.

TAKE LECTURE NOTES

By writing down what the instructor says in lectures, you are helping yourself become an active listener. You also are being realistic about the nature of human memory. Human beings quickly forget most of what they hear, no matter how much they would like to remember. Several days after hearing a lecture, most students can at best recall only about 10% of what was said. So, unless you tape-record the lectures or alternate note taking with a friend, you need to take notes at every lecture.

Some students don't take notes. They may be experimenting to see whether or not they can get by without note taking. These students may have reasons for wanting everyone to know they are not involved in the course. They may be trying to impress you with how smart they are. At any rate, if you ask a student who doesn't take notes to fill you in on something the instructor said last week, you quickly will learn for yourself how important note taking is for accurate remembering.

Use Lecture Notes as a Source for Exam Questions and Answers

You'll give yourself a tremendous advantage if you can think of your instructor's lectures as sessions that provide answers to important questions. When you actively use your notes to quiz yourself on critical questions that are likely to appear on your exams, you'll walk into your exams feeling really confident and well prepared.

Reduce Your Test-Taking Anxiety

Quizzing yourself over the questions you develop from your notes will dramatically reduce your test-taking anxiety. It only makes sense that if you have practiced the same behavior you will be tested on, answering questions, then you have less reason to be nervous.

Remember, use your notes to learn more and do better on your exams. If you remember the formula Notes = Exam Questions and Answers, you'll learn a lot, do well on your exams, feel less stress before and during exams, and live happily ever after.

Think Critically About Your Lecture Notes

Think of your lectures as textbook chapters. Just like a chapter, each lecture usually has a main theme and makes several important points. If you listen for the main points of each lecture, they will be easier to hear.

During lectures, most instructors answer several questions rather thoroughly. If your instructor only alludes to an answer, you'll have to turn to outside sources to get the information you need.

Your job during the lecture is to record the most important information given. Don't restrict your note taking to only the instructor's statements. Be alert to classroom discussions when the instructor asks students questions. After the lecture, use study time to develop questions answered by information in your notes.

Tips on Taking Notes

Keep a notebook for each course. Write your name, address, and phone number in each notebook. Use large pages for taking notes, and put the notes from each class session on separate pages. Write the date on each day's class notes.

Use an outline form whenever possible. The most commonly used outline form is this:

I. (Roman numerals for major topics)

    A. (Capital letters for major subgroups)

        1. (Numbers for supporting examples, people, points)

        2.

    B.

        1.

            a. (Lowercase letters for supporting details)

            b.

            c.

        2.

        3.

We encourage you to take lecture notes in an outline form. This habit will help you focus on listening for and recording main points that you can turn into questions and answers. We suggest the outline form because it helps create an orderliness to information that might otherwise appear confusing. Our chief concern is that you record all the information you need to develop good questions and answers. Larry Smith's work with thousands of students has proven that the following steps will help ensure that you listen for and record the main points of every lecture.

1.   Take notes in a spiral notebook, using a separate notebook for each course. Write your lecture notes on the right-hand page. Leave a wide margin on the left of this page for writing in probable test questions. Leave the left-hand page blank. Later you will use the back of each preceding left-hand page to integrate reading, lecture, and other notes while you are studying.

   Note: You will want to consider an important point about integrating your lecture and reading notes. You often will find yourself reading a book that presents information relevant to a topic covered in your lecture notes. You may say to yourself, "I ought to combine some of this information from the book with my lecture notes." The problem is that you don't really want to stop reading to do this. Here is a simple solution. You just need to write the page number that covers the important material from the book you're reading on the right-hand margin of the page in your lecture notes where similar information is covered. Later on, when you review your notes, you can flip open the textbook to the page you have noted. You then can integrate the information from your text with your notes.

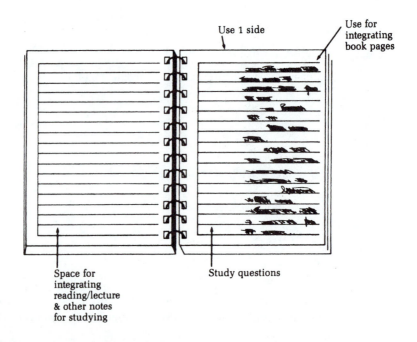

Use 1 side

Use for integrating book pages

Space for integrating reading/lecture & other notes for studying

Study questions

2.   Write down the major ideas and statements in the lecture. Don't try to write down every word, just key phrases and ideas. Underline points your instructor emphasizes.

3.   After the lecture, fill in missing ideas and key words and phrases. Underline headings that are of major significance. You also may wish to compare your notes with a friend's to see what you may have missed.

4.   After each lecture, take several minutes to turn your notes into questions. The main theme and subtopics can be turned into questions. Each lecture usually will supply three to seven good exam questions. The questions should be written in the left-hand margin.

5.   At least once a week, review the questions you have asked. Pretend you are taking a test. Give yourself an oral quiz, or, even better, practice by taking a written quiz. Then compare your answers with those given in your notes or textbook.

Remember: This procedure will help you make something meaningful out of lectures that often leave you in a quandary. If you are thinking critically, you'll attend each lecture with a purpose. You'll be looking for questions and their answers. If you leave each lecture with several questions and answers, you should be pleased. They're likely to be on your next test!

An Example of Note Taking

An example of notes taken at an introductory psychology lecture follows. The topic was operant conditioning.

Intro. Psych—Oct. 26
Notes

I. Topic: Operant Conditioning

    A. B. F. Skinner conducted pioneering research

        1. worked with rats and pigeons

        2. designed special cages—"Skinner boxes"

        3. believes "Behavior is determined by its consequences"

    B. Basis for operant conditioning

    (also called instrumental learning)

        1. a voluntary behavior is followed by a reinforcer—called a reward because some rewards do not act as reinforcers

        2. reinforcement increases the probability that a behavior will be repeated

        3. reinforcement variables:

            a. amount

b. schedule

1. 100% continuous

2. fixed-ratio and fixed-interval

3. variable-ratio and variable-interval

4. punishment can temporarily suppress behavior but seldom eliminates it

5. negative reinforcement—behavior increases when unpleasant stimulus removed

6. extinction of behavior

   a. from withdrawal of reinforcer

   b. after time lapse reappearance called spontaneous recovery

C. Application of principles

1. Behavior modification program

   a. terminal response or goal stated—must be observable and measurable

   b. current level of desired behavior observed—called baseline

   c. any baseline behavior directed toward the terminal goal is reinforced: all other behaviors ignored

   d. each small step is reinforced—is called:

1. shaping

2. method of successive approximations

3. tracking positives

4. Uses with humans—contingency management

   a. programs for brain-damaged children

   b. improve academic performance

   c. programs for psychiatric patients

   d. improve performance in business

Now that you've studied the example and read through the five steps for note taking, you're ready to apply what you have learned. Follow Steps 1–4 for taking notes in your next class. Discover how complete and efficient your learning can be while you also are becoming quickly ready for tests. Show several classmates what you are doing, and tell them what it feels like to use this method.

SUCCESSFUL LISTENING AND NOTE TAKING

Much discussion occurs these days about what good critical thinkers do as they learn. What many people wonder is, "How, when I am listening to someone, can I learn the most?" or "How, as I read information, do I learn the most?"

To process information so that you remember it better, you need strategies. Chapter 6 discussed critical-thinking and reading strategies. Chapter 7 has focused on note taking and listening strategies. Students with excellent listening and note-taking skills concentrate on asking and answering questions. As you sit in a meeting or class, you want to stay mentally alert. To do so you need to be an active learner. Listening for questions and answers will keep you alert and active.

Proficient learners also use several other cognitive or mental strategies in lectures and meetings to learn more and prevent boredom. Many students tell us it is difficult to sit in a classroom with 250 other students taking notes. They sometimes find themselves bored or distracted. They have a hard time staying mentally active.

Think about why you like small classes. You carry on conversations with your instructor and other students. You ask questions. Other students ask questions. The instructor asks questions. A continual dialogue occurs. In larger classes dialogue is impossible. It is a one-way conversation.

Not everybody can attend a small college with small classes. Even at small colleges, students attend large lectures. But successful learners find ways to keep themselves mentally stimulated in these large courses. They talk to themselves. Not aloud, but inside their head.

Researchers who interviewed successful learners tell us some interesting and valuable characteristics of students who carry out these mental dialogues in class. The students are constantly posing questions to themselves during the lectures. They make such comments as the following:

"What is the instructor trying to say?"

"How is she going to answer that question?"

"What kind of example can he give to prove that point?"

"Why would she expect us to believe that?"

"So that's what he's getting at!"

"Now that is a possible test question!"

"I see how that example relates to the question he raised earlier."

"I don't agree with the position he is taking."

"That example is biased. I could give several examples that prove the opposite point!"

"Now there is something I agree with."

Successful learners try to carry on conversations with the instructor and themselves. These conversations help highlight important points. Whether you agree or disagree with the instructor, you want to keep yourself alert to the points he or she is trying to make.

It is easy to remember ideas that conflict or agree with your own. These ideas have an emotional appeal. *Emotion* may be the key word. Information surrounded by emotion tends to be remembered. Whether it is positive or negative, emotion stimulates memory.

Think about sitting in a lecture with a friend. The speaker says something that really upsets you. If you were alone, you might say something to yourself such as "What a fool!" If you are next to a friend, you might whisper to her, "Can you believe he said that?" It is fun to go to a lecture with someone you like because you can comment to each other, give each other funny looks, and after the lecture you can talk about what you heard.

If you are attending a lecture by yourself, you can't talk with someone else during the lecture (without risking annoyance), but you sure can carry on a mental dialogue with the instructor. After the lecture you can talk to other students about what they heard. You can ask them about their feelings regarding what the instructor said. And, once again, you can look at your notes and make them more useful by turning them into questions and answers.

The key characteristic of these critical-thinking, listening, and note-taking strategies is that they require you to be active and involved. Talking to yourself in a lecture will keep you active. Talking with other people after the lecture will make you even more active.

COMBINING QUESTIONS FROM BOOKS AND NOTES

We discussed the strategies for reading books to gather questions and answers in Chapter 6. In this chapter, we have talked about listening and taking lecture notes to gather even more questions and answers. These questions and answers will be the bulk of what you use to prepare for tests. But you should consider a few other sources that will give you an even more complete set of questions and answers. Then you will be ready to prepare for your tests.

TEXTBOOKS

One of the most common behaviors of good students is the habit of taking notes from chapters. But the note taking of many students often doesn't make sense. The object of taking notes from a chapter is not to copy down every important point in a chapter. It is not to take a highlighter and highlight every main piece of information in a chapter. The object of taking notes is to create good questions and answers.

We often see in a student's book page after page of paragraphs that have been highlighted with yellow marker. If you ask the student the value of marking up the book, he or she will tell you, "I have marked things I want to remember." If you ask how the student will practice remembering this information, he or she will answer, "I will review the chapter and try to memorize everything I have marked." Now that doesn't sound very useful. Who can memorize everything marked in a book?

So let's forget about spending our time highlighting books and trying to copy down every important point. Let's use the SQ4R strategy of taking notes to develop questions and answers from books.

As you'll remember from Chapter 6, you put yourself at a great advantage when you read and answer the questions that precede or follow the chapter text. Such questions are included by authors because they believe students should be able to answer them after reading the chapter.

Many instructors take their test questions directly from questions in the textbook. Surprisingly, many students never look at these questions. They seem to feel that no instructor could be so stupid as to use questions similar to those found in the chapter.

Textbook authors usually try to help students, not trick them! If you are not in the habit of answering chapter questions, we recommend you use them as the starting point in your effort to organize a good set of questions and answers.

OLD EXAMS

Students often are made to feel guilty when they admit to having looked over past exams. The implication is that if you have looked over old exams, you have been cheating. Our answer to this is, bunk! Old exams tell you what an instructor thinks is important information you should be responsible for knowing.

Looking at old exams doesn't guarantee that you'll know exactly what your exam questions will be. Instructors change their lectures, textbooks, films, guest speakers, and even their opinions once in a while. Consequently, exams change from semester to semester.

Nevertheless, by looking at old exams, you may answer the following important questions:

1. Does the instructor have some favorite questions he or she asks every year?

2. Do test questions appear to be taken from material similar to what you are studying?

3. Do test questions come primarily from lecture notes or from a variety of sources?

4. What types of questions does the instructor prefer? Multiple choice, short answer, true/false, essay?

5. On which content areas does the instructor place the most emphasis?

These questions should help you see the value of reading and taking notes in the question/answer format. No one can guarantee the instructor will take most of the questions from the same source he or she used in years past. Yet it is surprising how similar the questions are from year to year regardless of the textbooks instructors use. They often choose new textbooks that give better answers to the same questions they have been asking for many years.

Equally important, few instructors make drastic changes in their course notes from semester to semester. Instead, instructors usually update notes. The questions you develop from course notes, textbooks, and other sources, combined with old exam questions, will be invaluable in your exam preparation.

STUDENT STUDY GUIDES

Student study guides that accompany many of your textbooks are excellent sources of exam questions. They are designed to show you what students using the textbook should know. Study guides often contain true/false, multiple-choice, fill-in, short-essay questions, and other exercises. Even if your exam is likely to contain questions that differ in style from questions found in the study guide, the questions in the guide are still extremely valuable.

You only have to relate the answers to the guide's questions to the questions likely to be found on your next exam. Study guides are designed to teach you important concepts and save you time. The time you save can be used for other important activities, such as watching television or taking a nap.

Note: The publisher of your textbook may have a study guide available even if your instructor does not require its use. Check this out—especially for introductory textbooks. Ask your instructor. If a study guide exists, you can purchase it through the bookstore or directly from the publisher. Sales figures from textbook publishers show that 7 out of 10 students using textbooks do not purchase and use the accompanying study guides. Yet, research has shown that students who use study guides tend to learn more and earn better grades than students who don't use the guides.

DISCUSSION GROUPS AND FRIENDS

Some of your best sources of test questions, yet often the most overlooked, are friends and fellow students. By talking with other students enrolled in the course or with students who have been enrolled in past semesters, you can judge the types of questions and answers you should be looking for. These students also can tell you where you should spend less time.

Many students believe it's difficult to organize formal study groups. Some students simply prefer to work on their own. This latter strategy can be self-defeating. By organizing the questions and answers from a variety of sources, you are in an excellent position to compare yours with those of fellow students.

Compare this process to the pastime of trading cards, collecting as many cards as you can and simply trading off your extras to build an even stronger set. Similarly, in a discussion group you find out what questions other students feel are important. You compare your answers to theirs to ensure that you haven't overlooked important information. Everyone comes out stronger. Everyone is better prepared to ask and answer intelligent questions.

By studying in a group or with one other person, you will help to ensure that you benefit in some important ways. Which of the following do you think would be a benefit to you of working with other people? Check off all that apply.

_____ I WOULD STRUCTURE A SITUATION WHERE OTHER PEOPLE ENCOUR-
AGED ME TO DEVELOP STUDY HABITS RECOMMENDED IN *STUDENT
SUCCESS.*

_____ I WOULD ASK AND ANSWER MORE QUESTIONS THAT ARE IMPORTANT
AND LIKELY TO BE FOUND ON MY EXAMS.

_____ I WOULD LEARN OF QUESTIONS I HADN'T PREDICTED.

_____ I WOULD REFINE MY ANSWERS WITH ADDITIONAL INFORMATION
SUPPLIED BY OTHER STUDENTS.

_____ I WOULD CREATE LONGER, MORE COMPLETE PRACTICE TESTS.

_____ I WOULD TAKE MORE PRACTICE TESTS.

_____ I WOULD DEVELOP A MORE EFFICIENT AND EFFECTIVE PROCESS FOR
PREPARING FOR EXAMS.

INSTRUCTORS

Your instructor is the best source of information on forthcoming tests. Many students find it difficult to ask instructors what the instructors believe is important. As we suggested earlier, most instructors are happy to tell you what they think is important. Give them a chance: Ask them!

Ask your instructors, "Could you make some suggestions about the areas we should concentrate our studying on?" or "What particular topics do you feel we should devote more time to than others?"

Whatever you do, don't ask, "What areas do you feel are unimportant?" or "Which of these chapters should we spend less time on, considering all that we have to study for this test?" If you ask such questions, the instructors may be so peeved they will assign the encyclopedia. Most instructors believe that everything they teach is important.

When you try to determine what is likely to be on exams, your goal is simply to encourage your instructors to narrow down all the important information they have told you to a precise statement of what your exam will cover and in what form. If you are pleasant and thank your instructors for their help, you'll be way ahead of the game. You even may find out the exact form of the exam and which questions are most important.

THE RESULT

Predicting questions and answers is the most useful critical-thinking strategy we have found to assist you to learn the important concepts covered in your courses.

Equally important, it will help you do well on your exams with much greater ease. If you have followed our suggestions, you will have collected exam questions from the following sources:

- Your textbook chapters
- Lists of chapter objectives
- Your lecture notes
- Old exams
- Lists of questions in your textbooks
- Lists of questions in student study guides
- Discussion groups and friends
- Your instructors

Once you have collected a good set of test questions, you will be better prepared to follow through with the strategies we suggest in Chapter 9 on preparing for and taking tests.

Is the purpose of education to learn how to answer instructors' questions and do well on tests?

Good question. The conflict between learning what you are curious about versus learning to do well on tests is an old dilemma. Fortunately, it is not an either/or choice. In most cases ways to accommodate the interests of both the learner and the instructor exist.

If you want to understand the experts and even progress beyond them, it is important to be able to ask and answer the same questions experts believe are important. If you're realistic, you know you have to meet the requirements of any course. If you learn what your instructor believes is important, you usually will learn a lot. If your instructor has a focus different from what you might choose, that shouldn't be viewed as a problem. You use the strategies we have talked about to learn everything you need or want to learn from the course.

How can developing questions for study help me if I'm afraid of being called on in class?

When you prepare questions and answers and practice answering your questions, you will be less afraid to speak in class. It is natural to be afraid if you are not prepared. Talk to yourself about the answers to questions your instructors are likely to ask in class. Once you have proven to yourself that you know the answers, you will be less fearful about your ability to answer similar questions in class. Language labs and discussion groups are useful places to begin to practice answering questions your instructors might ask in class.

If the fear comes from a general fear of everyone looking at you when you talk, find out what professional counseling, assertiveness workshops, or classes in verbal communications are available on campus. If you ask around, you will find that usually some professional counselors or faculty members are very good at helping shy people become more comfortable speaking in groups.

Is the key to critical thinking the ability to ask and answer important questions?

Thinking critically requires that when reading, listening, and recording information you believe valuable, you need to be focused. Chapters 6 and 7 have helped you see that an active learner is always thinking critically about the information presented to him or her. The world today requires that you read and listen to far more information than any people who have gone before you. To make sense of that information, we are showing you strategies to help you make information more meaningful and understandable. The result will be that you will remember what is important to you much better and far longer.

Now that you know how to improve your learning, let's focus on the area that students love to hate: preparing for and taking tests. We think we can make it much easier for you. Chapter 8 will tell you how.

ACTION REVIEW

Checklist for Successful Studying

Here is a list of guidelines that will help you monitor your studying and your success at using the learning strategies we've described in Chapters 6 and 7. Consider placing this list in a visible location where it can constantly remind you of the study habits that will lead to your success.

_____ I AM USING THE SQ4R STRATEGY OUT OF HABIT FOR LEARNING COURSE MATERIAL.

_____ I SURVEY MY READING FIRST, ASK QUESTIONS, AND THEN READ TO ANSWER QUESTIONS.

_____ I PRACTICE WRITING ANSWERS TO QUESTIONS AND DEVELOPING CHAPTER SUMMARIES.

_____ I DEVELOP QUESTIONS AND ANSWERS FROM LECTURES, TEXTBOOKS, CHAPTER OBJECTIVES AND SUMMARIES, STUDY GUIDES, OLD TESTS, DISCUSSION GROUPS, AND FRIENDS.

_____ I ASK MY INSTRUCTORS QUESTIONS THAT HELP ME DETERMINE HOW I SHOULD STUDY FOR THEIR COURSES.

_____ I KEEP A WEEKLY RECORD OF THE NUMBER OF QUESTIONS AND ANSWERS I DEVELOP FOR EACH CLASS.

_____ I REWARD MYSELF FOR DEVELOPING QUESTIONS AND ANSWERS.

ACTION PROJECT 1

Start Developing Questions and Answers

No better time than now exists to begin developing and answering exam questions! You will find it useful to count the questions and answers you collect from textbooks, old exams, lecture notes, study guides, discussion groups, classmates, and your instructors.

Create a chart that you can put in a highly visible location—if possible, in your regular study area. As you develop your questions and answers for each class, record your progress on your chart. Set goals for the number of questions you want to develop in each course, and reward yourself regularly when you achieve your goals. Show your success group partners what you are accomplishing. Talk about how it feels to use this study method.

ACTION PROJECT 2

Form a Study Group for Each Course You Take

Ask several students taking the same course to meet right after class or at a convenient time. Using your notes, review what was discussed in the lecture to determine what questions from that lecture may appear on the test.

From any lecture you are unlikely to find more than five to seven major questions that could appear on a test. Divide up the questions, and everyone write answers to his or her questions. Each member of the group will use whatever sources of information are necessary to develop what he or she thinks would be a complete answer to the question were it to appear on the exam.

At your next meeting, everyone will distribute copies of the answers to their questions. In addition, each person will take on several new questions from the most recent lecture.

It is important that the group establish criteria for a good answer. Answers should not take hours to produce. Develop answers that are complete and could be easily reproduced during the time allotted on the exam. Some students feel pressured to produce too much to ensure that the other group members will be impressed. Don't get caught in that bind. This activity is designed to teach you how to work as a team, to share responsibility, to learn from one another what makes a good answer, and to help each person save time.

SUCCESS GROUP ACTIVITIES

1.   Talk with one another about how well the SQ4R method is working for each of you. What difficulties do you have making it work? What successes have you had? What can you do to encourage and support one another's efforts to master

this study strategy? Does it help to modify or rename any of the steps? Is it more appealing, for example, to call one step "scan" instead of "survey"?

2.   Discuss the dilemma many students have at some time during college: Do you learn for learning's sake and the enjoyment of acquiring knowledge or for the sake of passing the instructors' tests? What are your thoughts and feelings about this question? Is it a big problem? A minor one? Do you care?

Chapter 8

Preparing for and Passing Tests Successfully

SELF-ASSESSMENT

Place a check mark by the statements that are true of you.

_____ I understand the relationship between making and taking practice tests and doing well on course examinations.

_____ I see the wisdom in always studying as though I am practicing to take a test.

_____ I have learned strategies that improve my test-taking ability.

_____ I understand steps successful students follow to develop and write the answers to essay questions.

_____ I know that developing and taking practice tests reduces nervousness about taking exams.

_____ I can reduce my anxiety during tests and improve my scores by making and taking practice exams.

GUARANTEEING SUCCESS ON TESTS AND REDUCING TEST-TAKING ANXIETY

Have you ever taken an exam that didn't require you to answer questions? Probably not. Some exams in music, physical education, art, and other classes where you perform are exceptions, of course. In most cases, however, your grades are determined by your answers to questions.

Your learning and success in college are dependent on an important skill. You have to be able to answer questions your instructors pose in class and on exams. That's why we've said that every time you read your course notes or textbooks, you should be looking for potential exam questions.

It makes sense that if you want to do well on your exams, you practice taking exams. You'll use the strategies described in Chapters 6 and 7 to develop exam questions from notes, textbooks, and other sources. You'll then use the strategies in this chapter to prepare for and take tests.

Most students don't prepare for exams by taking practice tests. They prepare for exams by reading and rereading their notes, textbooks, and other information sources. Have you ever had any instructors who asked you to come to an exam and read your notes or textbook to them? Absolutely not! Your instructors ask you to answer questions developed from their lecture notes, your texts, and other sources.

YOUR STRATEGY FOR SUCCESS

You want to develop the habit of creating exams just like the ones you believe your instructors will give you. Ask your friends to quiz you on exams they have made. Developing a realistic means of learning to pass exams is the key to your success. Just as orchestras rehearse for concerts and football teams play practice games, prepare for exams by taking exams. You'll find that when you prepare this way, your anxiety about preparing for and taking tests often will decrease dramatically.

PREPARING FOR TESTS

REVIEWING YOUR QUESTIONS AND ANSWERS

Now that I have collected a good set of questions and answers, how can I make sure I'll do well on the tests?

Periodically, review the questions you have developed to see whether or not you still can answer them. Avoid saying to yourself, "I know the answer to that one." Prove to yourself how brilliant you have become. Orally and in writing, practice answering your questions.

The habit of reviewing is easy to develop. You sit down between and after classes and talk out, think out, or write out answers to questions. Rather than sitting around wondering whether you are doing well in your courses, you prove to yourself that you can answer the future test questions.

QUIZZING YOURSELF

Periodically reviewing your questions and answers is a great habit to develop. The habit of actually quizzing yourself with practice tests is equally beneficial. The strategy focuses on several principles. Check off which of the following principles you regularly observe:

_____ USING THE QUESTIONS I HAVE COLLECTED, I MAKE UP PRACTICE TESTS.

_____ I TAKE PRACTICE TESTS UNDER CONDITIONS AS CLOSE AS POSSIBLE TO THE ACTUAL TEST CONDITIONS I WILL EXPERIENCE.

_____ AFTER I TEST MYSELF, I COMPARE MY ANSWERS WITH THE ANSWERS I DEVELOPED FROM MY TEXTBOOKS, LECTURE NOTES, AND OTHER SOURCES.

Using Your Notes

When you quiz yourself from the questions and answers in your notebook, cover up your answers with a blank sheet of paper. After answering each question orally or in writing, remove the paper and check your original answer to see how accurately you have answered your question. This system allows you to quiz yourself quickly.

Most students like this system because it gives them a central filing system of questions and answers. They don't waste their time fumbling through textbooks they have highlighted and trying to remember everything they have marked. They instead pull out their notebooks of questions and answers and practice answering their questions wherever and whenever they find it convenient.

Answering Math and Science Questions

What you have said about developing questions and answers sounds great for most students, but what about those of us who spend most of our time working problems in math and science? How can this technique help us?

One of the most important insights you can recognize is that success in a particular course is based on solving specific problems, especially in mathematics, chemistry, physics, and other courses with a heavy emphasis on computational and problem-solving skills.

Your reviews for math and science courses should be no different from those for other courses. To succeed, you need to practice working problems as similar as possible to those that will be found on your next exam. By working the sample problems from your lectures and textbook, you should be well prepared to solve the problems on your test.

When you prepare for tests that require problem solving, you want to do exactly that—practice solving problems. It will be especially helpful for you to work with other students in the course. You want to find out what types of problems they believe will be on your exam. Equally important, you want to see the steps they follow when solving the problems.

We can't overemphasize the value of working with other students to exchange problems. Other students will not only help you see what they believe are the important concepts and problems but also will give you an opportunity to see whether they are having the same difficulties as you in solving the problems.

Talking with someone who took the course before you will help you see whether the problems you predict may be on the test are in fact the same types of problems the instructor gave in the past. Looking at old tests is a very valuable strategy. The instructor will not give the exact problems used the past semester, but you will see what types of problems the instructor favors.

Preparing for Language Exams

How about students in foreign language courses? Should we review in the same way?

If you are taking a foreign language class, you have a very discrete set of skills to master. Your strategy for succeeding as much as ever focuses on preparing for tests by practicing answering important questions likely to appear on your next exam.

Language students must maintain basic vocabulary and grammatical skills if they wish to develop more complex language skills. By reviewing these areas, language students assure themselves of continued involvement in the basics that more complex skills are built on.

Your language courses will require you to quiz yourself on a daily basis over the vocabulary and structure of the language you are learning. Your language labs offer an opportunity to practice developing your language skills. Every exercise you complete—whether from your textbook, a workbook, or on tape—will require that you answer a question or demonstrate that you have mastered vocabulary or new language skills.

Although college students consider learning a language one of the most difficult tasks possible, preparing for language exams has one bright side. It involves little, if any, guesswork. What you are expected to know and be able to do are very discrete types of information and skills. Knowing vocabulary is the critical element. Once you have the vocabulary, the task of structuring the language can become second nature.

If one area exists that students can easily design practice tests for, it is the area of language learning. Your language textbooks are loaded with practice exercises, and most have workbooks that accompany them or are built right into the text. The language laboratory is the extra bonus. It is a "test preparation" center. It is where you go to practice answering many of the questions likely to appear on your exams.

MAKING AND TAKING PRACTICE TESTS

Making and taking practice tests will benefit you in many ways. One important benefit is that you practice exactly what is required of you in the testing situation: asking and answering intelligent questions. In addition, your practice tests will help you relax and build your confidence. After successfully passing practice tests, you are less likely to feel tense and uneasy. Taking practice tests is the key to managing your test anxiety. It is natural to feel a little tense about any test you are going to take. But the unnecessary anxiety you may have can be dramatically reduced by building your confidence on practice tests. You should sleep much better knowing you have studied good questions and answers.

Steps for Practice Tests

These eight steps will guide you through the process of making and taking practice tests.

1.   You first estimate the amount of time you'll be given to take your instructor's exam. Then, plan to take your practice test over the same length of time. Taking your tests under realistic time pressure is important. Once you know you can answer a reasonable number of questions in whatever time is allotted, you'll feel more comfortable when you're in the actual testing situation.

2.   Arrange the questions you've been accumulating from chapters, lecture notes, study groups, old exams, and other sources into practice tests.

3.   If you can test yourself with questions in the same format your instructor's test will offer (multiple choice, short essay, and so on), that's fine. But asking and answering questions is the important strategy. So don't get hung up on whether your instructor's test will be multiple choice. It is more critical that you can answer your instructor's questions no matter what the format. If all the questions you have developed from your notes and texts are short-answer questions and your test will be composed of multiple-choice questions, you needn't rewrite your questions to fit into a multiple-choice format. That would be a horrible waste of time.

If old tests are available, that's great. By practicing on old tests, you may feel more comfortable with your instructor's test. Study guides are also useful because guides contain many questions in a variety of formats.

By quizzing yourself on your questions, you will learn the information necessary to do well on your instructor's test, regardless of the format of the questions.

4.   Take your practice tests under conditions as similar as possible to those you'll be tested under. The classroom you'll be tested in is the best place to take practice tests. If it is not available to you, make sure you practice in a room where you won't be bothered.

5.   Try to answer your questions without referring to your textbooks or other information sources.

6.   When attempting to answer questions you need more information for, try to use whatever information you have to formulate a reasonable answer. Pretend you are in a real test and are trying to earn at least partial credit. This strategy forces you to take what you already know and to determine what might be the answer rather than saying, "I just don't know!"

Very few situations really exist in which you "just don't know!" Writing out an answer that makes sense to you, even though you don't remember exactly what was said in the textbook or lecture, is a reasonable approach. You often know more than you think. An imaginative answer may not answer the question you were asked, but your instructor may give you some points for trying to think the question out.

7.   Once you have completed the test, compare your answers with those you have in your own set of questions and answers.

8.   After noting the questions you have answered well and those in need of improvement, design a new test. Follow the same procedure we have outlined in Steps

1–7. Take the new test, and continue repeating the steps until you think you have mastered all the questions and answers likely to appear on your instructor's test.

Weekly and Final Practice Tests

When you take weekly practice tests in each subject, you'll find that exam panic, last-minute cramming, and test anxiety tend to be things of the past. It may sound like a lot of work to develop a weekly test or quiz for each course you are taking, but can you think of a better method of testing to see how well you are learning?

Before each scheduled real test, take a comprehensive practice test made up of sample questions from your weekly tests. You'll be pleasantly surprised at how much easier it is to pass your final practice test when you have been taking weekly tests. Taking weekly tests allows you to master small amounts of information each week and then to put everything together in a final practice test just before you take the real thing.

Advantages of Preparing for Tests by Taking Tests

But isn't this strategy very time consuming?

It may appear so, but students who collect test questions and answers, take weekly practice tests or quizzes, and take final practice tests spend far less time on irrelevant and wasteful studying. These students practice exactly what their instructors will require of them: asking and answering intelligent questions.

Such students also obtain a more solid education. They remember what they have learned much better than students who cram for exams. Research into forgetting, replicated many times, shows that people quickly forget most of what they learn unless they review and rehearse the material.

We have assumed in our suggested study strategies that you want to pass tests well and obtain an excellent education. Your success in life after college is a function of what you can do, not of your grades. When you go to an attorney to have a contract drawn up, do you ask, "What grade did you receive in contract law?" Or if you have a pulled muscle, do you ask the physician about his or her scores on anatomy tests? No. You seek help or services on the basis of what people know and can do.

To obtain learning that lasts, each of us must apply the basic principles of learning. Otherwise, we end up with average grades but little knowledge.

Does making and taking practice tests reduce test anxiety?

Yes it does. Exam panic and last-minute cramming are unlikely to occur if you follow our suggestions for studying and exam preparation. Most people are anxious about tests because they practice study behaviors and thought processes that are *not* similar to what will be required of them in the test. If people don't practice what will be expected of them, it makes sense that they will be anxious, especially when they walk into the room and see that everything they studied only faintly resembles what the test is asking.

For example, if you will be asked to work chemistry problems on an exam, you have to practice working problems as you prepare. If your English instructor will ask you to answer five short-answer essay questions about modern authors, you have to practice writing answers to short-answer essay questions.

If you try to predict test questions and practice answering your questions, it is unlikely you will walk into an exam room and find totally different questions from those you predicted. The minute you see that your instructor's questions resemble your own, your anxiety will decrease. The more you practice developing good test questions and practice taking tests, the faster you will see your test anxiety drop to a reasonable level.

TAKING TESTS WITH LESS STRESS

Now that you know how to prepare for a test, let's make sure you know how to relax and use your time wisely once you have the real test in your hands. These rules apply to all forms of exams.

GENERAL RULES

Survey Your Test

First read the instructions to determine the types of questions you'll be expected to answer. Then skim through the test to determine what it looks like and where you'll earn the most points. Don't spend much time reading questions. Quickly form a basic idea of how the test is set up and plan your attack.

Plan How to Spend Your Time

Divide your time to ensure that you schedule enough for all portions of the test. Otherwise, you'll devote too much time to the most difficult parts and will "choke" when you find you can't complete the whole test.

Figure Out Where and How You Will Get the Most Points

Before starting, determine whether or not answering the easier questions will earn you as many points as answering the more difficult questions. If so, complete the easy questions first. After answering them you'll have more confidence, and you then can tackle the more difficult questions.

Figure Out What Each Question Is Asking

As you take the test, make sure you understand what each question is asking. If the directions say, "Give several examples of . . . , " do exactly that. Give instructors exactly what they ask for. Don't twist questions into something else.

Don't Get Stuck on Difficult Questions

If you don't understand a question or find it extremely difficult, place an "×" by it and move on to easier questions. You can come back later. This procedure saves time and prevents anxiety. Most important, you may find the answer hidden in other questions as you move through the test. Don't waste precious time trying to dig out the answers from the back of your brain. Expect the answer to come to you as you work on other items, just as you do when trying to recall a person's name. Relaxing and expecting the name to come to you in a few moments works better than struggling to remember.

Leave Time to Review Your Work

Be sure to leave yourself a few minutes at the end of the exam to go over each section to see that you haven't forgotten to answer any questions.

TWO KINDS OF TESTS: RECOGNITION AND RECALL

Most of your exams in college will be structured in one of two ways. One requires you to recognize the correct answer to a question. The other requires you to recall from memory the answer to a question.

TESTS OF RECOGNITION

Three kinds of tests require you to recognize the correct answer to a question: multiple choice, true/false, and matching. The most popular is multiple choice. It requires you to identify the correct answer among four or five choices listed.

The next most popular are true/false tests that ask you to indicate if a statement is correct or not. Instructors don't use true/false items very much because you have a 50% chance of getting the answer right simply through dumb luck.

Another recognition test, less frequently used, is called matching. It requires you to match or pair off the items on one list with items on a second list.

Each type of recognition test requires a different test-taking strategy.

Multiple-Choice Questions

How and How Not to Answer Them.   Here are six good tactics to use when you take a multiple-choice test:

1.   Never leave an answer blank unless a penalty is given for guessing. Read questions carefully, but answer them quickly. If the answer is not immediately obvious to you, check off a tentative answer and come back to it. Later test items often give clues to the answers in earlier items.

2.   As you answer multiple-choice questions, always be sure to eliminate the obviously incorrect answers first. You will save considerable time, and it will help to reduce anxiety about choosing the correct answer.

3.   If, after reading the question and all options, the answer isn't immediately apparent, wait a second before you look at the options again. First, look at the question and try to develop an answer. Then look at the options to see if the answer isn't more apparent. Many students report that this is a useful technique.

4.   If a multiple-choice question doesn't make sense, read the question with each of the answers independently. By combining the question and the choices one at a time, you may figure out what the question is asking.

5.   If the question is quite clear but none of the options seems to make sense, try combining the question with each option one at a time. Reading all the options together may create confusion. But by combining them independently with the question, one may stand out as correct.

6.   When an "all of the above" option is available, be careful. Only when you can't eliminate one option will "all of the above" be correct. The same warning holds true for "none of the above." Unless you can find an obvious flaw in each answer, "none of the above" is not your answer.

Read Multiple-Choice Questions and Instructions Carefully.   If you don't read carefully, multiple-choice tests hold many pitfalls. Use the following five tactics to avoid falling into one of them:

1.   Be sure the instructor wants only one correct answer for each multiple-choice question. Few instructors develop multiple-choice questions with more than one correct answer, but be sure your instructor isn't the exception.

2.   Consider all options. Don't select the first one that looks good and forget to read the others. Sometimes instructors place a good, but not the best, option first to catch students who don't read each answer carefully. Read all options to make sure that you have chosen the best.

3.   Be cautious when an answer includes such absolute words as *every, always,* and *never.* In few situations is something always or never true.

4.   Read and answer each question quickly. Look for key words and phrases, such as "Which is not . . ." or "According to Skinner . . ." or "The strongest evidence. . . ." After you have answered all questions, go back to see that you have read them correctly. If you have time, reread them all. If not, reread those you marked with an "×" the first time through because you were unsure of your answers.

5.   Contrary to the popular advice about never changing answers, it can be to your advantage to change answers. The research evidence shows that when students have prepared well for an examination, the number of students who gain by changing answers is significantly greater than the number of students who lose by changing answers. Be cautious about changing answers, of course. But your second thought, if you have prepared well, may be more accurate.

True/False Questions

Don't waste time pondering true/false questions. Some students waste major portions of test periods on true/false questions. If you don't know the answer right away, don't become frustrated. Simply move on to the next question. One or two questions aren't worth that many points. They don't deserve the precious time that could be devoted to other, more important questions. Besides, the answers you don't recall on a true/false question may be remembered on another part of the examination.

Matching Questions

Check to make sure you have read the directions for matching questions carefully. Sometimes students believe matches are so obvious that they do exactly the opposite of what is asked. If the instructions say, "Match those that are different" or "Match those that are opposite," you'll feel rather foolish if you have spent much time matching those that are similar.

It saves time to answer the easy questions first. This tactic reduces the chance of guessing incorrectly on more difficult matches.

TESTS OF RECALL

Written examinations require you to recall the answer to a question from memory. Tests of recall are more difficult than tests of recognition. Written tests of recall include having you write long essays, write short answers to questions, or fill in the missing words in a sentence. A long-essay examination may ask you to answer only one question or perhaps two, three, or four, depending on how much time you are given for the exam. Long-essay examinations ask you to "Trace the development of . . ." or "Explain and provide supporting evidence for the theoretical views of . . ." Long-essay questions expect you to provide a detailed discussion of many facts and to demonstrate why those facts are relevant to the position you are taking in your answer.

In contrast, a short-answer essay exam has more questions. On it you might be asked to "Briefly compare and contrast . . ." or "What are the major characteristics of . . ." Your responses to these questions require a thorough answer but with fewer facts. You must make a strong case for the relevance of your facts to convince the grader of the accuracy of your answer.

To do well on any written answer test, you must pay careful attention to the key instruction in the question. The most common instruction terms are *define, compare, list, contrast, analyze, explain, outline, summarize, name,* and *describe.*

Short-Answer Essay Questions

Short-answer essay questions might ask you to do one of the following:

- Define each of the terms and concepts in a list
- Outline an experiment or study

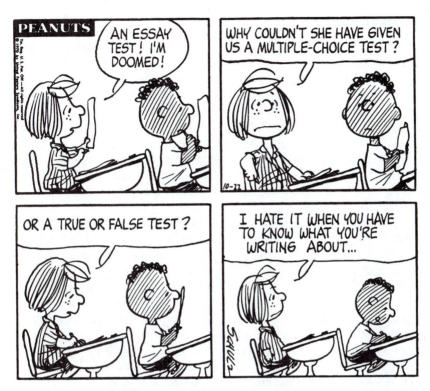

PEANUTS reprinted by permission of United Feature Syndicate, Inc.

- List the main points in favor of a theory
- Give three criticisms against a theory or report of a study
- Draw and correctly label a chart, graph, or structure (for example, a nerve cell)
- Name the basic steps or stages in a process

The answers to short-answer essay questions will be brief statements that are very much to the point. They may include lists that show you understand the main points. Good answers always emphasize your understanding of the definitions of terms and concepts referred to in the question.

Your aim is to show the instructor that you have a precise understanding of the answer to the question. Using examples that highlight the important characteristics of the topic is critical. For example, if the instructor wants to know what the features of George Washington's successful military strategy were, you need to tell him or her two things: what strategies Washington used and why they were important.

Hint: One thing we can't overemphasize is that for ease of grading, instructors appreciate clear, legible answers. Just think of the number of answers your instructor will have to grade. If your answers stand out as very easy to read, you'll gain points.

Long-Essay Questions

Long-essay answers must not only include facts but also demonstrate your understanding of broad trends, abstract concepts, and the like. You should be able to draw your own conclusions based on the factual data you possess. Because long-essay questions require more thought—and more information—they often pose problems for students taking essay tests. So where do you begin?

We cannot overemphasize the value of one strategy—to look at essay-question answers that have received A's. People always say a picture is worth 1,000 words. The same is true of good answers to questions and good term papers. This strategy has gained such popularity over the years that many instructors now hand out copies of sample questions and answers they want their students to evaluate and emulate.

A great teaching tool is to show a student a model of what you want and don't want. That is why art instructors have their students look at good and bad art. What is it that makes one painting so far superior to another? The same is true of answers to essay questions.

The Action Project at the end of the chapter provides a list of questions you should ask yourself when reviewing other students' essay answers. You will find that your English instructors may ask you to review papers that received A's and to compare them to papers that received lower grades. Follow this tip and make a practice of sharing your answers with other students. Don't be shy. Look at other students' essay answers, and figure out for yourself if the general guidelines that follow aren't a good model of what most instructors expect.

Winning Strategy for Writing Long Essays.

1. *Read the questions carefully.* Long-answer essay questions usually want you to write at length about several subjects or topics. Read each question carefully to make certain you understand exactly what the instructor wants you to include in your answer. Some students misunderstand the main purpose of a question and meander off into other areas. The reasons Napoleon lost the battle at Waterloo are primarily military. An analysis of his personality wastes time and earns no points.

2. *Outline your answers.* Outline your answer to a long-answer essay question before writing it. In this way you will ensure that you include key ideas that will earn points from the grader. The procedure saves time in the long run. You can organize your answer and can be sure to include everything important. You will feel more organized when you begin to write and will have few uncertainties about whether you have included all you should.

Put your outline right at the top of the paper before you answer the question. The outline will catch the grader's eye. The outline sends a message to the grader that you have thought out the answer, that you know what the important facts and characteristics are, and that you will try to convince him or her of the relevance of your facts. If you for some reason don't finish writing the complete answer, the grader may use the outline to give you partial credit.

3.   *Use an introduction.* Begin by describing the most important questions you intend to answer or the main ideas you intend to discuss in your essay. It can help if you pretend you are writing a short article and need an interesting opening.

4.   *Define terms.* Define the terms you use in your answer. Be sure to call attention to conflicting viewpoints or any uncertainties in your mind about the question asked. This approach often clarifies for the instructor why you have answered the question in a particular manner.

5.   *Use subheadings.* As you write, be sure to use subheadings for long answers. Subheadings show the reader the organization in your answer. Notice throughout this chapter how the subheadings "lead" you through the information. Imagine how difficult it would be to read without them!

6.   *Use examples and facts.* It is crucial to use examples to support your main points. You demonstrate that you really know what you are talking about if you can present examples to substantiate your position. Include facts, numbers, and details. Be specific. Instead of writing "Every student needs friends," write "According to Maslow, it is easier for a student who feels accepted by others to engage in personal growth and self-development than for a student who doesn't feel well accepted."

7.   *Draw conclusions.* As you discuss facts, show the importance of those facts. The grader will want to know why they are relevant. You want to summarize and draw conclusions about the relevance of your facts. The grader is asking, "How do these facts support the author's conclusions?" Be definite and positive.

As you draw conclusions, remember that no argument is one-sided. Facts also support the position that opposes the position you are trying to prove. It is important that you convince the grader that the facts you present outweigh the facts that would support opposing positions.

It is critical that you not be so one-sided that the grader says, "This person failed to consider any other facts or positions." Every position has at least two sides. Demonstrate that you are aware of the different positions or sides to the argument but that you favor one position because of the facts you have presented.

8.   *Edit your answers.* Above all, write legibly! After you have finished writing, pretend you are the grader. Ask yourself, "Have I misread or misinterpreted the questions? What did I leave out? Have I made any careless mistakes?" Allot time at the end to edit your answers for clarity, to add necessary points, and to deal with the more difficult questions you skipped over.

STRATEGIES YOU MAY NEVER HAVE THOUGHT ABOUT

ANSWER QUESTIONS YOU DON'T THINK YOU CAN ANSWER!

What can you do when you come to a question that baffles you? Try to remember that in your reading you're likely to have picked up at least some relevant information. And while you are taking the exam, other questions may provide some information related to the answer you need. Write down any possibility. You may earn a few points. A few points is more than you'll earn if you leave the answer blank.

If you can't figure out the exact answer, you can probably figure out an approximation. In math, for example, you may work out problems and get incorrect answers. You may not receive complete credit, but partial credit is surely better than a big zero. Instructors often review the process you used to solve a problem and award points for what you did correctly.

Using your imagination takes practice and even a little confidence. It is not the most important study skill we can recommend, but using it can be valuable at times.

WRITE COMMENTS ABOUT THE TEST

If, despite all your excellent preparation, you are still a bit nervous about the test, try imagining that written across the top is the statement "Feel free to write comments about the test items."

Wilbert J. McKeachie, a psychologist well known for his research on ways to improve teaching, discovered that when this statement was printed at the top of tests, many students did better. The students who were helped most were those who had stronger-than-average fears of failing. An interesting result was that it didn't matter whether students actually wrote anything about the test! Just the presence of the statement was enough to improve the scores of students who had strong fears of failing.

So, when you are taking a test, remember that you should feel free to write comments about the test items. If you believe a question is poorly worded, say so. But also go on to explain why and perhaps suggest a better wording. The whole purpose of the examination is to show that you know something about the subject. Note: If you have doubts about being allowed comments on the questions, ask!

ASK QUESTIONS DURING THE EXAM

Instructors know that their questions are not always clear. Sometimes the wording isn't as accurate as it should be. That's why most instructors will answer questions about test questions during exams.

Take advantage of this willingness. If one or two questions just don't make sense, go ask the instructor such questions as "I am a little confused by this question. Could you give me some assistance?" "The way this item is worded, couldn't it have several possible answers, this one and this one?" "I saw all the films but don't remember the one this was covered in. Can you give me any clues?"

If you are drawing a blank anyway, you have nothing to lose by seeing whether or not the instructor will give you some hints. He or she will not give you the answer, but a comment such as "That item is from the chart at the end of Chapter 6" may give you the clue you need. Try asking. Clues from your instructor can be worth several extra points on every exam.

ADVANTAGES OF THESE TEST-TAKING STRATEGIES

When you use the strategies described in this chapter, you become more confident about taking tests and achieve more points on any given test. When taking tests, you will find that you don't make those unfortunate mistakes that cause you to want to kick yourself and ask, "Why didn't I use my brain?"

You will read the questions carefully, plan your time well, determine the value of specific questions, and answer questions in ways likely to earn the maximum number of points. You will use test-taking strategies we most often observe in students who comprehend their course material and do well on exams. In essence, you will be a more successful student and will still have time for friends.

Experience proves that students who use these techniques seldom do any of the following:

1. Misread test questions or answer questions incorrectly
2. Waste time on questions that stump them
3. Waste time answering questions with irrelevant information
4. Run out of time and fail to complete the test
5. Lose points from changing their answers at the last minute
6. Have difficulty answering questions they didn't think they could answer
7. Develop exam panic when a test appears more difficult than they had predicted
8. Fail tests (they usually receive a B or better)

Furthermore, students who use these techniques report they do experience the following:

1. Get better grades on tests
2. Receive more points for answers than they would have predicted
3. Feel more relaxed and confident while taking tests
4. Know they haven't wasted their time while answering complex as well as simple questions
5. Feel better organized while taking tests
6. Seldom leave out important information from answers
7. Can complete exams in the allotted time
8. Get higher grades in their courses

Note: It is not necessary to play the "suffering student" game. Learning can be pleasant. Studying for exams can be efficient when you use the strategies we've discussed. When you prepare well for exams, the night before each exam you can relax and do one more very helpful thing: get a good night's sleep!

ACTION REVIEW

Checklist for Success in Preparing for and Taking Tests With Less Stress

_____ DO I PRACTICE QUIZZING MYSELF ON POSSIBLE TEST QUESTIONS?

_____ DO I MAKE UP AND TAKE PRACTICE TESTS?

_____ DO I EXCHANGE PRACTICE TESTS WITH OTHER STUDENTS IN THE CLASS?

_____ DO I PRACTICE TAKING TESTS UNDER CONDITIONS AS SIMILAR AS POSSIBLE TO THOSE I WILL BE TESTED UNDER?

_____ WHEN I TAKE TESTS, DO I USE THE TECHNIQUES SUGGESTED IN THIS CHAPTER?

_____ HAVE I MADE AN EFFORT TO LEARN FROM SUCCESSFUL STUDENTS HOW THEY STUDY AND TAKE TESTS?

ACTION PROJECT

Review an "A" Essay Exam

One of the best ways to learn how to succeed is to look at the products of people you want to emulate. A strategy we have found most useful to help students learn test-taking skills is to review and evaluate other students' essay tests that have received high marks.

We first recommend that you borrow several copies of "A" essay exams from friends, classmates, or instructors. Then use the following checklist to evaluate the test:

_____ DOES THE INTRODUCTION INCLUDE THE KEY IDEAS COVERED IN THE ANSWER? IS IT CLEAR WHICH QUESTIONS WILL BE ANSWERED IN THE ESSAY?

_____ ARE THE TERMS AND CONCEPTS CLEARLY DEFINED? DOES IT APPEAR THE STUDENT GOT EXTRA POINTS FOR HIGHLIGHTING ALL THE IMPORTANT TERMS AND CONCEPTS?

_____ DOES EACH PARAGRAPH HAVE A CENTRAL IDEA? IS THE CENTRAL IDEA SUPPORTED AND ILLUSTRATED WITH EXAMPLES TO PROVE THE POINT MADE IN THE PARAGRAPH?

_____ DOES THE CONCLUSION SUCCESSFULLY SUMMARIZE THE MAIN POINTS MADE IN THE ESSAY?

YOUR PORTFOLIO

Keep a record of your test scores in each course, with an outline of the material covered.

SUCCESS GROUP ACTIVITY

Interview Students Who Get "A" Grades on Exams

Invite several "A" students to meet with your group to answer questions about what they know about taking examinations. Ask them to tell you about their strategies for taking each kind of test. It is important to hear students you respect put into their own words what they do when they take tests. By comparing and contrasting their strategies, you will gain valuable insights into strategies for taking all kinds of tests in college and for jobs.

Chapter 9

Writing Excellent Papers: How to Use Your Library Well

HOW TO BEGIN YOUR RESEARCH PAPER

The successful way to write papers parallels the steps you take to prepare for and take tests. Begin by asking yourself the following questions when writing a paper for an instructor:

- "What important questions should I answer in this paper?"
- "What important issues do I need to cover to demonstrate critical-thinking skills?"

Students willing to approach writing from this perspective have found the process less difficult and less time consuming. More important, their papers are precise and accurate and receive top grades from instructors.

We now will discuss the steps to follow for planning and preparing your papers.

PICK AN INTERESTING TOPIC

Pick a topic you find interesting and that your instructor believes is important. By listening closely in class, you often will detect certain areas that are the instructor's favorites. Our students have found it best to choose topics that they and their instructors have enjoyed researching and reading about.

Instructors can supply bibliographies and other information about their favorite subjects. It may be helpful to talk with them after class or to make appointments to discuss your planned paper. Talking with the instructor will give you added insights on the advisability of writing about specific areas. It is also a good way to get to know your instructor.

When you have an assigned paper to write, our suggestion is that you prepare by selecting at least three possible topics. Have a preferred topic, of course, but include several alternative topics you would find interesting in case the first one proves unworkable. Make an appointment to talk with your instructor about your proposed topics. If you ask good questions during your discussion, it is amazing how often the instructor will suggest many approaches, useful ideas, critical issues, and key concepts to include. A good discussion can almost outline how your paper should be written. During this discussion, your instructor also can warn you about certain problems to avoid and which issues are either too simple or too complicated to attempt.

WRITE FOR YOUR AUDIENCE

Always keep in mind that you are writing to an audience of one person—your instructor. You are not writing an article for the *Saturday Review* or for your school newspaper. You are not writing a paper that will be published in a professional journal. Because your instructor is the person you are writing for, it is very important to take extra time to find out exactly what you need to do in your paper to get a good evaluation. If your instructor is vague or unwilling to talk with you about what you plan for your paper, talk to students who have taken the course in the past. Try to read papers other students have written for this instructor to gain an idea about what was liked and disliked.

LIST IMPORTANT QUESTIONS; COVER DIFFERENT PERSPECTIVES

Brainstorm a list of important questions you should answer in the paper. To demonstrate critical thinking, create questions that examine the subject from more than one viewpoint and that cover the pros and cons of each.

Your list will help you determine whether your topic is too broad or too narrow. Too often students find that they would have to produce encyclopedias to cover all relevant questions adequately. If you limit yourself to a few important questions, you will be in a better position to relax as you do the research and writing.

Begin your paper by indicating that you intend to deal only with specific questions and critical issues. Be humble and indicate that you recognize that other significant questions may exist but that you have chosen to limit yourself to several high-priority questions.

What if my instructor says I have missed an important issue? What do I do then?

This possibility is why we stress talking with your instructor beforehand to determine whether or not the questions and critical issues you think are important are the ones the instructor would like discussed.

What if I'm in a class of 200 and don't have access to the instructor or teaching assistant?

You have several alternatives. Many schools provide students with a writing skills center. During orientation you should have been told where writing help is available. Take advantage of this useful free service! It is there for all students, no matter their skill level.

Go to the library. Find a reference librarian. Reference librarians are wonderful people to know. They can help you find information sources you probably wouldn't think of. They know the research sources and can be extremely helpful.

Skim through the most recent books and journals that deal with your topic. Even new books can be several years behind the times, so it is wise to seek more up-to-date journals. By looking at what the experts are doing, you are likely to get a better idea of the important questions currently being investigated.

Search the Internet for useful sources. Be both creative and focused with the search words you use. Here are some of the better sites:

- *Britannica Online.* A limited version is available to nonsubscribers. http://www.eb.com/
- *Carnegie Mellon University On-line Reference.* The CMU computer science department has a general online reference page with several good links. http://www.cs.cmu.edu/references.html
- *Encarta Online Home.* The Encarta abridged encyclopedia has links to informational sites on the Web. http://www.msn.com/EncartaHome.asp
- *Encyclopedia.com from Electric Library.* A free encyclopedia with search, this site also provides links to pay services. www.encyclopedia.com
- *The Reference.* This is a free Web-based encyclopedia. www.thereference.com
- *Study WEB.* A collection of more than 73,000 "Research Quality" URLs, this site is searchable. http://www.studyweb.com/

- *World Book Encyclopedia.*
  http://www.worldbook.com/
- *Yahoo Reference listings.* This is a great place to start. Most listings are annotated.
  http://dir.yahoo.com/Reference/

Discuss your topic with students majoring in the subject. They may be aware of important questions you have overlooked.

DEVELOP AN OUTLINE

Now that you have a list of questions, take a minute to develop an overall picture of your paper. Try outlining the paper. First will be your introduction. Sketch one out. An introduction is usually one or two paragraphs. It tells your instructor which important questions you intend to answer. By stating the main points you'll be making, you will focus the reader's attention. He or she will know what to look for. Don't worry about making your introduction perfect. It may change dramatically after you have answered your questions. Just sketch an introduction that will lead you in the right direction.

Next, list in order the questions you will be answering. Make sure your questions are listed in a logical sequence.

The last part of your outline will be the conclusion. At this point, you haven't answered your questions, so you won't be in a position to draw any conclusions.

Your finished outline will include the following:

- A rough draft of your introduction
- The body of your paper—the questions you intend to answer, and the critical issues you intend to cover
- A statement about writing a conclusion after you have researched your questions

TALK TO YOUR INSTRUCTOR

After you have developed an outline, you need to ensure that you are heading in the right direction. Make an appointment with your instructor again. It will take the instructor only a few moments to scan your outline to see if you are focusing on the important questions and issues. He or she may give you a few hints about other questions you may wish to answer.

Now, off you go to the library to find out answers.

USE YOUR LIBRARY WELL

Libraries are wonderful places. In libraries you can discover extraordinary ideas, amazing information, and new worlds. You can find facts supporting impressions you have or data disproving opinions you don't like. To have these experiences, it is highly important to know how to use a library.

To use your library well, as we've said before, feel free to ask the librarians for assistance. Think of the librarians as resources! Librarians are paid to help students. More important, librarians want to be sure every student gets the most possible from the library facilities. Whenever you have a question about using the library, don't hesitate. Any question you have is a good one. The only poor question is the one you fail to ask.

Some colleges offer a credit course on how to use the library. If such a course is available, it would be extremely valuable to take it.

LOCATING BOOKS

The books housed in the library will be listed in the card catalog, the microfiche system, or the online catalog in the library computer system. The card catalog, of course, is the old system libraries used for many decades. Information about each book is typed onto a 3-by-5-inch card and filed alphabetically and by call numbers in drawers.

Microfiche is a piece of photographic film usually 4-by-6 inches. It contains information greatly reduced in size, so it has to be magnified for reading. One microfiche sheet replaces dozens of catalog cards. It saves space, is cheaper to produce, and can be updated quickly. To use the microfiche, you sit down at a magnifier, insert the card, and find the items you are looking for.

The online computer catalog is updated almost daily and may even show if a book has been placed on reserve or has been checked out. The library's computer system will be linked to regional and national libraries. Once in a while you may have to request that a book be sent to you through interlibrary loan.

Let's say you've heard about baseball's Mark McGwire using the muscle-building supplement androstenedione. Your paper is going to research athletic performance and the long-term effects of "andro" use. How do you find the facts?

With your questions in mind, you'll want to search the subject index. Libraries index their books in three ways: by subject, author, and title.

Use your imagination when checking the subject index. Look under every topic you can think of—steroids, enhanced performance, banned substances, nutrition, physical education, health science, and so on. When you compile your list of book titles and authors, always write down the complete call number of the book. The call number is the library's code telling you exactly where the book is shelved.

If a listing includes the statement "reference" or "reference desk," you will not find the book in the open stacks. An instructor probably has placed the book on reserve so that no one can check it out of the library. If you go to the reference desk, the librarian probably will let you have the book for several hours and in some cases for several days. At some libraries you can check out a reference book at closing time if you return it promptly when the library opens in the morning.

FINDING PERIODICALS

After identifying books related to your subject, look at the library's list of periodicals. All professional journals are called "periodicals" because they are published periodically every month, two months or quarter. As with books, periodicals may be listed in a card index, a microfiche index, and a computer index. Up-to-date information, especially scientific reports, appears in professional journals long before it is reported in books. Flip through the periodical titles, looking for journals that could contain articles related to your topic. For your paper on drugs and athletic performance, you'd cover all the physical education journals.

The journals of national professional groups are often titled *The American . . .* or *National Society of . . .* or *The Journal of the American. . . .* So be sure to look under "American," "National," and "Journal" in the alphabetical listings.

As you write down the call numbers for books and journals, you will begin to see a pattern. The books and journals with relevant information are clustered in two or three places in the library. When you go to these sections, you will discover other books and journals you didn't see in the catalog indexes.

GATHERING INFORMATION

Skim through the books and journals with information on your topic to get a general orientation. Skimming will help you identify the most useful books and articles to read carefully. When you find useful data or passages you may want to quote in your paper, be very accurate in your recording. It can be very frustrating later, when back at your computer, not to remember which author you quoted or if the statement in your notes is one of your own observations rather than a quote. Libraries have coin-operated photocopying equipment available. Save time by using it.

From the journal articles you will learn which authors are most highly regarded and most frequently cited as experts, and you will find clues about books to look for. Some professional journals publish book reviews of the latest books. You may learn about a book before the library purchases it. In such cases you might visit instructors in that topic area to see if one of them has purchased the book and will allow you to see it or borrow it.

From the books you will learn about which journals focus on your topic most frequently. You may learn about an older journal article that is exactly what you are after. You may discover, for example, that several articles on abnormal heart rhythms and steroids have been published in medical journals. Thus, another area of information opens up to you.

FINDING REFERENCE MATERIALS

You still haven't used your library well, however, if you ignore another source of useful information: the reference section. In the reference section you will find many resources, such as encyclopedias. Of most interest right now, however, is the *Reader's Guide to Periodical Literature.*

This index lists in alphabetical order the titles of articles published in the major popular magazines. If an article on steroids and athletic performance has appeared in any magazine, the *Reader's Guide* will list it. Some physicians and scientific researchers publish directly in popular publications, so don't discount magazines as information sources. Besides, the information is usually easier to understand than it is in professional journals and books.

Use almanacs as well. Almanacs sometimes can provide historical facts, statistics, names, and dates not available in encyclopedias or other sources.

Your reference librarian can update you on many technological resources. Your library may subscribe to the *Magazine Index,* available in microfilm, or *Newsbank,* on microfiche. In addition, it may subscribe to such computer information networks as Dialog or Datatimes. Some reference information is now available on compact disc and videodisc. Your college library has a wealth of information available if you learn how to gain access to it!

USING OTHER LIBRARIES

Explore other libraries in your area. Sometimes city or county libraries have books the college libraries do not have. Other colleges in your area may have references you cannot find in your own library on campus. You can use any library nearby, even the medical school library if one happens to be in your vicinity. These other libraries may not allow you to check out books, but you are welcome to walk in and use any materials they have.

You'll soon discover that by knowing the questions you want to answer, you can quickly cut through the massive amount of material that could otherwise distract you. By reading to answer your questions, you save precious hours you might otherwise lose meandering around, wondering how much you should include in your paper.

SEARCHING ONLINE

Knowing the questions you want to answer also helps keep you from spending too many hours on the Internet. Research in the library stops itself when you run out of books and articles on your subject, but Internet searches can be endless. The Internet is rich with possibilities for your research, but it takes self-control to stick to your specific subject and then stop.

HOW TO WRITE "EXCELLENT" PAPERS

GATHER INFORMATION; THEN WRITE YOUR ANSWERS

Gathering information can be the most time-consuming part of writing the paper. Once you have sufficient information, it is time to start writing the answers to your questions.

Write the answers to your questions as precisely as possible. Be brief. Don't include irrelevant information that clouds the issue. Make your point, back it with sufficient examples and data, state what you have proved, and stop.

Give precise references to your information sources in footnotes and in your bibliography. Give the reader all the information he or she would need to go to the specific publication and find the exact pages referenced.

Answers to questions are more believable when they are precise and well documented. Let your reader know that you've done research on the answers. Quote experts in the field. The more authoritative your examples, the better your ability to convince your reader. But don't overdo it. Several good examples are all you need to prove your point.

Brief, accurate quotations more effectively support your points than lengthy quotations or your own statements about what other people have said. Brief quotations, figures, and specific facts are more persuasive than vague generalizations.

ARRANGE YOUR ANSWERS

Once you have written your answers, arrange them in order so that they build on one another. Your next task is to connect them by writing the minimum amount of material between each answer. These transitions from answer to answer should be brief but serve their function.

REWRITE YOUR INTRODUCTION

Now that you have answered your questions and built the body of your paper, you are ready to rewrite your introduction. Many students try to start writing their paper by producing a perfect introduction for their outline. This is a mistake.

Once you have answered your questions, you'll be much better prepared to state exactly what your paper does and does not do. You may have found that several of the questions you originally thought you would answer were less important than other questions you discovered while researching your paper.

WRITE YOUR CONCLUSION

Your conclusion summarizes the major points you have addressed in your paper. You shouldn't include any new data, examples, or information, although you may wish to explain that your paper raises further questions that need to be answered at a later date. Essentially, your summary shows how all the pieces combine to prove a particular point. If the answers to your questions lead to a logical conclusion, you should draw that conclusion and leave it at that.

REVIEW YOUR WORK SO FAR

The material you've assembled constitutes the first draft of your paper. Stop a moment and review what you have accomplished. So far you've done the following:

1. Determined which questions you will answer in your paper

2. Developed an outline for your paper; written an introduction describing the intent of your paper and the questions you will answer

3. Asked your instructor to scan your outline

4. Answered each question as precisely and authoritatively as possible; provided examples to support your position

5. Documented your sources in footnotes and a bibliography

6. Put your answers in sequence so that they build on one another

7. Provided transitions from answer to answer

8. Rewritten your introduction

9. Written your conclusion

REWRITE YOUR PAPER

After you write your first draft, make an appointment to go over it with your instructor. Most instructors are willing to help you and will give you good feedback about whether you are ready for the typing or need to do more research.

Revising is where the real writing of any paper takes place. Most writers produce several rough drafts before attempting their final version. Plan from the beginning to produce a rough draft that you will then revise into your final copy. This way you can produce your first rough draft much more quickly and won't be wasting time by trying to edit, correct typing mistakes, and so on.

When you are in a position to rewrite your paper, do the following:

1. Have your instructor look over your rough draft.

2. Make sure you have clearly indicated which questions you will answer and which critical issues you will discuss.

3. Check to see that your transitions flow smoothly from answer to answer.

4. Vary the length of your sentences. Most of the writing in journals and research books is composed of long, involved, complicated sentences. Such sentences are typical of how academics think and talk. Long sentences do not make interesting reading, however. Likewise, you don't want to make your writing style too simple. The best approach is to mix both long and short sentences.

5. Correct any grammatical, punctuation, or spelling errors.

6. Rewrite or refine your answers if necessary.

7. Finish the paper with concluding comments and remarks. Include in this section statements about what you learned while writing the paper. State why it was a valuable experience for you. Also include questions, if any, that writing this paper has raised in your mind.

DEMONSTRATE GOOD EFFORT AND LEARNING

The grade given for a paper is influenced by four questions in the back of the instructor's mind:

1. Did the student put effort into this paper, or was it written with the minimum possible effort?

2.   Did the student learn anything, or is this paper just a collection of words?

3.   Is the paper original, or has it been plagiarized?

4.   Was this paper purchased from a paper-writing service?

If you can arrange to do so, glance through term papers written by other students. Certain quick impressions will begin to emerge. Some students turn in papers that show very little effort. You don't have to be an instructor to see that such students are trying to get away with the absolute minimum commitment of time, effort, and involvement.

Some students do more work, but they didn't connect with the topic. Their approach is to check out some books on the subject, sit down the night or two before the paper is due, and combine series of quotations: "In 1937, C. S. Johnson said. . . . His view was criticized by Smith, who said . . . , by Brown, who said . . . , and by Jones, who said. . . . But then in Eggland's 1949 book. . . ." Such a paper shows no learning.

What it Takes to Write an "Excellent" Paper

Demonstrate Critical Thinking With Questions

What does critical thinking mean to you? Does it mean to be highly critical of what someone has said or written? Not to college instructors.

One of the best ways to understand critical thinking is to ask, "What is the opposite of critical thinking?" When students are asked to describe uncritical thinking, they report the following:

"Accept without reservation what someone is saying."

"Believe that whatever is told to you is the truth."

"Not want to listen to another explanation or perspective."

"Believe that the thinking of one person or group is entirely right and good while the thinking of opposing persons or groups is bad and wrong."

To demonstrate critical thinking in a paper thus means to ask and answer questions that provide more than one perspective, viewpoint, or explanation—and to discuss the strong and weak points of each perspective. Your aim is to demonstrate that you can think in critical ways even about a theory, method, philosophy, or school of thinking you favor.

Remember Grammar, Spelling, and Neatness

Another set of suggestions is important, especially if your instructor requires that you submit typed or printed papers. You can safely assume that the instructor prefers this format, for most instructors do. Handwritten papers are difficult to read; they slow down the instructor and cause eyestrain. Your instructor reads hundreds of articles, books, and papers every year. It is a sign of consideration to present your writing in the most readable form. Make your printed copy as professional as possible. Use clean white paper, double-space the lines, and make a minimum number of corrections on the printed copy.

Above all, make sure your spelling is accurate. Use a dictionary whenever you are in doubt. If you have problems in this area and are using a computer, be sure to remind yourself to run the spelling checker. It also would be wise to have someone check your paper for grammatical mistakes. Regardless of the quality of your ideas, few aspects of a paper bother instructors more than poor spelling and bad grammar.

It has been shown in several studies that instructors usually give higher grades to neat and clean papers and those with correct spelling and grammar. Therefore, look sharp, at least on paper.

Note: Always keep a copy of your paper. The original could get damaged or lost. Some instructors keep papers. Play it safe. Keep a copy of computer-typed papers on disk and a hard copy for yourself before turning in the original.

FOLLOW INSTRUCTIONS

Always be careful to follow any directions your instructor gives for footnotes, bibliographies, references, or other requirements. Nothing worse can happen than devoting hours to a paper only to have it returned as incomplete. The consequences of failing to follow directions can be costly.

It can be a pain in the neck to follow the requirements your instructors assign. It may be one of the small sacrifices you have to make as a student. You may be dismayed to find that what your instructor wants for the form of a paper contradicts what your English instructor taught you to do. In the end, however, you'll probably find out your instructor had a good reason for the request. Go along with the suggestions, and you usually will be better off, both with the grade you receive and the level of your blood pressure after completing the paper.

DEVELOP GOOD WRITING SKILLS

While working with college students, we have observed some things that will help you. First, after you have written a rough draft, read aloud what you have written. Students often fail to find obvious mistakes because through silent reading they miss problems that would be obvious if they were to read their papers aloud.

Second, get someone else to read the paper to see if it makes sense. Listening to feedback from another person about your writing is often painful. But it is more painful to hear those same remarks from your instructor. Do the same for your friends. Read their papers. Learn to be a better writer from analyzing the mistakes of others. As you exchange information about one another's writing, be pleasant and give constructive help. Try to encourage one another.

Third, if you have difficulties, go to the writing lab. Get some tutoring. The English department has many helpful graduate students available to show you how to write good papers.

Fourth, the key to the whole task is to decide that you want to develop writing competence. Have you made that decision? Do you want to write well? Writing skills will help you your entire life, no matter what field you enter. They even can help you communicate effectively in your personal letters. Take advantage of this opportunity. Aim to become a competent writer and practice whenever you can. You'll never regret it.

DON'T PLAGIARIZE: ALWAYS DO YOUR OWN WORK

Once in a while, a student will copy long passages from a book or article and turn in the paper without mentioning the author's name or that it is quoted. Does this succeed? Rarely. An article an expert writes on a subject is not like a paper a student writes attempting to learn a subject. And, frankly, most instructors can spot the paper's style and point of view as those of a certain author.

It's human nature to consider taking shortcuts, but some efforts to save time involve high risks. The probability is high that the payoff will be the opposite of what is desired. That's why asking and answering questions works so well. An instructor reading your paper can see that your work is original, that you put genuine effort into it, and that you have learned something. Remember, an experienced instructor usually can recognize exactly what you did or didn't do to prepare your paper.

Some students unintentionally find themselves in difficulty because they do not know exactly what plagiarism is and is not. *Plagiarism* is a form of stealing. The act of plagiarism occurs when a student copies statements from a source and presents the material to the instructor as his or her original work with no credit given to the real author and no quotation marks.

Plagiarism takes many forms, all of them unacceptable, and can be grounds for disciplinary action:

- *Direct plagiarism* occurs when a passage is quoted verbatim (word for word) and not attributed.
- *Indirect plagiarism* is when the student paraphrases the original work without giving credit to the original author.
- *Paraphrasing* means to substitute certain words and alter some sentences while repeating all the main ideas. Even though the original work was not copied verbatim, the ideas and substance have been copied.
- *Purchasing a term paper* or report written by someone else is another form of plagiarism. This is a high-risk way of trying to get a passing grade. Don't do this. One of the main benefits from going to college is the maturity and self-confidence you gain from handling tough challenges. Besides, most instructors can spot papers not written by their students. If you get caught you will be in deep trouble.
- *Having another student write or rewrite your paper* also is plagiarism. Don't do it. Supportive, constructive feedback and fresh thinking on the subject are helpful, but don't ask someone to take over and do the work, and don't do anyone's if asked.

Plagiarism can cause you serious problems in the academic world. It is grounds for being flunked in a course, referred for counseling, placed on disciplinary probation, or even expelled from the college.

Remember: If you are in doubt about whether you are plagiarizing, take one of the following steps:

1.   See your instructor for guidance.

2.   Use quotation marks and footnotes.

3.   Make the effort to write what you've read in your own words, acknowledging the source of any unoriginal ideas.

ACTION REVIEW

Checklist for Success in Writing Papers and Using Your Library

1. Do I write papers using the question/answer format? ___YES ___NO

2. Have I asked the reference librarian for suggestions about where to look for information? ___YES ___NO

3. Do I use the card catalog and microfiche to track down good reference sources?

4. Do I get up-to-date information from professional journals? ___YES ___NO

5. Do I use the *Reader's Guide* to learn about useful magazine articles? ___YES ___NO

6. Do I use other libraries in the vicinity? ___YES ___NO

7. Are my quotes and references accurate? ___YES ___NO

8. When my rough draft is completed, do I ask the instructor to look it over and give me suggestions for improvement? ___YES ___NO

9. Do I check to ensure that my grammar and spelling are correct? ___YES ___NO

10. Is my written work clean and readable? ___YES ___NO

11. After my paper has been graded and returned to me, do I look for ways to improve next time? ___YES ___NO

ACTION PROJECT

Researching Research

1. Go to the library.

2. Locate the *World Book Encyclopedia*.

3. Read the chapter on "How to Do Research" in Volume 22.

YOUR PORTFOLIO

Keep copies of papers demonstrating good critical thinking, along with the instructor's written comments. Also record how you may have searched the Internet for answers to your questions.

SUCCESS GROUP ACTIVITIES

1.   Arrange to have one of the librarians show your group how to find the many resources available in the library. By now you have a general understanding, but what more can you learn about the library? Prepare for your special session by listing questions you would like to have answered. Include such questions as "What don't most students understand about the library's resources?" or "What do you wish students understood better about the library's services?" Find out about learning labs or computer rooms that may be available to you.

2.   Read one another's term papers. Trying to critique your own papers is one of the most difficult tasks you will face in college. You can read your own paper over and over, never sure of what you have overlooked or how well you have done. Another person reading it for the first time will spot things you've overlooked.

After you have developed rough drafts of your term papers, talk with one another about the questions that provide your paper's structure. Give and get positive suggestions from one another. Have you met the goal of the assignment? Are your grammar, spelling, and punctuation acceptable? What would you add or delete to improve the paper? How could the paper be improved without a total rewrite?

Suggestion: It can be helpful to summarize your paper to a friend. When giving a summary, you will often realize a better organization than you had for the paper. The summary is usually stronger than the paper itself. By summarizing what you've written, you gain a better idea of the topic and a better flow.

Part 3

Gaining Support From Instructors, Friends, and Family

Chapter 10

Erroneous Assumptions About Instructors

SELF-ASSESSMENT

Place a check mark by the statements that are true of you.

_____ It is likely that some of my assumptions about my instructors are inaccurate.

_____ It is possible that some of my inaccurate assumptions about my instructors will create problems for me.

_____ I know that many students have erroneous beliefs about instructors.

_____ I know that unrealistic expectations about my instructors can make me angry and disappointed.

_____ I know how to change my unrealistic expectations about instructors.

_____ I have noticed that some students act as though they want to give a bad impression to instructors and cause negative reactions.

_____ I am aware of biases some instructors have toward students.

_____ I am aware of how students' positive and negative behavioral patterns affect their instructors' teaching performance.

_____ I am aware of how negative student behavior toward instructors can cause negative reactions and hurt the students.

CONFRONTING ERRONEOUS ASSUMPTIONS ABOUT INSTRUCTORS

When you accept complete responsibility for learning as much as possible from your instructors, you're on the right track. You will get more than your money's worth from school. If, however, you assume your instructors are responsible for teaching you everything you need to know, you may become disappointed with your education.

A candid appraisal of instructors and of your assumptions about them will help you understand why many of your assumptions may be inaccurate. When we teach, we sometimes ask students to list their assumptions and expectations about instructors. Then we compare those assumptions and expectations with reality. In the pages that follow, you can discover which of your assumptions and expectations about instructors are erroneous and which are realistic.

We want you to learn about myths that may affect your expectations of what your instructors should be like. Most important, we want to encourage you to stop letting erroneous assumptions set you up to feel angry, disappointed, and discouraged.

After you have read the myths, we'll move on to Chapter 11 and talk about predictable conflicts between teaching styles and learning styles, some successful ways to gain as much as possible from a variety of different types of instructors, and how to avoid alienating your instructors.

In front of each of the following statements, you'll find two spaces. Before you read the "Reality," check off whether or not you agree with the statement.

MYTHS ABOUT INSTRUCTORS

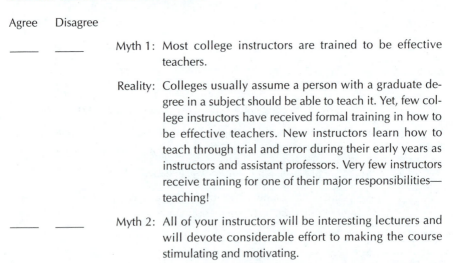

Agree   Disagree

_____   _____   Myth 1: Most college instructors are trained to be effective teachers.

Reality: Colleges usually assume a person with a graduate degree in a subject should be able to teach it. Yet, few college instructors have received formal training in how to be effective teachers. New instructors learn how to teach through trial and error during their early years as instructors and assistant professors. Very few instructors receive training for one of their major responsibilities—teaching!

_____   _____   Myth 2: All of your instructors will be interesting lecturers and will devote considerable effort to making the course stimulating and motivating.

Reality: Most of your college instructors would like to be interesting, stimulating, and motivating lecturers. But, you will find that your instructors vary widely in their ability to maintain your interest. Some of your instructors will be downright boring and uninteresting regardless of how hard they try to maintain your interest. These instructors still may be excellent at presenting the information you want to learn. They are just not entertainers.

Agree   Disagree

_____   _____   Myth 3: Your instructors will always be well prepared for each class you attend.

Reality: Most of your instructors will be well prepared for each class. Regardless of how much your instructors plan, though, sometimes a class won't work out the way they hoped. Sometimes, instructors' commitments and personal lives get in the way of their planning. They may come to class poorly prepared. Some of your instructors may even get to the point where they feel too confident and do little or no planning.

_____   _____   Myth 4: Most instructors will take a personal interest in you.

Reality: Some instructors will want to get to know you as a person and will devote a lot of time to you. They will enjoy talking with you after class, around campus, in their offices, and at social or athletic events. Some instructors, however, are so busy they just don't have much time for students. They are too busy with academic responsibilities, research, writing for publication, teaching classes, and various professional activities to have much time for anyone—even their own families. Still others are very private people. They prefer to keep relations strictly on a teacher to student basis and do not see that personal interest in students has a place in the classroom.

_____   _____   Myth 5: University and college instructors have little personal interest in students and should not be asked for assistance if a course is too difficult.

Reality: Many students are so awed by an instructor who has been transformed into a prestigious noun, such as "Doctor" or "Professor," that they assume such an instructor will have little interest or concern for a lowly student. Impressive titles and offices heaped with books and papers do tend to create distance between instructors and students, but most instructors are available and enjoy contact with students sincerely motivated to learn. Unfortunately, many students who could use help in a course do not seek assistance because of erroneous beliefs about instructors' attitudes.

_____   _____   Myth 6: Instructors want most ideas challenged and want students to present their opinions and views during class.

Reality: Many instructors will seek as much appropriate and useful student input as possible. A small proportion will

Agree   Disagree

have little or no interest in students' opinions and views. Other instructors will feel that they have limited time to present vast amounts of important information. These instructors are often rather dedicated individuals who don't wish to offend students but who very often discourage student input so as to maintain their schedules. For such instructors, getting through the course material is more important than letting students express their views.

_____   _____   Myth 7: The instructors' coverage of course material will be nonjudgmental, unbiased, objective, and comprehensive.

Reality: Many instructors use teaching as a way to advocate and promote their personal perspectives on their subject. They tend to play up why their approaches, conclusions, and methods are correct and why the views and teachings of some other people in the field are wrong. A few instructors make it clear, in their reactions to questions about opposing views or the works of certain people, that such ideas or works are not worthy of attention.

_____   _____   Myth 8: Instructors want you to accept obediently everything they say without reservation and to be able to regurgitate accurately on exams the truths they've taught.

Reality: Most instructors have two goals. One is for you to understand the basic facts and concepts in the field or subject they teach. The other is for you to learn to think for yourself. Once you understand these two goals, you can learn the content of the course while questioning basic assumptions.

_____   _____   Myth 9: Your instructors will be pleasant people.

Reality: Many of your instructors will be people who have entered the teaching profession because they enjoy having a positive effect on other people. These instructors often will be pleasant to know and will have a profound influence on their students. A small proportion of your instructors will be neither pleasant nor unpleasant. These instructors simply will be there to help you learn. A very small proportion of your instructors will be irritable, unpleasant, and boring. If you are asking the question "Do I like this instructor?" you are asking the wrong question. The right question is "Does this teacher know the subject well enough to teach me something?"

Agree   Disagree

_____   _____   **Myth 10:** Your instructors can answer all your questions about the subject.

                 Reality: Most instructors see education as an ongoing process for themselves as well as for their students. Being well educated includes learning what you don't know. Being well educated is to discover that some answers are partially true or only correct in certain circumstances.

Would you rather have an instructor who can give you what seems to be a definite correct answer about everything or one who says, once in a while, "I don't know" and then suggests a way to find the answer?

One of the results when you ask good questions and learn the answers is that you eventually run out of people who can answer your questions. Questions that no one can answer well are the forerunners of new knowledge, scientific advances, and exciting career directions.

_____   _____   **Myth 11:** Your instructors will know more than you.

Reality: If you've had a thirst for knowledge for many years, have read a lot, and have learned from life's experiences, you may find that you know more about some subjects than the instructor does. As disappointing as this may be to you, the fact is you may be too advanced for the class. If so, is that a legitimate excuse for anger at the instructor or the school?

One of the signs of having an educated heart as well as an educated mind is that you can handle those times when you discover that someone with an advanced degree knows less about a topic than you.

_____   _____   **Myth 12:** Your instructor must have firsthand experience to teach a subject well.

Reality: In trade schools, experience is essential. In many courses, however, sniping comments, such as "How can he know—he's never been there," only serve to rationalize not listening. An instructor in management can teach many practical ideas without ever having owned or run a business. A person can teach child development well without having had children. A psychologist can teach about mental disturbances without having been a mental patient. History teachers can teach well without having "been there."

Agree   Disagree

_____   _____   Firsthand experience is very useful, but not essential. In fact, many people with experience don't know how to teach what they do. Have you ever tried to learn from Granny exactly how she makes that special dessert the family loves? Asking "Has the instructor had firsthand experience?" is asking the wrong question. Asking "Can this instructor teach well?" is a better question.

DEVELOPING REALISTIC ATTITUDES

Feeling anger and disappointment because your predictions about your instructors are inaccurate can only hinder your success in college. By dispelling myths about your instructors, learning to accurately predict their behavior, and accepting instructional behavior you had not predicted, you'll avoid setting yourself up to feel victimized.

Developing realistic attitudes and strategies for coping with instructors' behavior may be an important step toward increasing your happiness and success in college. The Action Projects at the end of this chapter will provide you with guidelines for dispelling myths and for developing realistic attitudes about your instructors. Chapter 11 will help you see how changing your actions toward your instructors may enhance your success in the classroom and your general happiness in college.

GOOD ATTITUDES AND SUCCESS IN COLLEGE

When we talk to students about the myths versus the realities of college instructors, we hear disgusted, angry, impassioned, and sometimes humorous stories of students' feelings for and against instructors. We have no doubt your instructors' personalities and teaching behaviors will have a profound impact on your attitude toward learning and your performance in college.

What does all this mean for you? The reality of going to college is that you'll attend courses taught by instructors with just about every personality characteristic imaginable. You'll attend courses taught by highly competent instructors and less competent instructors. That is simply the way life works. Any student can learn something in a class an excellent instructor teaches. It takes an excellent student to learn well in a class taught by a less competent instructor or one not tuned in to your learning style.

> Remember: You are responsible for your learning. How well you do is up to you. Learning is the game, not teaching.

As you will see in more detail in Chapters 11 and 12, you can make your attitudes work for you or against you. You can attempt to get the most possible out of every course, regardless of your instructors' personalities or competency levels. Or you can complain and moan about your instructors and blame them for why you are not learning anything. It is all up to you!

ACTION PROJECTS

Dispelling Myths

1.   The way you react when an instructor doesn't live up to your expectations determines how good an education you will get. When you are disappointed, do you get mad at the instructor and the school, or do you find a way to make the course work for you?

Look at the list of myths presented in this chapter. Select one you agreed with, and challenge yourself to dispel that myth. Focus your attention on the reality of your instructors by answering these questions:

   a) Are my thoughts and beliefs about each instructor based on actual experience, or do they come from past experiences with other teachers or from statements other students made?

   b) Why is it reasonable and legitimate for instructors to be as they are even though I may be disappointed or upset?

   c) Can I learn something from an instructor who is less than ideal—who has weaknesses, flaws, and limitations?

   d) How can I change my habits and attitudes based on my assumptions? Why would it benefit me?

2.   Set a goal to dispel some other myth you believe in. Describe what you would do on a daily basis for the next month to demonstrate to yourself how erroneous your assumptions have been.

   A month from now, return to this space and write in exactly what you did the past month to change your habits and attitudes. How did you dispel the myth?

_____

_____

_____

_____

_____

SUCCESS GROUP ACTIVITIES

1.   Discuss with one another the erroneous beliefs you have had about your instructors and how certain myths may be having a negative effect on your

adjustment to college. What expectations did you have about college that have not been fulfilled? How have your false expectations created a problem for you? How can you work around it?

2.   Do group members have negative expectations about college that have not been realized to date? Discuss how if at some later point any of your negative expectations begin to appear true you can prevent them from hindering your performance as students.

3.   Have you noticed how you act when an expectation you have turns out to be untrue? Do you become upset? Angry? Depressed? Why do people become upset when their expectations are unfulfilled? How can you overcome this problem? Spend time discussing these issues. Your friends often will provide insights that are far more astute or beneficial than those of a trained counselor.

4.   Each of you make a list of how you could create a negative impression on an instructor if you actively set out to do so. Then compare one another's lists. Do the lists increase your self-awareness? Can you see how you and other students can sometimes create a negative reaction from instructors without knowing what you are doing?

5.   Talk together about what actions you can take to avoid causing negative reactions and to create more positive impressions on instructors.

Chapter 11

How to Improve the Instruction You Receive

SELF–ASSESSMENT

Place a check mark by the statements that are true of you.

_____ I know that students who make the effort to treat their instructors in positive ways learn more from their instructors than students who don't make an effort.

_____ I know that many students are unaware of the effects of their behavior on instructors.

_____ I know that students can increase awareness of the effect they have on instructors by listing ways to frustrate and irritate them.

_____ I know that negative student behavior can lead to negative instructor behavior.

_____ I know that I can get more from my instructors by complimenting them when they do something I appreciate.

HELPING YOUR INSTRUCTORS
IMPROVE THEIR TEACHING

If you say to yourself, "It's my job to help my instructors do well!" you can have a profound effect on your instructors' performance. As a student you can take many actions to make the lives of your instructors more pleasant and their performance more useful to you.

(Note: Years from now, during your working career, you will encounter similar challenges with managers. Take this opportunity to practice acquiring some useful life skills in a situation where your job is not at risk.)

MAKE SURE YOUR INSTRUCTORS KNOW YOU

No matter how large the class, find some way to introduce yourself, and tell the instructor why this course is important to you. Make an effort to help the instructor know you and recognize you. If you have special reasons for taking the course, let the instructor know what they are. Instructors need to know you are interested and motivated to learn from them.

REWARD YOUR INSTRUCTORS FOR GOOD TEACHING

When your instructors do something you consider effective, let them know you appreciate good teaching. Rewards for good teaching are few and far between. After a better-than-average lecture, tell your instructor what you liked about it. Most students are reluctant to compliment their instructors because they don't want to appear to be apple polishers. Your instructors probably will be excellent judges of sincere comments and will appreciate what you have to say. Don't hold back your compliments. Let your instructors know you like their teaching.

LEARN TO RECOGNIZE QUALITY TEACHING METHODS

Do you know exactly what makes instructors good? Can you clearly describe the specific observable behaviors that you know form the basis for quality teaching? Do you know what a student can do to reinforce good teaching or to improve teaching?

Develop a Positive Action Plan

Here are the basic steps to follow to answer the questions just raised.

Step 1. Take a few minutes to list everything good teachers do. List specifics. List observable behaviors.

In the following spaces, fill in a few specific, observable behaviors of good teachers, such as "listens attentively when I ask a question." Saying that a teacher "is nice" is not an observable behavior. When you are through, gather with several other students and compare lists. Discuss the lists and revise them.

1. _____

   _____

   _____

2. _____

   _____

   _____

3. _____

   _____

4. _____

_____

_____

5. _____

_____

_____

6. _____

_____

_____

7. _____

_____

_____

Do you believe students have a consensus as to the basic characteristics of good instruction? Compare your list to ours. Good instructors exhibit the following behaviors:

1. They clearly define their objectives for the course and each class session.

2. They clearly define course grading and testing procedures.

3. They encourage students to ask questions and participate in class discussion.

4. They answer students' questions during class.

5. They present informative and interesting lectures and class discussions.

6. They are organized and well prepared.

7. They periodically summarize the major points and issues presented in lectures and discussions.

8. They are considerate of students and treat them with respect.

9. They will admit when they are unsure of an answer.

10. They demonstrate a willingness to listen to and assess opinions that conflict with their own.

11. They are enthusiastic about teaching.

12. They provide students with assistance outside of class.

Our list of good instructional behavior is simply a starting point. We want to encourage you to consistently think about what your instructors are doing well. Equally important, we want to encourage you to reward your instructors for good instructional behavior.

Step 2. Brainstorm a list of everything you could do to reinforce a desired teaching behavior.

To brainstorm means to write out a list of ideas as fast as you can. The emphasis is on quantity, not quality. Be wild and imaginative. Be outrageous and funny. Do this with three or four other people and see how much fun brainstorming can be. Use the spaces provided here for your list.

1. _____

_____

_____

2. _____

_____

_____

3. _____

_____

_____

4. _____

_____

_____

5. _____

_____

_____

6. _____

_____

_____

7. _____

_____

_____

8. _____

_____

_____

9. _____

_____

_____

After about 5 minutes, stop and go through the list to see what things you could do. Note: You will continue to think of ideas for the list for a few more hours, so wait a day or so before finishing your basic list.

Step 3.   Type out a copy of your lists of desired teaching behaviors and teacher reinforcers and place it in your notebook.

Step 4.   Now look for the first possible opportunity to observe a good teaching behavior and reward it!

RESPOND POSITIVELY TO GOOD INSTRUCTIONAL BEHAVIOR

When your instructors are exhibiting what you consider good teaching skills, be very attentive. Nod, and even smile. Instructors' actions are determined to a large extent by the attention they receive from students. When you and the other students indicate your approval of your instructors' good teaching behavior, you'll encourage your instructors to do more of what you like and less of what you don't like.

If you don't see why your body language is important, imagine standing in front of a group of students who are nodding off to sleep, gazing out windows, carrying on private conversations, and generally acting disinterested. Would you be motivated to feel enthusiastic and to prepare well to teach this group of students?

If you have any doubt about the effect sincere attention and appreciation have on instructors, think about your own experiences. Think about the motivating effects sincere attention has had on you.

PROVIDE YOUR INSTRUCTORS WITH FEEDBACK

If your instructors encourage periodic evaluations of their classroom performance, be sure to fill out their evaluations. Let your instructors know what you like! If you want to tell an instructor that something needs to be improved, be sure to give an example of what you don't like and what you would like. Instructors find few things worse than students telling them to improve some aspect of their teaching behavior but not giving them clear examples of what the students would like them to do. For example, you might ask an instructor to give clearer instructions and to ask fewer personal stories.

HELP YOUR INSTRUCTORS BE CLEAR AND PRECISE

Encourage your instructors to clearly define their expectations of students. If an instructor is unclear when describing an assignment, pleasantly ask him or her to restate it. Don't hesitate to ask for clarification. If you didn't understand the assignment, more than likely other, more timid, students didn't either. You'll be doing yourself, your fellow students, and your instructor a favor by asking for clarification.

Regardless of how unclear an instructor's words may be, when you ask for clarification don't make a big deal about how confused you are. Don't make instructors look like idiots. Just ask them to clarify what they want and thank them for their help.

If you are still confused after asking for clarification about an assignment, don't badger the instructor. Try not to say things such as "I still don't know what you want!" or "You really haven't been clear about the assignment!" See if any other students understand what your instructor is assigning and ask them. If not, step up after class and pleasantly point out your confusion. Ask confidently; try not to act bewildered.

Unclear questions from instructors often turn students' stomachs. You're likely to think to yourself, "What is it she's asking?" Don't let your gut reaction show! Agreeably ask your instructor to restate the question. If your instructor's second attempt isn't any clearer than the first, nicely indicate that you're unsure of the answer. Again, try to avoid throwing your hands into the air and saying, "I don't know what you're getting at!"

PREPARE GOOD QUESTIONS BEFORE ATTENDING CLASS, AND ALWAYS TRY TO ANSWER YOUR INSTRUCTORS' QUESTIONS

As you read your assignments for class, decide what questions you want your instructor to answer. In class, listen attentively to see if your instructor answers your questions. If not, don't be reluctant to pose your questions to your instructor.

Most instructors want students to ask good questions. Too often, students sit back timidly, afraid to ask questions. Instructors then worry whether the students have any idea about what's going on.

Instructors prepare lectures hoping to stimulate students' inquisitiveness. If you sit back and fail to ask questions or turn your face to the floor every time an instructor poses a question, both you and the instructor will be losers. Give your instructors opportunities to demonstrate their intelligence: Ask good questions! Give yourself an opportunity to demonstrate your intelligence: Answer your instructors' questions!

ATTEND ALL CLASSES

Instructors work hard to prepare lectures. When you decide to skip a class, you are saying to your instructors, "I don't believe what you are doing is of any value!" Show your instructors by your attendance that you value what they have to say. If you must miss a class, do not show up at the next session and ask, "Did I miss anything important?" Don't remind the instructor you were absent. Just return to class and find out from a friend or another student what you missed.

TURN IN YOUR ASSIGNMENTS ON TIME

Late assignments often suggest to your instructors that you lack enthusiasm for their courses. Some instructors reciprocate with a lack of enthusiasm for your procrastination by deducting points from late papers. Do your best to show you care. Don't say it with flowers—say it with papers!

DEVELOP A FLEXIBLE LEARNING STYLE

The respected psychologist Abraham Maslow once stated that if you have clear goals, you can learn from even bad instructors. Recent research into learning styles shows, however, that the problem may not be that the instructor is bad. It may be that a mismatch exists between the instructor's teaching style and your learning style.

Auditory Versus Visual

Some people learn best by listening. Others learn best by seeing. An instructor with an auditory preference will talk a lot and not provide much information in writing. If you learn best from reading, you may see this instructor as doing a poor job.

If you learn best from what you hear, you will get along great with a talkative instructor but not well with one who relies on handouts, assigned readings, and frequent writing on the blackboard.

Left Brain Versus Right Brain

The human brain appears to be divided into two halves. In recent years, however, psychologists have shown that the two halves function so differently that the cerebral cortex can be considered two different brains: the left brain and the right brain.

The left brain makes possible the logical, analytical ways of talking and thinking. People who rely strongly on their left brain like facts, lists, charts, and objective, unemotional explanations.

The right brain is nonverbal, metaphoric, visual, sensual, and musical. People who function mostly out of their right brains live by the sights, sounds, and feelings of things. They talk with spontaneous free associations that have no apparent logical connection.

When a mismatch occurs between left brain and right brain styles, both students and instructors can be upset with each other.

Friendly Versus Distant

Instructors and students vary widely in terms of how friendly they want to be with other people and how much emotional distance they need to maintain. If you feel the instructor is too friendly or too impersonal, take a look at what this reveals about your preferred style.

External Versus Internal

Chapter 2 explained how people differ in their external and internal motivations. An instructor who uses an autocratic, controlling style will have a negative effect on students who are self-motivated. An instructor who uses a style effective with internally motivated students can cause externally motivated students to flounder.

In summary, the problems you experience with instructors will be typical of problems you will encounter throughout life with people you find it difficult to listen to, take direction from, and work with. During your career you will no doubt have a coworker, manager, or colleague you will find very difficult to work with. Instructors you find difficult to learn from provide excellent chances to practice conflict resolution skills, empathy, and tolerance for differences that develop your emotional intelligence and resiliency. Some *of the best lessons you learn in college are not in the assigned course content!*

THE GRAND SCHEME:
POSITIVE AND NEGATIVE EFFECTS

Students who get better teaching discover that *positive student behavior leads to positive instructor behavior and negative student behavior leads to negative instructor behavior.*

Students do not claim that reinforcing good teaching will turn an instructor from a Stephen King terrorizer into an angel. But, students who actively work to get better teaching are emphatic about the positive effects they can have on an instructor's performance. These students are equally emphatic about the profound negative effects students can have on instructors' behavior.

Students are wonderful at describing ways to destroy the best of instructors. Some students gleefully relate how they spearheaded a well-planned attack on a high school teacher they loathed. Their sadistic glee is often shared by other class members who remember a high school teacher who found ill-prepared, unmotivated, and uncaring students impossible to tolerate.

Strangely enough, when college students somewhat shamefully list their adolescent behaviors, they often realize what a damaging effect their behavior may have had on that disliked high school instructor. Some high school teachers literally find the inconsiderate, unmotivated, and lackluster students not worth the effort. These unhappy instructors eventually resign themselves to collecting their paychecks and enduring the daily task of teaching the "ungrateful."

The lot of the college instructor sometimes can be equally disheartening. College professors are known to complain of unmotivated, uncaring, and ill-prepared students. The causes of the professor's distress are often subtle and from, it is hoped, unconscious student behavior. In defense of themselves, college students often explain how unaware they are of the effects of their behavior on professors.

As is often the case, people are unaware of the effects their behavior has on others until it is too late. In your case, now is the best time to observe college students and the behaviors that create either dedicated and happy professors or those who become frustrated and often uncaring.

IT'S A TWO-WAY STREET

Just as student behaviors can have positive or negative effects on instructors, instructors' behavior can exert tremendous influence over how students perform in their courses.

Dr. Drew C. Appleby at Marian College in Indiana did an intriguing study in which he had students interview faculty. The interviewers asked instructors to identify which student behaviors irritated them. Appleby then asked his students to identify the instructor behaviors that irritated the students. He reported as follows:

> The purpose of the study was to identify perceptions that negatively affect the teaching/learning process. Certain student behaviors irritate faculty, and specific faculty behaviors irritate students, even though neither of these groups deliberately attempts to irritate the other. Faculty are probably unaware that some of their behavior irritates students, and students may be equally unaware that many of their behaviors irritate teachers. The quality of the teaching/learning environment might be significantly improved if both groups become aware of the impact of these behaviors and decrease their frequency.

The results of these interviews are truly enlightening and should guide both student and instructor behavior. Appleby found that "(a) teachers are irritated by students who act bored, (b) students are irritated by teachers who are poor communicators, and (c) both groups are irritated by behaviors that they interpret as rude or disrespectful."

A clear consensus arose among faculty about irritating student behaviors. An equally clear consensus arose among students about irritating instructor behaviors. Appleby's research supports the notion that a circular causal relationship exists between student and instructor behavior. When students act negatively, instructors in turn respond to students negatively, which then leads to more negative student behavior.

This research tells us we must learn to be aware as students and instructors of the effects of our behavior on one another. Equally important, we must learn to act appropriately toward one another and sense when our behavior is having both positive and negative consequences.

BEHAVIORS GUARANTEED TO FRUSTRATE INSTRUCTORS

As you read the following behaviors, ask yourself these three questions:

1. How often have I behaved this way to an instructor?
2. What effect would this behavior have on me if I were the instructor?
3. If I were the instructor, how would I respond to students who act in such ways?

By taking the perspective of your instructors, you may discover why it's academic suicide to behave inconsiderately toward them. You may appreciate how easily professors can become disheartened by nice students who simply aren't aware of what it's like to deal with well-meaning but unthinking students.

ARGUE ANGRILY WITH INSTRUCTORS, ESPECIALLY OVER EXAMS

Students consistently describe instances when frustrated classmates verbally attack instructors' statements. You have a right to your opinion. But regardless of how seriously you differ with your instructor, you needn't argue. A huffy, heated attack on your instructor's position will gain neither of you anything but a mutual dislike.

Useful Alternative

Learn to present your difference of opinion assertively but without anger. Ask questions to find out why the differences exist. Turn the conflict into a learning experience.

TREAT CLASSES AS SOCIAL HOURS OR AS UNWANTED OBLIGATIONS

For a variety of reasons, students often carry on private conversations, act bored, show up late, sleep, leave early, or simply play the fool in class. You wouldn't be paid for sleeping, playing cards, or socializing with your best friend if you were working. Instructors are justified in feeling that you don't belong in their courses if you appear disinterested in learning.

Useful Alternative

Save all socializing for before and after class.

BE A KNOW-IT-ALL STUDENT

We've all experienced know-it-all students who act as though no one has anything of importance to say but them. Know-it-alls are universally disliked. Our students have heard comments directed at know-it-alls such as "Oh, we don't get to hear from you again, do we?" or "You're so smart! You always have the final word!"

Useful alternative

If you treat other students as valuable people you can learn from, you'll be way ahead of the game. Assume everyone has something valuable to say. Acknowledge other students' contributions. If you always try to prove that your instructors and fellow students know less than you, you are only wasting your time.

TELL EMOTIONAL OR PERSONAL STORIES LEADING NOWHERE

Students often become so involved with class discussions that they diverge into personal stories that typically have little value to anyone. Instructors are just as guilty of overpersonalizing their courses. Sometimes our personal experiences are relevant to the focus of class discussion. We simply urge you to always ask yourself, "Will the personal comment I'm going to make add to the class discussion, or do I just want to tell people about myself?"

Periodically, the focus of a class discussion can lead people to become heated, angry, elated, joyous, or just about any emotional state imaginable. When you become emotional in class, if you're like most people you may tend to allow your mouth to run off with your emotions. Students often define such emotional behavior as "spilling your guts." We've all spilled our guts at times. We're all human. But learn to ask yourself, "Do I really want to say what I am going to say when I feel like this? Do I want to think about what I am responding to and be sure that what I have to say has value? If I do say something, need I be emotional?"

Useful Alternative

Learning to think about what you're going to say and why you're going to say it is a skill everyone needs to practice. In your case, the crucial questions are "Will what I say have value?" and "How can I say what I want to ensure it will be most useful to other people?"

EXPECT YOUR INSTRUCTORS TO BE OUTSTANDING EVERY DAY

All of us have days when we'd prefer to avoid contact with other people. Professors do not have the luxury of hiding in a closet until a bad mood passes. If they haven't had time to prepare for class, they still have to show up. Allow your instructors some bad days.

Useful Alternative

Show a little compassion. Don't expect the impossible. No one can be outstanding every day. If your professor appears to be having an off day, do your best to make the class a good one. Be more attentive than ever. Ask good questions. Nod and smile at everything your instructor does well. (A word of caution: Don't overdo it. You needn't look like a smiling Cheshire cat. Just be positive.) After class, if you liked your instructor's performance, go out of your way to say so. It's doubly important on tough days for instructors to know that they can ride out a storm.

TELL OTHER STUDENTS WHAT YOU DISLIKE ABOUT THE INSTRUCTOR, NEVER GOING DIRECTLY TO THE INSTRUCTOR

It is easy for you to complain to other students about a particular instructor. The problem is that your complaints won't help your instructor teach better or your classmates learn more. Your complaints may result in students responding negatively toward your instructor, which will surely hurt his or her performance. So why make classes tough for your instructor, your fellow students, and yourself?

Useful Alternative

Encourage other students to get the most out of instructors' courses. Never downgrade your instructors to other students. Try to help your instructors, not hurt them! Encourage yourself and other students to look for the good points about your instructors. As we've stated throughout this chapter, try to create a climate that encourages your instructors to do an even better job.

If you decide you just don't have the time or interest to help your instructors improve their performance, at least keep your negative comments to yourself. Don't make other students suffer who are willing to try to help your instructors.

BE IRRITATING TO AN INSTRUCTOR WHO IRRITATES YOU

Don't cut class, drop the course, or transfer to another class when you have an instructor you find irritating. Instead, attend class and do things such as these to communicate your negative opinion:

- You take a paperback book to class and read it while the instructor lectures.
- If you knit, take your knitting to class and work on it instead of taking notes, clicking the needles loudly if you can.
- You sit back with your arms crossed and refuse to take any notes while everyone else is writing furiously. You scowl and sneer at those who are taking notes.
- You use class time to clip your fingernails.
- Just as the instructor leads up to an important point in the lecture, you lean over and whisper loudly to a classmate. You include muffled laughs and snickers. You keep it up, pretending not to notice how distracting your whispering is to the class and how angry the teacher is getting.

None of these actions accomplish anything but irritating the instructor.

Useful Alternative

Be responsible for your feelings. When you blame others for your feelings, you are letting other people control you. Try to determine exactly why you find the instructor so annoying. Consider this as information about yourself and try to learn a lesson.

TALK DOWN TO INSTRUCTORS YOU THINK ARE "LOSERS"

Like most students, you probably will feel that one or two of your instructors are excellent, most of the others are adequate, and that one is "not so great." You might wrongly consider this a good opportunity to sneer at, be sarcastic with, and show open contempt for a teacher. You may think this proves to other students that you are so tough you can put down instructors to their faces. But, how does this attitude satisfy your learning goals and those of other students?

Useful Alternative

If you can't avoid being sarcastic, then consider not saying anything at all. It is tough enough being an instructor, especially when you know that some of the students openly dislike you. Instructors have all the fears you might have if you had to make useful presentations to the same group day after day.

Remember, too, that it is a function of your human nature to like one of your instructors the best and another the least. If you really wanted better teaching, you could give the instructor a sincere compliment after a better-than-average lecture. You could take the various actions we recommend at the beginning of this chapter to encourage good teaching. If you are critical of teachers in a way that is neither helpful nor useful to them, you are focusing on a target for your disgust more than on your need for good teaching.

Ask Your Instructors to Be Personal Counselors

It's natural for you to want to be friendly with your instructors, but, unfortunately, some students expect too much of them. These students expect their instructors to be terribly interested in all their personal ideas, interests, and problems. Most instructors want to be friendly with their students but are not in a position to be all things to all students.

The difficulties begin to arise when students start dropping in all the time to talk, to unload about their personal problems, and generally to cut into the rather tight schedules many professors work under. Professors often feel uncomfortable discouraging such calls. Few professors want to be known as uncaring or uninterested in their students. Instructors want the best for their students and are usually willing to try to help. It's simply unfair to ask professors to spend their time socializing on the job or solving your personal problems.

Useful Alternative

Try not to ask your instructors to do more than they are professionally equipped to handle. If you need help with personal problems, see the professional counselors at your college, or talk to your best friends.

Demand That Your Instructors Give You Special Favors and Consideration

We've known students who missed half of the semester and then asked if they can somehow get the information from the instructor. We've known students who asked instructors if they could take the midterm 2 weeks late because they were leaving early on spring break for a vacation in Florida. Our favorite is the student who called an instructor at 8:00 A.M. on Saturday to find out if he missed anything important during the week of classes he missed while vacationing in South America. These minor special requests are unfair both to the instructors and to other students.

Useful Alternative

Most of your instructors will be people who are interested in your academic and personal well-being. Instructors understand that you may run into financial, transportation, health, or numerous other problems that interfere with successful performance in class. Don't be afraid to let your instructor know when an important event drastically alters your performance. If you're ill with the flu for 2 weeks, let your instructor know why you're missing class. Instructors appreciate knowing why students aren't coming to class.

Minor problems should be kept to yourself. If your car breaks down and you miss class, don't come in with a big song and dance, expecting your instructor to pray for your car and give you lecture notes. Accept the bad with the good. Borrow notes from someone in the course. Don't expect your instructor to repeat an entire lecture for you.

In short, if something of tremendous importance necessitates asking a favor from your instructor, don't hold back! But if life's minor irritations have made your student life a bit miserable, assume you'll recover. Don't throw your personal problems at your instructor. You'll probably find that you'll live happily ever after if you forget the past and proceed with the future.

HOW TO SALVAGE A BAD GRADE: DIPLOMACY AND WILLINGNESS TO WORK

If you are likely to receive a D or F in a course, you often can salvage a bad grade. But you have to learn to be diplomatic and pleasant to deal with.

Too often, students having academic problems approach instructors with unbelievable stories, rather than accepting that a straightforward approach is best. Talk to your instructor and ask for a chance to make up or improve your work. Go with a plan. Offer to make up or retake exams. Ask if you can write an extra paper or rewrite the project you threw together the night before it was due. Explain why you are willing to do extra work.

Instructors are much more likely to give students a chance to make amends if the students accept responsibility for their poor state of affairs. If you get caught in this situation, you need to acknowledge responsibility for having done poorly. You need to acknowledge that you are willing to turn over a new leaf rather quickly.

Most instructors will give you a chance. Bad grades are not permanent unless you allow them to be. For example, if you do poorly on the midterm or final for reasons other than that you just didn't study, then it is fair to ask to take a makeup exam. Ask for a chance to show you do know the material. Maybe you didn't prepare correctly or you were ill. The situation has changed now, and it may be appropriate to ask for a chance to redeem yourself. Even if the instructor says you can't take the test to change your grade, ask to take it anyway just to see for yourself if you can do better. Assuming you get a better score, this will have a positive psychological effect on you and possibly the instructor.

If you anticipate a bad grade in a course because, for legitimate reasons, you haven't been able to turn in all the work, consider asking the instructor to submit an "Incomplete" on the grade sheet. Your instructor may be willing to follow school policies that allow students to complete course work after the course is over. At most schools you have several weeks into the next semester to complete the work.

You can change the past if you want to. A sincere request for another chance, a specific plan about what you will do, and a commitment to do it may influence the sternest instructors and deans.

GETTING HELP FROM SCHOOL SUPPORT SERVICES

Students often are unaware as to why they are facing difficulties. You may need professional instruction in reading and study skills that is offered from academic support programs on campus. You may have personal problems getting in your way. Your college will have professional counselors to offer guidance. Sometimes students just need a break from college, which in many colleges is called "stopping out." Your adviser may see a need for this and may be able to arrange for you to take a leave of absence and come back later.

It is critical to know that colleges want you to succeed. But it will be up to you to seek help. The help is usually available if you seek it out.

Whatever you do, don't just quit. If your college courses are overpowering you, you don't have to become a dropout. Don't just disappear or not show up for registration. Talk to your advisers, and explore several possibilities.

SEEING INSTRUCTORS AS HUMAN BEINGS

The discussion of "Behaviors Guaranteed to Frustrate Instructors" is not meant to convey the message that instructors are special people who have to be treated with kid gloves. Absolutely not! Instructors react to pressures, demands, problems, stresses, and all the other factors that complicate our lives.

Instructors are human beings just like you. They prefer to be treated nicely. They want you to come to their classes and learn everything you ever wanted to know. Most instructors will work overtime to help you. If you'll look for the positive in your instructors and try to make their classes pleasant and enlightening, most of them will do everything humanly possible to make your life as a student just as satisfying.

But remember, if you ask too much of your instructors, cut into their personal lives, appear disinterested in their courses, or generally make a pest of yourself, you'll encourage them to be sullen and angry individuals. You'll hear instructors complain about not having enough time to get their work done. You'll hear professors gripe about students who don't show up for class, don't ask good questions, don't seem to be interested in learning, and all in all are no joy to teach.

Accept that you will have great instructors, mediocre instructors, and some who are less than desirable. What we're suggesting to you is the simple fact that you can make a difference! You can choose to help your instructors be better instructors who enjoy teaching. In contrast, you can choose to behave in ways that cause instructors to be unhelpful and boring. Instructors who carry a chip on their shoulders often are created by students who don't appear to care about their education. The choice is yours. We suspect you'll want to do your best to help your instructors do their best for you and your fellow students.

ACTION PROJECT

Turn a Negative Instructor to Student Relationship Into a Positive One

STEP 1. WHAT BEHAVIORS OR HABITS DO YOU EXHIBIT IN A CLASS YOU DON'T PARTICULARLY CARE FOR THAT MIGHT RESULT IN YOUR INSTRUCTOR DEVELOPING A NEGATIVE ATTITUDE TOWARD YOU? LIST THEM BELOW:

_____

_____

_____

STEP 2. WHAT COULD YOU DO INSTEAD TO DRAW MORE POSITIVE REACTIONS TOWARD YOU? LIST THE BEHAVIORS BELOW:

_____

_____

_____

STEP 3. PRACTICE YOUR NEW BEHAVIORS FOR A MONTH. THEN RETURN TO THIS SPACE AND DESCRIBE HOW YOUR BEHAVIOR HAS CHANGED IN THE CLASS. DISCUSS WHETHER OR NOT BY BEHAVING DIFFERENTLY YOU HAVE DEVELOPED A DIFFERENT ATTITUDE TOWARD THE CLASS AND THE INSTRUCTOR. WRITE YOUR ANSWER BELOW:

_____

_____

_____

STEP 4. IF YOUR BEHAVIOR IN A CLASS CHANGED, DID YOUR PERCEPTION OF THE CLASS CHANGE? WHAT DOES THIS TELL YOU ABOUT THE

PEANUTS reprinted by permission of United Feature Syndicate, Inc.

EFFECTS OF YOUR HABITS ON YOUR ATTITUDES? WRITE YOUR ANSWER BELOW:

_____

_____

_____

YOUR PORTFOLIO

Keep a record of how you successfully handled a situation with an instructor you found difficult. This is essential information for future employers because you are bound to encounter difficult managers. Describe how you problem-solved the challenges, your proactive plan, the outcome, and what you learned.

SUCCESS GROUP ACTIVITIES

Getting Better Teaching

With your friends and success group members decide which of the following strategies would be the best for all of you to try. Try not to take on too much.

You want to figure out which would be best for you and focus on doing them well.

1.   Take some time with several classmates to develop a list of what good teachers do. List specific, observable behaviors.

2.   Look at how your learning style might differ from the instructor's teaching style. Clarify what you might ask the instructor to do that would be useful for you.

3.   List everything you might do that could reward an instructor.

4.   Observe each instructor to see how much or how little your desired teaching behaviors occur.

5.   List everything students do that can irritate, bother, or upset instructors and make teaching an unpleasant experience.

6.   Observe how you react when a teacher is less than what you would like. Ask yourself, "Do I do any of the things that upset and frustrate teachers?"

7.   Track positives. When an instructor scores low in giving you good teaching behaviors, look for any little signs of improvement and immediately reinforce them.

8.   Compliment and reward instructors who do many of the things you list as good teaching. Be specific. Let instructors know what you appreciate. Remember: The more quickly you reward a desired behavior, the more effective your reward.

9.   Ask yourself, "Am I a rewarding person to have in class?" If you aren't, then here is a good chance to practice. Remember: Trite as it is, the old idea of "an apple for the teacher" is wise to follow!

10. Talk with one another about the results of your efforts. What went well? What did you learn? Compliment one another in the process.

Help a Teaching Assistant

Many teaching assistants (TAs) report feeling nervous about their roles. Few TAs have ever taught before and are anxious to make the class go well.

With your success group, decide on a few actions all of you can take to help your teaching assistant provide better instruction and feel more comfortable with your class. Choose a few things everyone in your group can do consistently. For example, if your TA appears to be interested in students' questions, make sure you regularly have several questions about the readings or lectures. If your TA lectures, group members should take good notes you can develop questions from. Show you pay attention to the lectures by asking for just a few minutes to review with the TA the questions you have developed.

Naturally, this procedure will work better with TAs who are interested in students' opinions. You may run into a TA who doesn't want to be bothered, who just wants to lecture and not be interrupted by students' comments or concerns. These TAs tend to be few and far between. Don't devote much extra time to these instructors. Give your added attention to the TA who is really concerned and could use a little encouragement from students, especially well-prepared and interested students.

Chapter 12

How to Develop Friendships and Gain Support From Your Family

SELF–ASSESSMENT

Place a check mark by the statements that are true of you.

_____ I am lonelier in college than I had thought I would be.

_____ I understand that loneliness is a problem for many college students.

_____ I know how to increase the number of friends I have.

_____ I enjoy having the opportunity to meet students from other cultures and backgrounds different from mine.

_____ I have found it difficult to mix with others in college who are very different from me.

_____ I know what to do if I feel unworthy of friendship.

_____ I am pretty good at getting emotional support from my family.

FRIENDS ARE ESSENTIAL IN COLLEGE!

Graduating seniors from nine colleges were surveyed to find out what factors contributed significantly to a successful and satisfying college career. The seniors ranked "personal contacts with other students" far above every other factor.

Friends can help you maintain your enthusiasm for studying. It is hard to be enthusiastic about studying and learning when you feel homesick or lonely. Little energy is available for studying and learning when the need to be accepted and liked dominates your thoughts and concerns.

Friendships are a great antidote to the stresses and strains of college. Evidence is accumulating that people who spend time talking with friends have stronger immune systems and remain healthier than those who don't.

Friends help protect you against vulnerability to the opinions and manipulations of strangers. Friends can lessen the effects of bad grades, of being dumped by someone you like, and of other discouraging or upsetting experiences.

Fortunately, you can do many things to increase the number of friends you have and the amount of warm support you get from your family. It is not necessary to struggle through school with a rather lonely existence, hoping that life will improve later on.

GUIDELINES FOR DEVELOPING FRIENDSHIPS

As with success in college, you can choose how many friends you have. It is not a matter of luck, of having money, or of possessing a great personality. Friendships develop between people due to a combination of variables you can influence.

HAVE FREQUENT CONTACT WITH OTHERS

Research into the sources of friendship feelings shows that the main contributing factor is frequency of contact. That is partly why we have emphasized so often in this book that a realistic plan for succeeding more in school should include frequent opportunities to spend time with friends.

Research in college dorms, apartment houses, and neighborhoods shows a consistent relationship between friendship and how often people contact one another. One study of married students in campus housing, for example, showed that couples living in certain apartments developed friendships more frequently than would be predicted by chance. These people were living in apartments at the foot of the stairs. Observation finally revealed that the couples were seen more frequently because the garbage cans were located near the bottom of the stairs!

Many such studies show that, in general, the closer you live to someone, the more likely he or she will remain a close friend. Once you understand how frequency of contact influences friendship, you can see why certain conditions predict that some students will have fewer friends at school. Don't take a lack of friends personally if any of the following apply to you:

- Living at home instead of in student housing
- Not a fraternity or sorority member
- Married to someone who is not a student
- Working full-time while attending school
- Studying all the time
- Training full-time for individual athletic events, such as swimming or long-distance running
- Being a quiet loner who rarely talks to anyone

To have more frequent contact with other students, get involved in one or more of the many extracurricular activities on campus, such as the following:

- Committees for student body activities such as Homecoming Weekend
- Intramural sports
- Environmental causes or social-action groups
- Special-interest clubs and groups, such as the psychology club, ski club, foreign students' club, or photography club
- School newspaper
- Church-sponsored social activities near campus

A wide variety of activities is available to bring you into contact with other students with similar interests. Keep in mind that it is not unusual for a beginning student to feel lonely. Loneliness is a normal experience when in a totally new situation without contact in person with old friends and family.

If you feel homesick, phone home. Write letters or e-mail messages or exchange audiocassette "letters" with your family. Get a cassette tape recorder and make a short tape to send home. Your family would like to hear from you. Sending tapes from time to time also will help them make the transition with you as you assume your new role as an educated adult.

Stay in touch with several good friends from high school. Exchange e-mails, letters, or cassette tape messages with them. Exchanging tapes probably will feel better than writing or e-mails because you gain much more from hearing a familiar voice. Besides, people often will say things on tape about personal experiences they wouldn't want to put into e-file or letter!

BE MORE OUTGOING

Can you walk up to someone who looks interesting and initiate a conversation? If you are in the cafeteria, can you go to a stranger, ask permission to join that person, and ask several questions that will help you get to know each other? Can you voluntarily offer your opinions or thoughts in a way that lets others get to know you?

Once you decide to take some initiative and to make a reasonable effort to create what you want, you will find that your life works better in all areas. One of the important lessons of life is to learn how to develop friendships, how to be a good friend, and how to gain the support of other people. It could be that learning how to develop and maintain friendships and gain support will prove to be one of the most valuable abilities you learn in college.

What Is Not Useful

If you sit around passively and hope others will go out of their way to make friends with you, you are likely to be disappointed. Shyness does not have to be a terminal condition unless you want it to be!

If you feel you lack assertiveness, we recommend reading several books on becoming more assertive. They will provide excellent advice and examples on how to behave in ways that will help you improve your interaction skills.

BE A GOOD LISTENER

People like being listened to. They feel friendly toward a person who has a sincere interest in them. How do you accomplish this? Ask questions and listen with an open mind.

Dale Carnegie, the famous author of *How to Win Friends and Influence People,* states, "You can make more friends in two months by being interested in other people than you can in two years by trying to get other people interested in you." Why should other people be interested in you if you aren't interested in them?

So do not work at being liked. Work more at finding out what is likable about each person you have contact with. Good listeners have a wide range of acceptance for what they learn about others. This is why so many people feel friendly toward a person who is accepting and tolerant. Your behavior is contagious. Positive behavior creates positive reactions; negative behavior gets negative reactions.

Be Open Minded

If the person you are listening to has attitudes and opinions you dislike, the chances are poor that you will become good friends. You can have empathy for the individual, but you probably will not have much in the way of friendship. A quick way to become more open minded about other people and less judgmental is to develop the habit of mentally responding "That's okay" when you learn about another person's thoughts and attitudes.

What Is Not Useful. A judgmental person, even though remaining silent, eventually communicates through facial expressions, body language, and other reactions the attitude of "no one should think that" or "that's sick."

If we compare observing, open-minded people with those who are more judgmental in their reactions, the ranges of acceptance and rejection look like the scales shown here:

Open minded

accept	neutral	reject

Judgmental

accept	neutral	reject

Notice that the open-minded person has not only a wider range of acceptance but also a wider neutral range where new information is neither accepted nor rejected. People respond well to this trait. If instead you constantly have a judgmental attitude about the ways other people think and live their lives, frequency of contact with others will make very little difference and will not lead to close friendships.

LET PEOPLE KNOW YOU

If you want people to accept you and like you, you must let them know what you feel, think, and do. If people have very little sense of you as a person, you give little for them to relate to. Accept that when some people learn about your feelings and thinking, they won't like what they hear. That's okay.

No matter what you are like as a person, someone is going to dislike you. That is the way the world works. Trying to avoid being disliked will prevent you from being liked. Allowing people to know more about you is the only way to gain the friendships and acceptance you need.

What Is Not Useful

Putting on an act that impresses others creates a barrier to friendship. How? Because when people smile and show that they like you, a part of you knows it is your act they like. This makes their response emotionally dissatisfying. You tend to question how much you can really respect anyone who falls for an act such as yours. And you still end up feeling lonely because you have private thoughts and feelings others don't see. No, trying to invent the perfect act is not the way to avoid feeling lonely. It is guaranteed to make you stay lonely behind a happy front.

BE EMOTIONALLY HONEST

Did your parents raise you to be honest? Probably so. And did they raise you to hide certain feelings? Were you told, "Don't get angry, don't be selfish, don't complain, don't brag," and so forth? If so, you were raised to be an emotional liar. You were raised to deceive people into believing you do not have such feelings.

Your parents had good intentions, of course, because people who constantly express such feelings are very difficult to be around. The problem is that people who try never to feel angry, selfish, negative, or proud are also very difficult to be around. Expressing such feelings either too much or too little makes friendships difficult.

FEEL WORTHY OF FRIENDSHIP

If you do not feel worthy of friendship, none of the recommended actions will work for you. How do you react when people like you? Is it enjoyable, or do you get embarrassed? When people tell you they like you, do you say "Thank you," or do you feel uncomfortable?

What is your opinion of people who like you? Is it positive or negative? Do you respect them, or do you question their judgment? If you believe that anyone who likes you is a person of questionable judgment, you definitely have a problem!

If you feel uncomfortable when people make efforts to befriend you, take a little time to make as long a list as you can in answer to these questions: What are all the good reasons people would enjoy being friends with me? In what ways am I a nice person to be around? What are all the things I like and appreciate about myself?

If you are uncomfortable about attempting to answer such questions, you may have been raised to avoid feelings of self-esteem. Conscious self-esteem is necessary, however, to function well in the world. As was discussed in Chapter 2, self-esteem allows you to accept people's praise and affections as legitimate.

Remember, it is not conceited to think well of yourself. Conceit means to feel superior to others and informing them about it. Self-esteem means to feel basically good about yourself even though you still have a lot to learn.

VISIT THE COUNSELING CENTER

Let's say you have frequent contact with others, listen well, are open minded, express your feelings honestly, and yet are still shy and lack friends. The counseling center has books and cassette tapes on how to overcome your shyness.

You may want to have a few sessions with a counselor to talk about why you are so shy. It is possible you want to be cautious about not revealing to others something from your home life. Adult children of alcoholic parents, for example, are often guarded and try to present a cheerful front rather than revealing themselve easily. Go find out.

FRIENDSHIPS WITH STUDENTS FROM OTHER CULTURES AND BACKGROUNDS

One of the most exciting discoveries about attending college, for many, is that students learn about cultures very different from the one they know. As a college student, you have some rich opportunities for multicultural experiences. You have many chances to learn how to live and work successfully with people who may be different from you.

Which of the following statements reflect your expectancies about how your college experience would prepare you to live and work with other people? Check off those that apply.

_____ I EXPECTED THE COURSES AND INSTRUCTORS TO EXPAND MY
KNOWLEDGE OF THE PEOPLE WHO INHABIT THE WORLD.

_____ I LOOKED FORWARD TO THE OPPORTUNITY TO MEET PEOPLE WHO
HAD RELIGIOUS PHILOSOPHIES VERY DIFFERENT FROM MY OWN.

_____ I HOPED TO MEET AND GET TO KNOW PEOPLE OF ALL RACES.

_____ I HOPED TO MEET PEOPLE WHOSE SOCIOECONOMIC STATUS WAS
VERY DIFFERENT FROM MY OWN.

_____ I LOOKED FORWARD TO MEETING PEOPLE WHOSE LANGUAGE AND
BACKGROUND WERE DIFFERENT FROM MY OWN.

_____ I HAD HOPED THAT BY MEETING AND GETTING TO KNOW PEOPLE
DIFFERENT FROM MYSELF, I WOULD INCREASE MY ABILITY TO WORK
IN POSITIONS THAT REQUIRE CROSS-CULTURAL SKILLS.

The opportunities you have in college to meet and interact with people very different from yourself bring you many unexpected benefits. The observations of college graduates and their employers reveal many useful payoffs. Comments from graduates follow:

"College helped me get rid of many of my stereotypes of what people who are different from me are like."

"Learning to work successfully with all types of people was as important as anything I learned in college."

"The world is changing so fast. It is getting smaller by the day. I really needed to learn to understand what people from other parts of the world were like and how they saw life."

"College really opened my eyes as to how little I knew. It is not that I have changed my values so much. What has happened is that I have a better understanding of why other people think and act as they do."

These are some comments from employers:

"My company can't afford to hire people who can't listen to and appreciate another person's views. After all, we are selling to an international market. We must understand what people want and why they want it. Our salespeople must know how to work with people who are very different from themselves."

"The number one thing our company looks for is intelligent people who can communicate. That means they can read, write, and learn effectively. Learning is a key. They must be able to get along with all types of people and learn from them. It isn't a matter of being a company person. What matters is that you are enthusiastic about meeting and working with all types of people."

"No matter how you cut it, a person in our line of business has to be people-oriented. You have to be able to get along with other people. That doesn't mean you can't have your own opinions. You have to appreciate the value of other people's ideas and be willing to learn from them."

The comments from directors of personnel, directors of training, office managers, owners of private businesses, and CEOs abound with this message: Success in life requires that you appreciate the other person's perspective.

It is really rewarding to talk with college freshmen who have stayed up until 3:00 in the morning in discussions with dorm mates. We typically find that many freshmen say these discussions are more enlightening than some of their courses. That is what college is all about.

GAINING SUPPORT FROM YOUR FAMILY: BARBARA'S STORY

It is easy to think, "If only my parents were different, things would be much nicer for me." That might be true, of course, but such thoughts are not likely to lead to much improvement.

You have the ability, if you want to use it, to improve your relationships with your family. Once you develop the intention to change things and start looking for ways to make small improvements, you can get some positive results. Here is one example of many that we know about.

Barbara was starting her sophomore year in nursing school when she took introductory psychology. For a course assignment, she was required to do a behavioral-change project. The project involved using principles of behavioral change with a person she had frequent contact with in daily life.

Other students in the class went to work on younger sisters, a neighbor's child, bus drivers, talkative roommates, boyfriends who drove too fast, smokers, overweight friends, and other available subjects. Barbara decided to use her father as the subject for her project.

Barbara lived at home, and her relationship with her father was very poor. She described the situation as follows:

> We were always looking for ways to cut each other. He enjoyed saying rotten things about nurses to me. If he'd say "Good morning" to me, I'd say "What's good about it!" If I came home from school excited about something and wanted to talk about it, he would just sit there in his chair and keep on reading. He didn't care about anything that was happening to me. Once when I was trying to talk to him about school, he got up and walked out of the room. Didn't say a word. Just walked out.
>
> He is retired, so he is usually home during the day. I know he likes it if when I'm home at lunchtime, I make a bowl of soup for him. I'd go into the kitchen and make myself something.
>
> He would get his hopes up and then be disappointed when he saw I only fixed something for myself. Chocolate cake is his favorite, so when I baked something I made sure it was not chocolate cake.
>
> When we were assigned the project, I decided to see if I could improve my life at home. It is hard enough getting through nursing school without always having a big hassle at home. I've been dreaming about going into nursing for a long time. It's exciting! I wanted my family to care!

BARBARA'S PLAN FOR HERSELF

Barbara decided that each time her father responded pleasantly or positively, she could be pleasant to him and do something special to show her appreciation for his interest in her. She would immediately attend to the slightest positive gesture from him. She would try never to overlook the slightest improvement, no matter how small or weak. Her goal was to increase the number of times her father showed interest in her and also the depth of his interest.

Following the procedures recommended in class, Barbara outlined these steps:

Desired project goal: Father to greet me cheerfully each morning; show interest in what is happening at school; talk with me about school.

Current level of desired behavior: Seldom looks at me or listens when I am talking about school; never asks about school.

Reinforcements to father for increase in desired behavior:

- bowl of soup at lunch
- bake cookies and chocolate cake
- smile and say "Thanks for talking with me"
- kiss on the cheek.

Three weeks later Barbara reported the results of her project to the class:

My first chance to use a reinforcement was during a lunchtime. I talked with Dad for several minutes, and he listened without looking at his magazine. I didn't try to push my luck by going on too long, so I got up and asked him if he would like for me to fix him a bowl of soup. His face brightened up. He smiled and said "Yes."

In the morning if he said hello to me, I'd smile and say "Hello" and kiss him on the cheek. Mornings are much more pleasant now.

After about three times fixing him soup at lunch, he began showing more interest and would ask questions. Then one evening he asked me to tell him about a book I read, and we spent almost 20 minutes talking. I immediately got up and went out to the kitchen and baked him a batch of cookies.

Last Friday afternoon I got home about 1:30. He got up from his chair as soon as he heard me come in and came over and said "I've been waiting for you. I would like to know more about what you are doing in school if you have time to talk." Did I ever! We spent 2 hours talking. That is the longest my father has had a conversation with me in my whole life! It was great! He was really interested. When we finished, I gave him a big hug, said how great it was talking with him, and went out and baked him a chocolate cake.

[Barbara suddenly grew quiet. Her eyes started to water, and she struggled to hold back tears. Her voice choked up a little as she went on.]

Something happened this morning that isn't in my written report. I was getting ready to leave for school, and Dad came up and put his arms around me. He said, "Barbara, I want to take you out to dinner next week. I want to get to know you better before it's too late."

Like many people who want their lives to improve, Barbara discovered that by changing how she interacted with her father, he changed in ways she had hoped for. She took steps to improve how she and her father got along, and he responded in positive ways.

When you are willing to try something different and are open to altering old habits, you can change your life. Knowing how to modify your behavior on your own by learning directly from your life experiences is an essential skill to develop, because you always will have problems and challenges in your life that no one prepared you for and that no one can teach you how to handle well. You have to learn some skills all by yourself—and that is the focus of the next chapter.

ACTION PROJECTS

Gaining More Support From Your Family

Most students want and appreciate support from their families. Yet students often report that they receive less praise and recognition for their academic accomplishments than they hoped for. In fact, it is not uncommon for a family member to be critical or to make discouraging remarks about academic pursuits.

If you have an upsetting conflict with a family member and would like to make relations more pleasant, review "Barbara's Plan for Herself." Then develop a plan of action that has a realistic chance of leading to an improvement.

To improve your contact with your family, however, you also may have to engage in some uncomfortable self-examination. Can you admit to yourself that you have been acting in ways that maintain the conflict?

If you have no big problems with your family members except lack of interest and support, develop a plan of action for yourself based on the principles described in this chapter. Think about how you would like relations to be between yourself and your family, and then take the necessary steps.

Developing More Friends

Review the chapter, outlining the principles related to creating friendships. Then select someone to test the principles on. Choose a person you feel equal to, someone likely to have attitudes and interests similar to yours. To increase your chance of success, select a person who is easily available to you. Then you'll have more opportunities for frequent contact. Follow these steps:

1. Start by having frequent but brief contacts with the person. Develop the habit of saying "Hi!" as you walk by. Wave to the person as you pass. Nod and smile whenever you have an opportunity. Find out the person's name and say hello, using this person's name, every time you have a chance.

2. As you sense feelings of friendly recognition developing, be ready for an opportunity to ask the person one or two questions about himself or herself. Be

specific. Ask, "How are your exams going this term?" or "What do you think of the president's announcement yesterday?" Be willing to reveal your private attitudes or feelings briefly, and then quickly focus your attention back onto the other person. Don't be overly quick to like a person; don't be too eager, not at first.

3.   Be a good listener. Listen with interest and an open mind. Try to learn what it is like to be the other person. Try to discover what is unique about this individual. Then, as you find out what he or she is really like, let yourself warm up more.

Don't be overly concerned if at first you feel you are manipulating the situation or doing what is so obvious that the person will see through it. People will be flattered you are making the effort. You're really acting as people do who have good friends. When you conduct yourself in a new way, at first you are very aware of it. But as you practice and see that it works, it gradually becomes a habit. You become unaware of what you're doing, and it becomes more natural for you.

Helping Someone Who Wants a New Start

Do you feel concerned about someone who uses alcohol and other drugs too much? Would you be available to help that person if he or she wanted to stay sober and drug free?

These are important questions to think about because students working with other students is the key ingredient to every successful rehabilitation program on college campuses. Many universities have made significant improvements in reducing student alcohol consumption. The key in every program is new friendships—and that is where you come in.

A Friendly Challenge

Do you want to undertake a worthwhile challenge? What if your success group, or you individually, offered friendship and some good times together to a fellow student wanting to get off drugs and alcohol?

If your campus has a program, how about volunteering to help out? If it doesn't, consider doing something on your own.

Our nation has a problem with drugs and alcohol. It is a problem in schools, on the highways, in the workplace, and in homes. But healthy, responsible lifestyles cannot be legislated. The solution to the problem of alcohol and other drugs is friends. Strong friends. Quality friends.

You can do something about the problem. You can make a difference. Here are some guidelines to follow:

Guidelines for Living and Associating With Substance Abusers

1.   Don't ask drug and alcohol abusers why they use the substances. An explained or justified behavior is more difficult to change. Don't listen to explanations.

2.   Focus on feelings. Ask them how they feel when high. Ask them how they feel when they don't use alcohol or other drugs. Use information covered in

Chapter 14 about positive and negative thinking. Discuss with substance abusers the positives and the negatives of taking drugs. Then discuss the positives and negatives of not taking drugs.

3.   Don't be judgmental. If you moralize, put them down, diminish them, or try to make them feel guilty, they'll go back to their old friends. Practice liking people while disliking one of their behaviors.

4.   Make a rule. You will never meet with them or go anyplace with them if they are high or on drugs. No exceptions.

5.   Expect relapses. They occur. Don't take it personally.

6.   Don't chase them down. Don't forgive them. If they miss a chance to get together with you, it is their loss. Don't feel responsible for their recovery. Bob Meehan, of the Palmer Drug Abuse Program, says that 31 different efforts were made with him before the 32nd time succeeded.

7.   Schedule sessions with them to cover the following key areas in *Student Success:* self-esteem, effective study skills, how to develop friendships, and how to gain strength from adversity. Overcoming weakness and ineffectiveness in these areas will replace the need for substance abuse with better experiences.

8.   Be sure to stay in regular contact with your own support group. It also would be smart to let a counselor or someone with the drug and alcohol program know what you are doing just in case anything goes wrong. It is reassuring to know that if you get in over your head, you can call or see someone with professional training as a backup resource.

Develop Friendships With Students From Different Cultures

1. List the names of students different from you whom you would like to know better while attending your college:

   _____

   _____

   _____

2. Describe the situations, places, and opportunities you will have to learn from them:

   _____

   _____

   _____

Your learning may take place in classes, dormitories, fraternities and sororities, religious organizations, and student groups and clubs and from the many different types of social groups and organizations on your campus. Try to empathize with students from different cultures. How would you feel trying to live in a place full of strangers who act, think, dress, and eat in ways different from what you have ever known?

YOUR PORTFOLIO

Create a record of various ways you have worked and associated with students from other cultures and diverse backgrounds. Diversity in the workplace is a major challenge for organizations competing to attract and retain quality workers. Any evidence that you can work well in multicultural settings will be a big plus.

SUCCESS GROUP ACTIVITIES

1.   Talk with one another about what a good, solid, lasting friendship is like. Do you agree that the ability to get angry at each other at times helps make the friendship better? How do you recognize a good friendship?

Discussions about quality friendships identify the following as some important features. Look over the list and see what you agree with, what you would reword, and what you would add or change.

- Friends feel equal to each other. Friendship cannot exist when you feel superior or inferior to someone.
- Friends are comfortable being seen together, letting people know they are friends.
- Friends reveal private thoughts and feelings to each other that they usually don't reveal to others. Their openness with each other is natural and spontaneous. They laugh together.
- Friends can be trusted with confidential information. One of the fastest ways to destroy a friendship is to tell other people something you've been told in confidence.
- Friends accept each other as they are. If you have a close friend, you allow that person to see you as you really are. You do not contrive or attempt to manipulate the friend's perceptions of you to get him or her to think of you in a certain way.
- Friends see each other as unique. A friend says that no person on earth is quite like his or her close friend.
- Friends have the freedom to disagree with each other. They can become irritated or angry if that's how they really feel. You don't feel truly close to someone who is never angry at you. In any relationship the strong, positive feelings tend to disappear if negative ones are controlled and suppressed.

2.   Compare as a group the inner psychological factors affecting friendships with the information about your inner resources in Chapter 2. Do you find similarities? Can you see how the ways you think and feel can affect both your success in school and your friendships?

3.   Discuss the process for developing friendships. How do people become good friends?

4.   Does each of you believe good friends can get angry with each other and still remain friends? Discuss the steps described in Chapter 14 for handling anger between friends. How do the suggestions feel to you?

SUGGESTED READINGS

Bry, A. (1979). *Friendship: How to have a friend and be a friend.* New York: Grosset & Dunlap.

Glasser, W. (1976). *Positive addiction.* New York: Harper & Row.

This book has been around for a while and is available in paperback. It will give you some good insights into the desirability of healthy, "positive" addictions. Glasser describes how and why drug and alcohol addictions shrink a person's world and trap him or her in it, while positive addictions expand a person's world and increase effectiveness. (This was written before research into endorphins occurred.)

Hearn, J. (1979). *Making friends, keeping friends.* Garden City, NY: Doubleday.

Meehan, B., with S. Meyer. (1984). *Beyond the yellow brick road.* Chicago: Contemporary Books.

Read this book. It is highly informative. It will give you a good feeling for dealing with substance abusers from the viewpoint of a recovered drug addict who is very successful at rehabilitating young drug users. It will provide you with practical ways to be helpful.

Part 4

Surviving the Nonacademic Tests in College

Chapter 13

Surviving Hazards and Dangers in College

SELF–ASSESSMENT

Place a check mark by the statements that are true of you.

_____ I have taken a realistic look at all the dangers I'm exposed to in college.

_____ I know that feeling depressed is normal for college students.

_____ I can recognize signs of addiction to alcohol and other drugs.

_____ I know that young adults are frequently not honest with each other about possible exposure to AIDS.

_____ I am having more unpleasant experiences in college than I expected.

_____ They made a mistake admitting me here. I may flunk out.

_____ I cope well with adversity.

_____ I know how to learn useful lessons from difficult experiences.

_____ I sometimes think about dropping out of college.

_____ I know that serendipity is a talent that can be learned.

SERIOUS HAZARDS AND DANGERS IN COLLEGE

College is a more dangerous survival test than many students realize. Too much stress, depression, suicide feelings, alcohol and other drugs, exposure to AIDS, and poor driving judgment can ruin your life and health or kill you.

To succeed in college and in life, you must be conscious of the many dangers that can do you in. Survival requires examining the negative side of situations as a first step to taking preventive actions. It requires minimizing risks.

Events do happen, of course, that are out of our control. Christa McAuliff, the teacher killed in the *Challenger* space shuttle explosion, died in an unpredictable accident. Each of us, however, can take action to reduce the predictable risks to our lives, health, and well-being.

OVERWHELMING STRESS

It is normal to feel overwhelmed by college during the first few weeks. You left a familiar world with people you knew to enter an unfamiliar world filled with strangers. You changed status from being a successful senior in high school or from working at home or for pay to becoming a naive freshman.

Life at college is complex, ambiguous, challenging, and fast paced. Protective adults do not save you from irresponsibility. You now make choices and decisions every day that affect your life.

Instructors load more work on you the first month of classes than you had to do in a year in high school. You may get lower grades than you are used to and may feel inadequate for college. You may get homesick, but going home is not a choice because your younger brother or sister has taken over your room.

The freedom you may have to eat or not eat as you wish or to sleep or not sleep whenever you desire can throw your physical health off balance. Your old friends aren't around. You may have broken up with your high school sweetheart or ended a marriage, or, worse yet, maybe you've been dumped because your partner found someone new.

Typical signs of overwhelming stress and depression include the following:

- Feeling sad, discouraged, and helpless
- Feeling guilty for letting family and former high school teachers down
- Sleeping 12 to 16 hours a day or hardly sleeping at all
- Withdrawing from friends; spending most time alone
- Inability to concentrate; can't study; grades dropping
- Increasing use of medications, other drugs, or alcohol
- Having emotional outbursts—crying, anger, temper extremes, constant self-criticism
- Overeating or losing appetite for eating
- Feeling lonely, unhappy, unlovable, unlikable, unaccepted all the time
- Feeling that all chances for a good career are shot
- Considering suicide as the way to escape from the pain and distress

It is important to understand that unhappy experiences, loneliness, embarrassments, and awkwardness are all necessary for personal growth. These experiences are a normal part of your maturation and emotional growth. People who self-medicate with drugs and alcohol to avoid unpleasant feelings remain immature!

Thousands of entering college students have unhappy feelings. Most of them survive this difficult period, learn valuable lessons, and develop more character from their unhappy experiences. Some do not. Suicide is the second leading cause of death among teenagers. (Accidents, mostly driving, are the leading cause.)

Note: If you think of suicide as the only solution for you, tell someone. No matter how hopeless, worthless, or deeply distressed you feel, talk to someone. Agree to meet with an experienced suicide counselor. He or she will listen and coach you on how to find other solutions.

Research shows that people who are stress resistant usually do the following:

1.   They talk with family and friends about what they are experiencing. They do not withdraw from the people who care for them. They verbalize their feelings and are receptive to love and support from people who care about them.

2.   They locate and use available resources. At college this means talking with the counselors in the counseling center, in the health service center, or in one of the church-sponsored student centers.

3.   They accept that life has painful periods. They expect that somehow they will find a way to get through this. They tap into inner resources and problem-solve the situation.

People in the Counseling Office Can Help

No miracle pills exist that *eliminate* distressing feelings, and the people in the counseling office offer something much better. They can show you how to get through unpleasant periods while your natural emotional self-healing processes work for you.

Self-referral for counseling is difficult for almost everyone, especially if you are afraid or concerned about giving people a bad impression. Try to remember, however, that it is normal to have down or lonely periods and that it is entirely okay to get assistance for overcoming them.

If your car gets stuck someplace from a dead battery, do you ask someone for a jump start? You'd have to do something. So if you ever get bummed out and can't pull out of it, ask for help. Talk with counselors. They know ways to handle situations that seem hopeless to you. You don't have to try to handle them by yourself. It is not a sign of strength to mask your feelings with drugs or to put on a false front of happiness. Emotional strength develops from feeling whatever you feel and letting another human being be close to you when life isn't working perfectly.

ALCOHOL AND OTHER DRUGS

A freshman wanting to be accepted and liked by other students is easily led into frequent bouts of drinking and drug use. According to Eugene Hakansen, director of a college counseling service, "The greatest instigator of alcohol and drug use in college is a friend. Roommates get roommates to try drugs, older students influence freshmen to drink and use drugs."

Bob Meehan, a recovered addict and alcoholic, agrees. According to Meehan, a founder of the Palmer Drug Abuse Program that has helped thousands of teenagers and parents, "Teenagers do drugs to gain acceptance." He says, "Peer pressure to take drugs is so strong that one teenager in two will say he gets high before he actually does."*

The National Institute on Drug Abuse conducts nationwide research into the use of alcohol and other drugs by high school and college students. Their studies find that approximately 20% of college students use marijuana in a 30-day period. About 7% use cocaine or crack. About half of the male students and one third of the female students frequently engage in heavy weekend drinking. The researchers found that the reason given most often for using any substance is "to have a good time with my friends."†

The Center on Addiction and Substance Abuse at Columbia University reports two important facts. First, freshmen drink the most, seniors the least. Second, a direct correlation exists between amount of drinking and grades. "D" and "F" students average 10.6 drinks per week. "C" students average 7.6 drinks. "B" students average 5.5 drinks, and "A" students average 3.6 drinks per week.

The picture is clear. Freshman students have such a strong need for acceptance and friendship that many of them drink and use drugs in ways detrimental to their academic goals.

Surveys show that very few students understand that alcohol, cocaine, and marijuanna can be very addictive. Here are some indicators that a person is addicted:

Signs of Substance Abuse or Addiction

- Using the substance with increasing frequency
- Developing a tolerance for it (needing a bigger dose to experience the effects; effects lasting a shorter time)
- Feeling "off" when not using it (shaky, anxious, edgy); feeling physical discomfort without it
- Having little awareness of how much is used; believing usage is normal and under control
- Experiencing personality changes; going from feeling happy, up, social, and self-confident to unhappy, grumpy, withdrawn, depressed, fearful, and paranoid
- Causing concern among friends, family, and acquaintances; being encouraged to use less or stop
- Repeatedly saying "I could stop if I wanted to; I just don't want to"
- Rationalizing, blaming other people or events for substance abuse
- Becoming unmotivated at work or school; deteriorating in performance
- Having more auto accidents, alcohol-related traffic tickets
- Not remembering what happened the night before
- Receiving warnings from officials, notices of delinquent payments

---

* Meehan, R., with Meyer, S. (1984). *Beyond the Yellow Brick Road,* Chicago: Contemporary Books, p. 17.

- Trying to borrow money; making excuses for not repaying loans; selling off belongings; stealing money or items to sell
- Promising to improve when confronted; asking for another chance; asking to be trusted

As we've noted, most campuses have alcohol and drug counseling available. Keep in mind, also, that with some people alcoholism is hereditary. The evidence is strong that people with alcoholism have a biochemistry different from social drinkers. Their bodies metabolize alcohol differently, but it is a condition that can be managed with medications and other treatments.

SEX, HONESTY AND STD RISKS

If you are sexually active, your risk of getting a sexually transmitted disease (STD) is quite high. As reported by the American Social Health Association, 1 in every 3 sexually active persons will contract an STD by the age of 24.

New cases of STDs each year are estimated at*:

20,000 HIV

70,000 Syphillis

77,000 Hepatitis B

650,000 Gonorrhea

1 million Herpes

3 million Chlamydia

5 million Trichomoniasis

5.5 million Human papilloma virus

(Trichomoniasis is an STD without visible symptoms that can cause infertility. Human papilloma virus, usually symptom free, can cause genital warts and genital cancers. Both of these STDs can be detected by medical tests when requested.)

Of great concern is a research report by Susan Cochran in which sexually active young adults were asked how honest they would be if a potential sexual partner asked them about recent sexual activities with others. About 40% of the men and 20% of the women said they would downplay or deny sexual contact with others if asked by a potential partner.

Centers for Disease Control report that the highest risk comes from intravenous drug use. These cases occur mostly in people living in poverty in AIDS epicenters. AIDS is spreading throughout the entire population, however, and the likelihood of contracting it from heterosexual activity is increasing.

The message is clear—if your health is important to you, use good judgment and intelligent precautions.[‡]

---

* Meehan, R., with Meyer, S. (1984). *Beyond the Yellow Brick Road,* Chicago: Contemporary Books, p. 17.

[‡] Data source: *U.S. News & World Report,* December 14, 1998, P. 74.

How to Gain Strength From Dangers, Distress, and Difficult Experiences

What do you do when you must deal with a side of life you wished did not exist? when the realities of campus life do not match up with your dreams and hopes?

A college campus has many opportunities for people who prey on others. For instance, you have to guard your credit cards against thieves who make charges or get cash advances against them.

It can be distressing to suspect that a dorm mate may have stolen money or personal items from you. Or you return to your room and discover that your computer and stereo have been stolen. Students with automobiles have their car windows smashed in by thieves who steal cassette tapes, car stereos, athletic gear, or other items.

On many campuses women need to walk in groups or to ask campus security or friends to escort them at night because of attacks by rapists. Women must be cautious about going on a date with someone new because of the risk of date rape or of being given "date rape drugs" while drinking.

You hear about students who cheat on exams or purchase a term paper and then brag about it. You hear about intolerable things that instructors, administrators, and coaches sometimes do or say to students.

You hear that someone is saying horrible things about you to others. A student that you've just met may dislike you and make cutting remarks.

You discover that someone you've been dating, a person you really like, is going out with someone else. You feel devastated. You wonder if you will ever find true love.

When, as your mom may have said, you are "not a happy camper," the best way to handle the situation is to accept that you are enrolled in the school of life and must learn better survival and coping skills. Your ability to learn important lessons directly from life's experiences will make the difference between how poorly or how well your life goes for you.

How good are you now at learning from life's experiences? When you find yourself in a bad situation, do you let yourself become a victim and blame others, or do you learn valuable lessons and find a way to cope?

Learning What No One Can Teach

Life's best survivors have a knack for turning difficulties into growth experiences. This is why viewing life as a school is practical and useful. The academic program in college is a *structured learning environment*. The nonacademic survival tests are an *unstructured learning environment*. When trouble develops, you gain strength every time you struggle to cope with something upsetting or difficult.

For example, in Chapters 10 and 11 we suggested using difficulties with your instructor as a way to learn to handle people better. Throughout the book, our approach has been to show you how to handle any difficulty in a way that makes you a stronger, more capable person.

Self-Managed Learning in the School of Life

Here is an old saying: "Good mariners are not created by calm seas." The Outward Bound program, in fact, started from the observation that when ships were sunk in the North Sea during World War II, the oldest sailors were more likely to survive the icy ordeal than younger, stronger sailors. Conversely, students who use alcohol and other drugs frequently remain stuck at the same emotional level as when they started. They miss the emotional struggle that is part of important learning.

Throughout *Student Success,* at the end of each chapter you have found activities designed to help you stay in touch with learning on your own. Here is the recommended sequence for learning lessons in the school of life:

1. After any difficult experience, reflect on it. Replay the whole thing in your mind. Relive the feelings, actions, body language, and words as they all happened.

2. Put the experience into words. Write it down, tell a friend, or talk to yourself about what happened. Do this as an observer. Avoid either justifying or blaming.

3. Ask yourself, "What can I learn from this? What is the lesson here?"

4. Think to yourself, "The next time I'm in a similar situation, what will I do?"

5. Rehearse handling such a situation well. Imagine yourself doing what it would take to get the outcome you desire.

Life is a never-ending school. Difficult experiences offer many valuable lessons. Self-managed learning develops self-confidence in your ability to survive and pass nonacademic tests in college and in life.

You get better and better as you learn how to learn from experience. You become increasingly competent, resilient, and durable. You survive major adversity better, enjoy life more, and develop a talent for serendipity.

Journalist Terry Anderson, for example, was held as a hostage in Lebanon for almost 7 years. He was subjected to many hardships. At the press conference after his release, he was asked how he felt about having so many years of his life wasted. "They weren't wasted years," he said, and talked about many positive results from the experience. His older sister, sitting next to him, nodded agreement. "He is different. He is better," she said.

ACTION PROJECTS

Develop a Talent for Serendipity

You can learn how to gain strength from adversity by developing your inborn talent for serendipity. To turn unpleasant difficulties into valuable learning experiences and to convert misfortune into good luck, ask yourself serendipitous questions such as the following:

SELF-ASSESSMENT

How Resilient Are You?[§]

Rate yourself from 1 to 5 on how well the following qualities found in highly resilient people apply to you: (1 = very little, 5 = very strong)

_____ Always curious, ask questions the way children do. Want to know how things work; conduct experiments.

_____ Adapt quickly to change, highly flexible.

_____ Think up creative solutions to challenges, invent ways to solve problems. Trust intuition and hunches.

_____ Constantly learn from experience and from the experiences of others.

_____ Good at making things work well for myself and others.

_____ Play with new developments, find the humor, laugh at self, chuckle.

_____ Feel comfortable with paradoxical or opposite inner qualities.

_____ Optimistic and yet good at anticipating problems and avoiding difficulties.

_____ Develop stronger self-esteem and more self-confidence every year.

_____ Listen well. "Read" others well. Excellent empathy skills.

_____ Non-judgmental. Easy acceptance of individuals from different and diverse backgrounds.

_____ High tolerance for ambiguity and uncertainty.

_____ Manage the emotional side of transitions in healthy ways. Grieve, honor, and let go of the past. Start new life activities with eagerness.

_____ Expect tough situations to work out well, keep on going. Help others cope. Bring stability to times of uncertainty and turmoil.

_____ Have a talent for serendipity. Find benefits in accidents, bad experiences, or misfortune.

_____ If you scored 60 or higher, you handle life's challenges very well. If you rated yourself 30 or below, you need to develop more resiliency and better coping skills! A good place to start is learning how to learn lessons in the school of life.

[§] "How Resilient Are You?" Adapted with permission from Al Siebert's Web site: http://thrivenet.com.

- Why is it good for me that this happened?
- What can I learn from this?
- How might I turn this around and make everything turn out well?
- What would be useful for me to do right now?
- Do I have an opportunity here that I never expected to have?
- What is amusing about this?

Questions such as these are the best way to organize your energies toward having situations turn out well. By developing a talent for serendipity, you learn that when you are hit by adversity or misfortune, you have a choice. You can dwell on your version of "If only other people would change, my life would be much better," or you can make things better for yourself.

Because you are a human being, you have an inborn capacity to learn what no one can teach you. To develop this talent, select a problem you are trying to handle right now. Ask the serendipitous questions, and take your time looking for answers. Write your questions in a diary if you like, and talk with yourself about what answers you discover. By doing this, you may learn how to convert a major difficulty into the best thing that ever happened to you!

Talk With Role Models

Talk with several classmates who are happy, stable, and capable and who seem to be good survivors. Find out what their lives have been like. Ask them to talk about several of their worst experiences. Perhaps someone was physically abused, had an alcoholic parent, or grew up in an unusually hard situation. Find out how these classmates learned to cope. Do they say they gained or learned anything from what they endured?

Maintaining a Positive Attitude in Stressful Situations

You can develop the ability to cope with seemingly impossible situations. Much depends on your attitude. To help yourself get started, follow these steps:

1. Make a list of everything you experience as negative or stressful. Discharge your feelings. If necessary, cry, yell, and get mad.
2. Next go through the list, item by item, asking these questions:

    a) *Could I do something about this? How direct is my contact?*

    b) *What if I ignored this or avoided contact?*

    c) *Could I change the situation in some way? Who could coach or help me?*

    d) *What if I changed my reaction to it?*

    e) *Why is this good for me? What can I learn from this?*

    Next time, what will I say or do?

3.   Now, review and reflect on pleasant experiences, and make a list of what is positive and revitalizing in your life.

4.   Think about how to repeat, increase, or have new positive experiences, asking questions such as these:

   a) Am I ignoring or taking for granted some positive aspects of my life?

   b) What do I enjoy doing? What am I enthusiastic about?

   c) What would I like to do that I keep putting off?

   d) Whom do I enjoy sharing good experiences with?

5.   Take steps to decrease negative experiences and increase positive, revitalizing experiences.

YOUR PORTFOLIO

Keep a record of how you encountered a very difficult personal challenge, how you overcame the difficulty, and what you learned or gained from the experience. Some job interviewers are asking, "What was one of the worst experiences you've ever been through, and how has that affected you?" They listen to find out if you coped well and can give an example of gaining strength from adversity.

SUCCESS GROUP ACTIVITIES

1.   Have any of you known a student who talked about or attempted suicide? What are your feelings about that happening? What would you do if you felt so badly that you contemplated suicide? What would you want your friends to do?

2.   Discuss with one another these questions: What are the worst feelings you've ever felt? your worst feelings as a student? How do you manage to bear emotionally difficult times?

3.   What are some of the group's concerns about AIDS? What facts do you have available? Have you ever associated with a person with AIDS? What are your concerns about sexually transmitted diseases? What precautions, if any, do you think a person should take?

4.   Do any of you know anyone who has had to deal with date rape? Is this a subject students or instructors discuss?

5.   Discuss with one another your attitudes toward alcohol and drugs. Do you know anyone who shows signs of addiction? Can you confirm from your own experience the role that friends play in the use of alcohol and drugs?

6.   How good are each of you at learning valuable lessons from bad experiences? Ask one another for examples.

Chapter 14

Developing Your Emotional Intelligence: Mastering Anger

SELF-ASSESSMENT

Place a check mark by the statements that apply to you.

_____ The people I am meeting and living with in college are about what I expected.

_____ Living with a roommate has turned out to be more difficult than I thought.

_____ I sometimes get angry when things happen that I did not expect.

_____ I can recognize and verbalize my angry feelings.

_____ I feel irritated by students who gripe and complain all the time.

_____ Sometimes I can't study because I am so upset.

_____ I entered college fearful that I would not succeed.

_____ I worry about living up to other people's expectations for me in college.

_____ Sometimes I think about transferring to another college where college life would be more what I had expected.

DIFFERENT REACTIONS TO COLLEGE LIFE

Most students find college very different from what they expected. This makes some students very happy. For them, college life is better than they predicted.

Other students are happy sometimes but unsettled at other times. They feel unsettled when college is unpleasantly different from their expectations.

A surprisingly large group of students feel unhappy much of the time. College isn't what they expected in ways they don't like. Classes are not interesting. They couldn't get the classes they wanted. Their living situation is uncomfortable. They aren't adjusting socially. Friends are hard to find. They don't like the food. They have to work too hard. All in all, college life isn't real great.

ENERGY-DRAINING EMOTIONAL REACTIONS

It is in our human nature to react to upsetting events with angry words or actions. These reactions come with the rest of the equipment. They are the emotional equivalent of the "fight-or-flight" response to danger.

Learning how to handle anger is essential, because this emotional state can be very disturbing when you are trying to study and learn. If you have ever spent an evening in the library and accomplished nothing because you were too upset to study, you know what we mean. Thus, to survive in college you must pass tests in one of the major unofficial courses—"Emotions 101: Learning How to Handle Anger in Yourself and Others."

Remember that it isn't the situation that counts; it is your reaction to it that determines your success in college. The first step to learning effective coping methods is to observe and describe what is bothering you.

UNMET EXPECTATIONS, DEMANDS, AND FRUSTRATION

Why do so many college students express unhappiness, frustration, distress, and "pure" anger? They have a number of reasons, but most boil down to these frequently heard comments of students:

"Things at college just aren't what I expected."

"People are placing too many demands on me!"

"I am not happy!"

When you hear comments similar to these, they are often accompanied by anger. Few students recognize anger as a chronic problem. Most students think of anger as happening only when they are subjected to other people's ill-conceived acts, stupidity, and general carelessness.

Psychologist Daniel Goleman, author of *Emotional Intelligence,* says that learning how to verbalize anger in the right way at the right time is a major learning challenge and determines a person's emotional intelligence. For college students, an excellent perspective on anger and how to learn to deal with it comes from an unpublished book manuscript, *The Anger Habit,* coauthored by professor emeritus Donald E. P. Smith, one of the world's foremost authorities on college reading and learning skills, and Carl Semmelroth.

Different Forms of Anger

Smith's research demonstrated that college students have learned to react with anger to many different situations and express their anger in a variety of forms.

Which of the following would you interpret as ways of expressing anger? Check off those you think apply.

_____ CRYING

_____ SWEARING

_____ TELLING JOKES ABOUT OTHERS THAT PUT THEM DOWN

_____ THROWING AND SMASHING THINGS

_____ LEAVING YOUR ROOM MESSY

_____ WALKING AROUND FEELING DEPRESSED

_____ HITTING A PIECE OF EQUIPMENT THAT DOESN'T WORK

_____ FEELING SAD AND LONELY

_____ NOT SAYING "HELLO" TO SOMEONE WHO SAYS "HELLO" TO YOU

_____ LEAVING A FRIEND OUT OF ACTIVITIES

_____ THROWING TRASH ON THE STREET

_____ YELLING AT OTHER DRIVERS WHEN YOU ARE DRIVING

_____ LEAVING A BATHROOM DIRTY

_____ NOT PUSHING IN YOUR CHAIR IN THE LIBRARY

_____ EATING BY YOURSELF IN THE LIBRARY

_____ MAKING NASTY COMMENTS ABOUT YOUR ROOMMATE

_____ NOT GOING TO CLASSES

_____ NOT READING CLASS ASSIGNMENTS

_____ USING DRUGS WHEN OTHERS ASK YOU TO STOP

_____ NOT PAYING ATTENTION IN CLASS

_____ PUTTING OTHERS DOWN

Unless a person is very overt, loud, antagonistic, and generally difficult to deal with, we don't classify his or her behavior as anger. But, as we said, students express anger in many different ways. All of the items just listed can be ways of expressing anger. Anger can be expressed in ways so indirect the person is not conscious of feeling angry. This happens because many children are made to feel guilty about feeling or acting angry. Instead of becoming a person who never expresses anger, however, they let their anger seep out indirectly.

It is important to recognize that anger is normal and healthy. It is also important to understand that if you don't learn to handle your own anger well, you will not handle other people very well when they are angry. Their lack of control will overwhelm your shaky controls.

To understand the situation better, let's look at how anger can get triggered.

Unmet Expectations and Anger

Anger is usually the result of situations not occurring as you expected and desired. When you feel angry, you are reacting to something that wasn't what you had predicted or wanted.

Examine your expectations of college. How are instructors and courses different from what you imagined? If you live in a dorm or apartment, how is living with a roommate different from your expectations?

Here are some examples of what students report to us about situations with their roommates that made them angry. Do you identify with any of these experiences?

"I like having my roommate gone while I study, but she's so popular I have to take over a dozen phone calls each evening!"

"My roommate is a slob!"

"When I was trying to study for an exam, my roommate had his friends in to watch TV and eat pizza until after midnight. I was fuming."

"My roommate borrowed my car without asking permission."

"My roommate and her friends ate my food. When I told her I didn't like that, she said in her home the rule was 'finders eaters.'"

"I came back early on the weekend and found a stranger in my bed *sleeping on my sheets*. My roommate had told a friend of a friend it was OK."

In all of these instances something happened that the student had not expected and did not like. What do you do about these and other incidents? One solution is to take time to realign your expectations so that your expectations will be more accurate. The other is to learn how to express your anger in healthy ways and to learn how to resolve the conflict.

How to Verbalize Your Anger and Resolve Conflicts

You learn to deal with anger by learning to make more accurate predictions about what you can expect from other people and objects—like that car of yours, which you expected to start on a cold day and which failed miserably—and by taking steps to avoid having the problem happen again.

Keep in mind that it is not bad to feel angry. Your anger can help you learn what to expect next time. You can regard anger as feedback. Feedback is information that tells you how accurate your thoughts and behavior were in a situation. Your anger often says to you, "Dang! I hadn't expected that. I've got to change things!"

Before we cover what to do, however, take a moment to think about ways of expressing anger that make things worse and ruin friendships. Have you ever done any of the following? Has someone acted this way with you?

Unproductive Ways to Express Anger

- Catch the person by surprise just as she is going out the door on a date or starting to fall asleep.
- Blame him for your feelings. ("You really upset me . . .")

- Accuse her of bad motives. ("You're trying to make me fail my courses.")
- Turn him into a no-good noun (a nerd, paranoid, pervert, sleazebag, etc.).
- Decide she is so bad and defective that she has no hope for improvement. ("I will never again go anyplace with her again.")
- Refuse to talk face-to-face. Refuse to reveal your feelings if he asks what is wrong.
- Tell others how bad the person is. Gossip destructively.

If you want to express your anger in productive ways, to improve the situation, and to maintain a good relationship with the person, the following steps will be useful to follow:

How to Verbalize Your Anger Productively

1. Ask for time to talk about something that is upsetting you. Warn him that you feel angry. Let him say when he is ready. (He will listen much better this way.)

2. State your feeling first, and then describe the behavior that triggered it. "I feel angry because I saw you on campus wearing my best sweater." "You . . ." statements are often hurtful, make the person defensive, and can lead to a permanent loss of friendship. "I feel . . ." lets you express your feelings and gives you a chance to work things out.

3. Ask questions. Ask why she did what she did. Ask if she is aware of the effect of her actions on you. "Don't you know that my aunt bought me that sweater in Italy and I only wear it at special times?"

4. Ask for what you want. "Please never again wear my clothing without my permission."

5. Discuss possible solutions. "I want you to agree that in the future you will ask first."

6. Thank the person for listening.

Does the idea of verbalizing your anger directly to someone you like make you nervous? Have you heard the term *codependent? Codependency* is a term developed for partners of people with alcohol and drug dependencies. The codependent partner always forgives even physical abuse and makes excuses for the abusive partner.

In other words, "turning the other cheek" when you feel upset and abused can be a fine quality, but if practiced as a rule instead of an option, it can get you treated like a punching bag or a doormat. Part of being an emotionally strong person is being able to speak up to express angry feelings when you are bothered by what another person has done.

The main challenge, however, is learning what triggers your angry feelings. According to Smith, "The feeling of anger is automatic and a necessary part of learning. But the rest of the anger experience, all the ways in which we express it, all the damage we do with it, to others and to ourselves, all of these follow-up events result from learning."

One of the thorny problems with learning to have angry reactions to unexpected events but not expressing your feelings is that when you suppress (or "stuff") your feelings, you become a candidate for cardiac problems, ulcers, migraine headaches, and several other health problems.

We've covered how to handle your feelings in healthy ways when they occur, and we'll later show how to handle other people when they get angry. Now let's go back to the matter of what triggers the anger reaction in the first place.

ANGER: A LEARNED HABIT

Feeling angry is natural, but you don't need to acquire the habit of continually feeling angry whenever your expectations are unmet. You can learn to deal with unmet expectations in better ways. You can reduce the amount of time you act in angry ways.

Just as we learn to expect certain things—the car starting when you turn the key or a friend greeting you pleasantly when you say "hello"—so can we learn to deal with unpredicted events.

Example

Let's say you've been invited out by someone you are very attracted to. You hope this relationship can blossom into something greater than a mere friendship. You anticipate a pleasant romantic evening alone with your date. Your date arrives. He or she comes to the door, and you see a car parked outside with another couple inside. The show and dinner you thought the two of you would enjoy alone will now include another couple. Ugh! Do you act disappointed? cold to the other couple? miffed that you didn't know more of the event's particulars? Do you place demands on your date? Do you tell him or her that in the future you would prefer knowing if the plan includes more than the two of you? Do you tell your date that you do not want to go to this particular restaurant or show?

Why do we ask these questions? Because most of us deal with our unmet expectations by getting angry and placing demands on other people. We expected certain things. They didn't occur as we had predicted. Now we get angry and start making demands. We are determined to control someone or something so that our predictions can be met, if not now, in future situations.

Reasonable Alternative. In the dating situation we described, rather than feeling angry and placing demands on others, do you have another alternative? You might say to yourself, "I didn't think they'd be coming along. Next time I'd like to know exactly what's happening. I'll make the best of tonight. The next date can possibly be more to my liking." If you can find a way to have a nice time, you may discover that these are your date's best friends and you are the person they've been looking forward to meeting. You might enjoy their company.

UNLEARNING THE ANGER HABIT

Everyone picks up habits from living with their parents. In some families the parents' way to get cooperation is to make threatening demands: "You'll eat what I give you, or I'll really get mad at you." The child may learn that making angry demands is the way to get people to act differently.

Sometimes the child learns that the only way to get attention is to have temper tantrums. In some families an alcoholic or abusive parent is the only role model for the child.

Whatever the origins, reacting with anger is a learned habit. It is also a habit that can be unlearned.

Do you recognize the anger habit as common to you? Do you often get angry when things don't go as you expected? Do you often respond to your unmet expectations with excessive anger? Do you see yourself as a person who starts placing a lot of demands on other people when things don't go your way? If so, welcome to the club. You have nothing the matter with you. You are just another person who can learn why people act angry and who can take a better approach to dealing with unmet expectations.

How would you feel and how would you respond to people who said or did the following to you?

- *Situation 1:* You are late to pick up a date. When you arrive, she or he says to you, "Just why can't you get here on time? I feel embarrassed standing out here in the lobby. People think I am being stood up!"

- *Situation 2:* Your roommate says, "Why do you always keep the room such a mess? I keep telling people what a slob you are. Would you please try to keep this place more orderly? After all, I live here too! I am really embarrassed when people come into the room!"

- *Situation 3:* You are late to class. The instructor looks at you coming in the door and says, "Mr./Ms. _____, I would really appreciate your arriving on time. It is very disconcerting to start a lecture and having people interrupt!"

As you answered the foregoing questions, you might have thought to yourself, "The person had a right to be miffed, although they could have been more diplomatic." The mistake they made was acting angry. People are late, and people are sloppy. But trying to control them by placing demands on them just results in more anger. Many people feel attacked when we place demands on them.

The anger occurs when what people predict doesn't happen. The result of the anger is the demand or attack. This habit of getting angry when our expectations are unmet and then attacking other people or ourselves leads to much unhappiness. A reasonable alternative exists. That alternative requires you to look at yourself and ask the following 10 questions:

1. How can I learn to accept that anger is not a problem?
2. How can I learn to accept that my unmet expectations may lead to anger, that anger is part of the learning process?

3. How can I learn to respond to the anger that develops by not placing demands on other people or attacking them?

4. What are reasonable responses when my expectations are unmet?

5. What expectations do I have about college that may be unreasonable?

6. How have I responded to my unreasonable expectations?

7. Have I placed many demands on other people? Do I spend a lot of time attacking other people?

8. How should I respond, rather than placing demands or attacking?

9. How can I learn to gather the information I need so that I can establish realistic expectations about the people I live with?

10. How can I gather the information I need to develop realistic expectations about my courses and professors at college?

DEALING WITH YOUR ANGER

Feeling angry and trying to control people through anger and demands are common to many people. As we've said, once you learn to recognize your unrealistic expectations, you can learn to change your expectations and reduce your anger. You also can learn to recognize that anger is a normal human emotion. The aim is to develop choices about your thoughts and behaviors. You needn't always react with anger to people or place demands on them. You can make other, better choices to deal with situations and people who don't act as you had predicted.

After you are angry and act in ways that make you feel uncomfortable, do you say to yourself, "I didn't like acting that way. Why did I act that way?" If so, that's a good sign. Now you know that you have unrealistic expectations that are unmet and you get angry. It is no big deal. You simply learn to recognize your anger and act in more appropriate ways, such as those we have suggested.

DEALING WITH ANGER IN OTHERS

Think back to how you have reacted when someone is angry at you. What have you learned is *not* a useful way to react if you want to improve the situation? Here is what people say does not work:

Unproductive Ways to React to an Angry Person

- Get angry, and argue back. ("You're not easy to live with either!")
- Interrupt the angry person to give him your explanation. (Anyone can create excuses and rationalize what they do.)
- Refuse to listen. (It is not a sign of strength to refuse to listen.)
- Use negative body language. Cross your arms, clench your jaw, and look out the window.

- Tell her to not feel angry. (First the person is angry, and now you are telling her to not feel what she is feeling.)
- Feel frightened or overwhelmed.
- Believe that when he says he is angry at your behavior, he is really saying you are a bad person.
- Tell her she's wrong.
- Say "Yes, but . . ." This is one of the first games psychiatrist Eric Berne spotted in his research for *Games People Play.* To say "Yes, but . . ." is saying "I've let you talk for a while, but now I'm going to explain how my view of all this is the correct one."

If you want to frustrate people so that they tell many others what a royal pain you are, then do what we just listed. If, instead, you want to handle conflict so that it leads to a good outcome and keeps your relationships healthy, then follow the steps provided next.

Develop Empathy Skills

The most important thing to accomplish with an angry person is to give him or her the experience of being well heard. An angry person calms down fairly quickly when you show empathy and make a sincere effort to understand what you might have done wrong. Here are the steps to follow:

1. Ask, "What is wrong?" "What are you angry about?"
2. Listen. Listen with the intent of being able to repeat back what she says.
3. Ask clarifying questions. "Have you been upset about this before?"
4. Listen.
5. Repeat back. The one time an angry person will be quiet is to see if you have heard him accurately.
6. Validate feelings. "I can see why you are so upset. I would be too." Learn how to validate feelings even when you don't agree with the facts.
7. If she's right, then apologize. "You're right; I should have left a note on your desk saying your father wanted you to call home right away. Just because I thought I'd see you in the library is not a good excuse."
8. Thank him for telling you face-to-face about his feelings. If you aren't a good listener, he is going to tell 10 other students about you. Better to have it in your face than around campus.
9. Find out what she wants. "What is your request if something like this happens again?"
10. Talk about a better way to handle a similar situation in the future.

These steps are not guaranteed to work every time, but they increase your chances of resolving the situation and help you maintain control when others lose control. Keep in mind that repeating back what people say to you is a powerful way to let them know you heard them. This is how to exhibit empathy when it really counts. We want to help you learn ways to develop successful relationships with people and make college a great experience.

ACTION PROJECT

Managing Your Anger

Step 1: Write out a brief description of a recent situation that made you angry.

_____

_____

_____

_____

Step 2: What expectations did you have that were unmet? Were your expectations realistic? How did you show your anger?

_____

_____

_____

_____

Step 3: What would have been a more reasonable response?

_____

_____

_____

_____

Online Research

Emotions and Emotional Intelligence. This Internet site includes an introduction to the concepts, links to related sites, and a bibliography in the area of emotions and emotional intelligence and describes current research findings and notes of interest.

http://trochim.human.cornell.edu/gallery/young/emotion.htm

The Emotional Intelligence Home Page. Take a free empathy test. Check out a list of the hottest careers and how much emotional intelligence is required for each.

http://www.virtent.com/eq.htm

Developing High-Level Emotional Intelligence

Here is an optional effort that can take your emotional intelligence to a level achieved by only a few humans. To do this will require self-directed research, empathy skills, self-esteem, and critical thinking.

Your challenge, should you choose to accept it, is to research what psychologists know about a mental phenomenon called "attribution error." It is a human predisposition to attribute the actions of other people as evidence of bad motives while explaining our actions as having good reasons. Attribution error is almost always present in statements two groups in extreme conflict make.

After your research, try reversing your explanations the next time you find yourself perceiving the actions of someone in conflict with you as due to bad motives. Try viewing what that person is doing as though you were a very empathetic friend, and try explaining how his or her bad perceptions of your actions are legitimate. Notice what happens after you do that.

YOUR PORTFOLIO

Keep a record of incidents when you handled your anger in a productive way and handled well someone who was angry at you. Examples of your ability to have "a thick skin" and resolve conflicts effectively will make you very desirable as an employee or colleague. Organizations need someone who can handle angry people well; they terminate people who drain energy by dumping angry emotions on others.

SUCCESS GROUP ACTIVITIES

1.   As a group, list some of your original expectations about college that may have proven unrealistic. Then discuss with one another these questions: Did you react with anger to having your expectations not met? How will you change your expectations? In the future, when you recognize anger developing due to unmet expectations, how might you prevent yourself from placing demands on other people and acting in unproductive, angry ways?

2.   Talk with one another about the problems that develop if a roommate comes from a family where it is OK to borrow dad's car, wear a brother's good shirt, or take $20 from mom's purse without permission. What can roommates do when habits that were all right at home are now intrusive, upsetting, and a violation of another person's space?

Chapter 15

Making Athletic Goals and Academic Goals a Winning Combination

SELF-ASSESSMENT

Place a check mark by the statements that are true of you.

_____ I know that freshman athletes get grade point averages slightly better than nonathletes.

_____ I know about the academic support services available for freshman athletes.

_____ I understand the NCAA guidelines for athletic department support services for athletes.

_____ I know how to devise a winning game plan for success in college.

_____ I have considered the possibility that I could become an academic all-American.

REACHING ATHLETIC GOALS AND ACADEMIC GOALS

Some of the best athletes in football, basketball, baseball, soccer, track, volleyball, swimming, and other sports can compete while also doing very well academically. At a national level many of these athletes are recognized as "academic all-Americans."

It is true that a few colleges with highly competitive sports programs let a few marginal student athletes slip by to keep them eligible to play. The average athlete, however, does as well in college as his or her classmates.

A study of the academic effects of freshman participation in varsity athletics, conducted by the Educational Testing Service and the American College Testing Program, showed that "on measures of persistence and grade point averages, the athletes did as well or better than a matched group of nonathletes at the end of the freshman year. This finding held true across the 57 participating institutions, despite their diversity in size, selectivity, and athletic prowess."

This report, *Athletics and Academics in the Freshman Year: A Study of the Academic Effects of Freshman Participation in Varsity Athletics,* was developed for the American Association of Collegiate Registrars and Admissions Officers and the American Council on Education. The report was prepared with the assistance of the College Board.

A most revealing finding is that athletes who were predicted to have a grade point average below 2.0 in their first year did better than nonathletes who had similar preparation for college. The athletes' grades "were higher than predicted—and higher than the grades of the nonathletes against whom they were matched. In fact, relatively few athletes earned grade point averages that were much below a 2.0 regardless of their SAT or ACT test scores or their high school grades."

Why do student athletes do so well, considering the extra demands on them? Among the many reasons are the following:

- They work closely with their academic advisers.
- More than other students, they use academic support services.
- Athletes know they have little time to waste. They apply themselves well in the limited time they have for studying.
- They get special attention from the coaches, who constantly encourage them in their academic studies.
- Their motivation to succeed and their ability to persist with hard challenges help them.
- They respond to failure and defeat by trying harder. Many bright students give up too easily when they encounter failure.

ACADEMIC SUPPORT SERVICES

Do you know what support services you need as a student athlete? If so, do you know how to get the help you need? Research has shown that students who use academic support services are more likely to succeed in college. Use the following checklist to indicate what resources you need. Check off the items you could benefit from.

_____ ADVICE AND HELP FROM AN ACADEMIC ADVISER WHO
     UNDERSTANDS MY SPECIAL NEEDS

_____ BETTER WRITING SKILLS

_____ TUTORIAL ASSISTANCE WITH DIFFICULT COURSES

_____ IMPROVED READING AND STUDY SKILLS

_____ HAVING A PERSONAL MENTOR TO TALK WITH

Academic Advisers

Does your athletic department offer the services of an academic adviser? If so, seek advice. Consult him or her regularly about the courses you are interested in taking.

Academic advisers to athletic departments usually have unique backgrounds that equip them to deal with your academic and personal problems. They have talked to hundreds of student athletes. They know which courses will best suit your interests and skills. They also can help you with special scheduling arrangements. Did you know, for example, that you might be able to take some classes in the evening with continuing education students?

Reading and Study Skills

Does your athletic department provide financial support for courses in reading and study skills improvement? If so, sign up right away.

By using the information and skills in *Student Success* and taking a course or two that encourages you to practice these skills, you will get the best possible start in your career as a student athlete.

Courses in reading or study skills improvement will serve the same function as your athletic practice sessions. Such courses will encourage you to try new techniques that will make an immediate difference in your reading speed, comprehension, and efficiency as a student.

The National Collegiate Athletic Association (NCAA) guidelines allow athletic departments to financially support reading and study skills courses. If your athletic department hasn't started this type of program, ask your coach or academic adviser in the athletic department to investigate the possibility.

If a course is available but your athletic department can't supply the financial support, consider investing your own funds. Most reading and learning skills centers offer inexpensive courses. You even may find that the courses are free.

Writing Improvement

If you didn't know already, your college admissions tests showed you how good your writing skills are. Good writing skills are very important in college. They are closely related to college success. If you know you aren't very good on written assignments, papers, or answers on essay tests, make your improvement in this area a high priority.

Most colleges require freshman composition courses. Many of the instructors who teach these courses will not have a tremendous amount of time to give you individualized instruction. It will be to your advantage to seek additional assistance from someone who can assess your strengths and weaknesses and spend the time necessary to help you improve your writing skills.

Check with your academic adviser to determine if individualized writing instruction is available from the athletic department, a campus tutorial program, or the English department.

If you can't find a writing instructor, make arrangements with a friend to critique each other's papers. A close friend often will tell you things about your writing that other people will not. This is no time to be sensitive. Get all the help you can.

Tutorial Assistance

A tutor is an especially skilled person available to work with you privately. Does your athletic department offer tutorial assistance? If so, try to find tutors who are either upper-level undergraduates or graduate students. Ask other members of your sports team for recommendations of outstanding tutors.

You want tutors who will teach you how to study for courses rather than tutors who simply want to reteach the course content. By picking up the study skills and tricks of the trade successful students use, you may decrease your need for future tutorial assistance.

Mentors

Does your athletic department have a mentor program? Mentor programs are established to help students adjust to the demands of attending a university.

If you participate in a mentor program, a faculty or staff member at your college will volunteer as your personal link to the university community. Your mentor will be available to talk with you about your personal concerns and will introduce you to social and cultural aspects of university life that might otherwise escape you.

Mentors are like friends or relatives away from home who help you orient yourself to a new city. Once you are comfortable, you may see them less often, but you always know they are available for assistance.

We have found that mentors often become good personal friends with student athletes. They help you adjust to the demands of university life while showing you a university often never seen by many students.

THE OVERALL GAME PLAN

Your college may offer support services other than those we have mentioned. Making immediate use of support services may be your key to a successful college career. Receiving academic support is no different from receiving daily instruction from your coach.

Very few first-year student athletes can step into the starting lineup without at least a year of college coaching. Academically, you are probably in a similar position. To crack the academic lineup, find out where you need help, and get the best assistance offered. Often you will find that with a little help, you soon can adjust to the academic demands that initially appeared insurmountable.

Eliminate Self-Defeating Actions

To win a sports competition, you know you have to avoid costly mistakes and errors. In sports the turnovers can kill you. Many contests are determined by the loser making too many mistakes, errors, fouls, or turnovers. That's why you spend part of your practice time working to eliminate self-defeating mistakes.

When you show up for the game or contest, you dress and act like a winner. You dress and act with confidence and enthusiasm. What would your impression be of a team that showed up late for a game, with many members wearing sweatsuits, and with the players slouched around on the benches not paying attention to the coach? What if during the game they shrugged off turnovers and missed chances to score. What would you think?

If this description amuses you, try running through your memories of student athletes in their classes. Do you recognize any of these self-defeating actions?

Do You Create a Bad Impression With Your Instructors?

Instructors sometimes have negative opinions and biases about students. Have you ever had to take a class from a teacher who had a bad impression of you? It's no fun. Once a teacher has a negative opinion about you and your work, it is very difficult to change it.

Some students, however, seem to go out of their way to create bad impressions. Too often we have seen students act in ways that cause instructors to believe they are unmotivated, irresponsible, and inconsiderate. Some student athletes act like college would be great if only they didn't have to study and attend classes!

The negative first impression some students trigger in classmates and instructors frequently results in a negative stereotype that is hard to overcome. For example, here are some ways student athletes create negative impressions. College instructors and professors were asked, "What biases do you have against student athletes and how did they develop?" Some of their responses follow:

- "When students come to class wearing their athletic shirts and sweat clothes, they stand out from other students. If I were their coach, I would discourage athletic garb. It sets them up to be discriminated against by people who don't care for college athletics."

- "Some athletes sit at the back of the room. Often they talk to one another during class. I assume they aren't interested in what I have to say. They just want to be as far away as possible and wait for the hour to be up."

- "Athletes tend to sit together, seldom mix with other students, other than talking occasionally to attractive girls. They seem to be uncomfortable with other students. Maybe this is a sign that they don't feel they fit in. I would like to see them mix with other students."

- "Athletes sit near the door with their jackets on. They don't appear to be taking notes. I wonder how they think they'll do well in the course."

- "One fellow attends class about 50% of the time. He never tells me why he was absent. When he learns that he has an overdue assignment, he acts as though I am being unfair because he won't receive full credit."

- "I set up an appointment with two players. They walked in 45 minutes late. I had another appointment in 15 minutes and couldn't do much for them. They acted as though it were no big deal, then asked if they could see me the next day."

- "Some students who are athletes never ask questions. I wonder if they read the assignments."

- "One group of athletes, whom I really like, unfortunately continually come in late. I try hard not to let this upset my routine. It is disturbing. I must have mentioned this to them three times. They don't seem to get the picture. They are fine once they are in class. I just wish they weren't late."

- "Several athletes frequently miss my Friday class at 1:00 P.M. I know they are often on the road on weekends. They must assume I know their schedule. They are polite enough to come in on Monday and mention they were on the road. Why not let me know beforehand?"

- "Several of the football players let their beards go all week. On Friday they look like bums. I don't care what they look like. But the other students appear to be joking about them. I think this hurts their image."

- "A big lineman drags himself to my morning 8:00 o'clock and falls asleep at least once a week. Having a 280-pounder sleeping in class is a bit of a distraction."

- "One jock turned in a paper the other day that looked as though it was scratched out on a notepad while he was watching television. The paper was wrinkled, dirty, and torn off a pad with jagged edges."

The bad impressions given by a small percentage of student athletes serve as an example of how any student can cause negative biases in instructors. Whether or not you are a student athlete, ask yourself if any of the behaviors described apply to you. Some working students, for example, come into class late wearing dirty work clothes. The capacity to create a bad impression is available to everyone!

ACTION PROJECT

Become Conscious About How to Create and Reverse Bad Impressions

A successful game plan often includes thinking about what *not* to do. First, start with a reverse play. Answer this question: "If I purposefully wanted to cause instructors to develop negative opinions and biases against me, what would be my plan of action?" Write down your answers on a sheet of paper. Have fun thinking about the outrageous things you could do.

After you've imagined your plan for self-destructive actions in the classroom, use it to increase your self-awareness. Ask yourself, "Do I ever do any of the things that would be part of a purposeful plan to create bad impressions with instructors?"

Your answer to this question can tell you how to avoid or improve some bad impressions you may have created without knowing it.

Second, list what you could do if you wanted to create a better impression of yourself in class. Write down your answers on a sheet of paper.

Some athletes who read early drafts of this chapter and developed action projects to create more positive impressions reported these activities:

- "I would get to class early. As I walked in the door I tried to make eye contact. I wanted the instructor to be reminded that I was there early."

- "I tried to sit at the front of the class. I always take notes and try to keep eye contact with the instructor."

- "I never sit at the back of the room. I try to sit with people I don't know, so that I avoid talking with anyone during class."

- "If I arrive late for class, I always apologize to the instructor after class."

- "During discussion sessions, I try to raise questions over the readings. I make sure I am not always the first one to ask a question, but I find the teaching fellow always looks in my direction."

- "If I haven't had enough sleep, I always have a cup of coffee. I don't want to look sleepy in morning classes."

- "I made up questions from my notes. I made appointments with my discussion leader and asked him to look at my notes and questions to see whether I was looking at the important ideas. At first I felt funny doing this, but I found that the instructor appreciated my interest in his opinion."

- "Every paper I turn in I have somebody proof. I know my spelling and punctuation need improvement. Also, every paper is typed."

- "I try to make friends with one person in the class who isn't an athlete. When I have to miss class, I make arrangements to borrow that person's notes. I always let the instructor know when I am going to miss and that I have borrowed notes."

- "I have one instructor who always likes to talk to the students before class starts. I make it a point to get there early. He likes to talk about sports and he always wants to find out about the last game."

These statements from reports of action projects emphasize how to be realistic about what can work for or against you. We should add, however, that many students figure out these things for themselves. A senior athlete who reviewed this chapter said:

- "One thing that I did my entire career was never to wear my letter jacket to class until I took several exams or turned in several assignments. Even though I had a 3.8 average I was wary of professors who might discriminate against me because I was an athlete. After the instructors found out I was a good student, I would wear my letter jacket to class. By that time I felt I was on safe ground."

By now you should be convinced your actions affect your instructors' opinions of you as a student. In the following spaces, write five actions you can take that will show your instructors you are serious about learning as much as you can in their courses:

1. _____

_____

2. _____

_____

3. _____

_____

4. _____

_____

5. _____

_____

NCAA Rules You Should Know

If you intend to participate in Division I athletics as a freshman, you must register with and be certified by the NCAA Initial-Eligibility Clearinghouse. Here is where to find information online about this:

http://www.americaeast.org/ncaarule.html

YOUR PORTFOLIO

Keep a record of any times when you had a bad relationship with an instructor and the steps you took to turn it around.

Also keep a record of times when you had a leadership role in sports and times when you coached another player on how to perform better. Evidence of your good team leadership and of having coaching skills will give you a significant competitive advantage over other job applicants.

SUCCESS GROUP ACTIVITY

Get together with a few athletes who want instructors to have a better impression of them as students. Help one another develop a personal action plan (outlined previously) to use. Coach and encourage one another.

Report to one another regularly on what you did and what result you got. Strategize and help one another plan and run more "plays."

Give a final report on your progress at the end of the course, and celebrate one another's successes!

Chapter 16

Surviving and Succeeding as an Adult Student

SELF–ASSESSMENT

Place a check mark by statements that are true of you.

_____ I suspect some of my fears about attending college are unrealistic.

_____ I know instructors enjoy teaching adult students and that adult students often get high grades.

_____ I know colleges and universities go out of their way to help adult students survive and succeed.

_____ I know students do not compete for grades the way they used to and instructors now encourage students to study together and help each other.

_____ I know I can seek cooperation, support, and encouragement from employers, family, and friends.

GOING TO COLLEGE AFTER YEARS AWAY FROM SCHOOL

If you are older than age 25 and feel like a misfit in college, that is not your problem. Colleges originally were designed and run to handle teenagers coming directly from high school into college life. The recent high school graduate is called the "traditional" college student. That is why somewhat older students may be called "nontraditional," "reentry," "older-than-average," and "returning" or "adult" students.

Even though more than 40% of all college students enrolled in college courses today are age 25 or older, many colleges still don't quite know what to do with a student who is more mature and has a "real life." One adult student, age

47, told us that the rules at her college required the staff to mail her grades to her 73-year-old mother each semester instead of to her. If you feel out of place at your college, it isn't you—the college is out of touch.

OVERCOMING COMMON FEARS AND CONCERNS OF ADULT STUDENTS

If you have felt or thought any of the fears and concerns listed next, you are typical of most adult students starting college. As you read the list, ask yourself, "Is my fear realistic?" In the past you have overcome fears and difficulties by facing up to them and seeking information. You can do the same now.

I haven't studied in years. I'm out of practice. My brain feels rusty.

Reality: No evidence has been found that students out of practice can't learn and remember as well as younger students. You can pass tests as well as any younger student.

I was always nervous taking tests. I'll be too upset to do well.

Reality: Student Success is designed to show you how to reduce your anxieties about taking tests. Study skill centers provide help for students who need to learn techniques of test taking. Check around. Expert help is available.

I won't be able to compete. Only a few smart students receive high grades.

Reality: In the past most college courses were competitive. Instructors usually graded "on the curve." They gave high marks to the few students who scored better than others in the class. Now, however, colleges are centers for learning. Most instructors grade students on how much learning they accomplish during a course. This means that you and other students in a course can work together to master the material and all get excellent grades.

I won't fit in. I will be an outsider in a world much different from my own.

Reality: You have as much right to be in school as anyone else. In fact, your tax dollars may have helped build the place. The students, faculty, and administrative members of any college will be far more friendly and helpful than you ever imagined. Many young students enjoy having older friends they can learn from and exchange views and experiences with. Making friends like this can be some of the most enriching of your educational experiences.

Instructors won't like having adult students in their classes.

Reality: You may be close in age to many instructors and have a lot in common with them. Most instructors enjoy and welcome adult students. These instructors welcome the life experience such students offer to a class. They often find communication is easier with you than with younger students. Returning students are frequently more motivated to learn and pay closer attention to the instructor. Studies show adult students tend to get better grades than younger students.

I have young children to raise and can't afford the cost of child care.

Reality: Colleges are accommodating the needs of students with children. Child care referral services are found at many colleges and women's resource centers. Many campuses offer low-cost child-care services for students. Colleges are doing much to assist people who have children. Many student parents trade baby-sitting with other students. To work out a cooperative schedule, one student takes day classes and the other nighttime or weekend classes. Some student parents vary days of the week—with one taking classes on Monday, Wednesday, and Friday and the other on Tuesdays and Thursdays.

It will take me years to earn a degree, since I cannot attend full-time. How can I possibly take that long to finish a degree program?

Reality: Once you adjust to student life and gain confidence, you probably can take more courses each term. In some cases, your life experiences and skills can be counted as credit toward your degree. Most students say their college careers go much faster than they thought possible.

My friends and family will suffer. I will have to spend so much time with schoolwork that others will feel rejected. What if my spouse or friends feel threatened by my attempt to improve myself?

Reality: Your family and friends are quite capable of supporting you in your new role as a student. It's up to you to explain to them why you need to return to school. Show how your success will benefit all of you. Give others a chance, and they probably will support you, especially after they see the positive results.

I have a heavy load at work and it's not getting any lighter. I'd never have time to take courses. I would have too many pressures.

Reality: Saying that you'd never have time is realistic only if you're unwilling to give up an evening a week to take a course. Employers often are willing to adjust workloads for employees in college, and some offer educational benefits. Practice the time management tips in Chapter 3. For guidelines on dealing with stress and pressure, read Chapter 13.

I won't have enough time for my family, friends, or outside interests. I can't take courses, study, and still have time for anything else.

Reality: It is true that you won't be able to do everything you used to do and also be a college student. You have to make some changes. But millions of people have gone to college while working and maintaining active personal lives. You are no different. If you follow the guidelines for succeeding in college, you'll do just fine and still have time for other important things.

I won't know anyone, and I'm afraid to start out on my own.

Reality: Finding another student to study with will help you overcome those feelings quickly. It will not be long before you have supportive friends in each class, friendly fellow students who will help you feel you really belong and can succeed.

If You Want to, You Can Find a Way

As you can see, many fears of adult students are unrealistic. When you have other fears or concerns, here are the steps to follow:

1. Clarify the worry. Be very specific about exactly what it is. Write it down, or try to explain it to someone who is a good listener.
2. Ask yourself, "Is my worry based on rumors or opinions, or is it a result of known facts?"
3. To deal with potential problems and difficulties that might occur, ask people who have been through it about their experiences. Find out if your fears are real.
4. With serious problems, seek the advice of experts. Develop a realistic action plan for improving or solving the problem. Remember, don't be afraid to ask questions!

The College Wants You to Succeed

Going to college is an exciting challenge. It will take hard work and some sacrifices, but the benefits are worth the effort. The main point to understand is that you are not alone. Many people and many resources are available to you. The world wants you to succeed in your effort to better yourself!

In the past few years a change has occurred in higher education. Colleges are trying to attract and keep adult students. Colleges arrange financial aid, employment, transportation (car pools and buses), housing, child care, personal counseling, medical coverage, and classes on how to study efficiently and pass courses. They provide counselors and advisers, recreational activities, and much more. They want to attract and retain students. Students of any age who want an education, advanced skills, or new careers can find support, resources, and encouragement.

ACTION PROJECT

Create a College Success Support Group for Adult Students

Get together with a few other adult students. Urge any such students you know to come along. Create a success group by taking the following steps:

1. Meet in a place where you can sit comfortably and talk with one another, perhaps in the college cafeteria.

2. Introduce yourselves. Keep repeating and checking that you have one another's names correct as you talk and listen.

3. Take turns talking about your feelings, impressions, and experiences starting college. Find out why you each decided to go to college. Ask about difficulties that have to be handled. Talk about your dreams and plans for the future.

4. Discuss the courses you are each taking and what program each person has selected or is considering.

5. Discuss the benefits of having a small support group. Talk about why it will be useful to get together to study for tests, to read one another's papers, to problem-solve difficulties, to encourage one another, and to applaud your successes.

6. Talk with one another about the list of fears and concerns covered in this chapter. Discuss how realistic they are.

7. Make certain each person feels heard. By the time you finish, make certain each of you feels "A few of my classmates know about me and understand what I am feeling and experiencing right now."

8. Plan to meet again soon to discuss what you are learning in this book about how to succeed in college. Read the chapters, for example, on ways to increase self-confidence and on how to gain support from family and friends.

9. Exchange telephone numbers. During the first weeks it will be useful to telephone one another daily and meet frequently.

10. Congratulate one another for having the courage to take this exciting, important step in life.

YOUR PORTFOLIO

Keep a record of working with students of different ages. Employers have a variety of problems stemming from age differences between workers. You gain points for showing that you can work well with people much different in age from you.

FINAL ACTION PROJECT

Review Your Self-Assessments

As you finish *Student Success,* it will be useful to review how much you've learned about how to succeed in college. Look back through the self-assessment checklists at the beginning of each chapter. Check off the items you left blank the first time.

Appreciate yourself for how much you have learned in such a short time!

FINAL SUCCESS GROUP ACTIVITY

1.   Now that you've had some weeks together, discuss how much having a friendly support group has helped you. Could you have done as well in your learning efforts without your support group?

2.   Compliment one another on what you've seen one another accomplish! Have each person take a turn receiving compliments and appreciation from each of the others in your group. Is a celebration of your successes in order? Do something to reward yourselves. You deserve praise and appreciation for what you've accomplished.

3.   Each of you write a letter to give to each person in your group describing what you liked, enjoyed, and appreciated about having the person in the success group. In addition to giving you practice giving compliments, this letter also will give the person a written record for his or her portfolio about how well the person works in a successl group.

4.   Show one another your portfolio! Do a "show-and-tell" with one another and congratulate yourselves.

5.   Have a party. You have earned it!

A Concluding Observation

You are living in a world much different from what your parents and teachers grew up in. To survive and thrive you must find ways to orient yourself quickly to new circumstances.

You probably will have three or four careers during your life. By the time you graduate, fewer that 50% of people in the country will have full-time salaried jobs. You may start and run your own home business.

National boundaries are blurring. To succeed in your career or profession, you must be able to work with people from different cultures. Critical-thinking skills will be essential for handling rapid changes, conflicting perspectives, changing values, and unexpected developments that carry both opportunities and dangers.

In this book we have done more than provide practical ways to handle the challenges of surviving and succeeding in college. For every challenging situation, we talked about how your reactions and strategy for interacting with something new and difficult usually can determine the outcome.

In other words, we know the guidelines for surviving and succeeding in college can serve as a model for how to continue to cope well and improve throughout your life.

We wish you well!

APPENDIX

The Accomplishments Portfolio

by Barbara Ritter, M.E.D.

WHY CREATE A PORTFOLIO?

1.   The traditional portfolio was used by artists, photographers, and architects to demonstrate samples of their work. Unlike a cover letter, résumé, or application form, *a portfolio demonstrates how one's skills, experiences, and history* match a position.

2.   Today, *with many applicants for each job opening and with the necessity of screening individuals efficiently and effectively,* the portfolio is emerging as an excellent tool to accomplish this task. A one-page list of the "Portfolio Contents" sent with your cover letter and résumé allows the employer to screen your qualifications quickly and then request items from your portfolio, if desired.

3.   The *cost of training and maintaining excellent employees* is high, both in terms of financial resources and time. A portfolio is a visible means of proving that one is well-matched to a specific position in an organization. Employers know that in the long run, time, energy, and resources will be saved by making the first choice the right choice.

GUIDELINES TO BUILDING A PORTFOLIO

When one is ready to seek a job, it is common to think ahead to the future: What will the job require in terms of skills? What will I need to know? What will I be doing? Rather than think of future requirements, building a portfolio is best done by *concentrating on one's past:* What have I done? What skills have I mastered and practiced? What experiences do I have that have made me the quality person I am? What do I know? What have I done well?

By answering these questions and then aligning items that demonstrate the answers, an "accomplishments to date" of one's past is created. This will serve as a material, visible presentation to a future employer. It will also put the owner of the portfolio in better control of an application and interview situation because the material to be discussed is chosen and familiar to the holder!

Another added benefit is that it is simpler to *narrow the focus of one's desires in future employment.* That is, rather than applying for all kinds of openings that may look interesting (a very time- and energy-consuming and sometimes defeating process), one can apply only for positions in which both that applicant and the employer will find true success and satisfaction.

Steps in the Guidelines

1. *Ask and answer the questions that follow.* Leave nothing out in this brainstorming look at yourself. Don't try to do it all at once, but take several days to return to your list and jot other items down as they occur to you. You may always trim your list down, but you don't want to omit important characteristics that really are the essence of you!

- What paid employment have I had?
- What unpaid work have I done? (Volunteering, service, informal helpfulness all count.)
- What courses have I taken (particularly a category, such as writing classes or acting classes) where I have gained skills and felt successful?
- What training have I had? This might include informal classes, seminars, groups of friends that gather with common interests (such as book groups), or specific programs.
- What life experiences have I had that I enjoyed, felt successful, and learned? This includes such things as travel (even family vacations growing up), living situations (such as summers on the water where boating or swimming were a part of the experience), a talent for cooking or baking, special collections of interest, and hobbies that have yielded you information, such as hiking in the woods that taught you about wildflowers, animals, and preparing for weather changes.
- What skills do I have that make me capable of accomplishing tasks? This includes abilities such as organizing, speaking, writing, driving, care giving, sensitive listening, dancing, woodworking, using tools, following directions, and noticing details, for example.

2. *Collect items* that correspond to your answers to the questions. *Gather materials* by scouring through your old school records, awards bestowed upon you for volunteer work, collections of hobby items, certificates, and photographs. Again, leave nothing uncovered! Faded newspaper articles that highlighted your achievement can be rewritten or copied. Collections too big to put into a portfolio can be photographed. How to fit something into the portfolio should not eliminate any materials at this point.

Once these items are collected, it becomes important to *categorize them according to theme, skill, or qualification.* It is at this point where you can start to see how one thing you have done is related to other things, or how one skill has built upon itself.

3. *Select how your items might best be displayed.* Some items lend themselves to easy display; a certificate or diploma, for example, can be copied and shown. Some items are more difficult, but with creativity can be shown. A collection can be photographed. A collage of photographs can be copied. A videotape can be edited with highlights of oral speeches, presentations, and dance or

athletic competitions, for example. With computers, scanning and editing can be done to nicely demonstrate many performance-type achievements. Professional videographers, copy centers, and computer whizzes are available for consultation or to format this work.

After you have gathered your materials and selected how you want them to be demonstrated, *decide which (if any) are simply not important or relevant.* However, do not eliminate anything from your portfolio that you consider an essential element of you or your achievements. When you present your portfolio, it does not have to be done in whole. For a specific position, you may want to include only 4 of 6 portions, for instance, if that is all that seems relevant to that job.

4. *Demonstrate that you have a demonstration portfolio!* This may sound like double talk, but it means that you need to *indicate that you have a portfolio and what kinds of materials it contains.* You will not be handing your portfolio out to many people at one time, but you need to let them know what you have. This could be done in the form of your résumé, a personal brochure, or cover letter. You might have a heading in your résumé that is called *Portfolio Contents,* for instance. Then, by category, you could list the items it contains. Or you may choose to include a paragraph in a cover letter indicating you have a portfolio containing specific items that you will be glad to review with them at their request.

Compile a list of what the portfolio contains by category. This contents may be included inside the portfolio and also as an attachment to your résumé or cover letter. You may wish to write a cover letter that describes some sample highlights from your portfolio and then note the portfolio may be requested in whole or part. In doing this, you have shown an ability to organize, confidence in your past accomplishments, proven demonstration of your skills and achievements, and a willingness to be helpful and available to a future employer.

5. *Duplicate your portfolio one time.* Be sure you have *two complete portfolios* in case one is loaned temporarily. However, unlike a résumé, you need not duplicate your portfolio many times. *It will be loaned, not given,* to future employers. In some cases just listing what is contained in the portfolio is sufficient to secure an interview.

6. *Select a container for your portfolio.* This may vary as your portfolio builds. Office supply stores carry many inexpensive containers that would serve this purpose well. Accordion folders, small briefcase-type holders, or other similar carrying pockets are available. A portfolio does not have to be expensive, but does need to be lean and neat.

7. *Update your portfolio periodically and keep it current.* As you accomplish new tasks, keep material demonstrations of them. Once you begin thinking in terms of creating and keeping a portfolio, it becomes natural to think, *"How can I include this in my portfolio?"* You will begin to photograph, record, and collect proof of your work in many displayable ways.

8. *Use and enjoy your portfolio!* This is a *tangible picture* of you—your skills, experiences, accomplishments, qualifications, and interests. Use it to reflect on your past, know yourself, and move to your future!

9. *Internet resources.* If you conduct a Web search for "student and portfolio" or "portfolio and student" you will find several thousand sites. Many universities have Web pages for students to have their portfolios online. One basic resource is the following:

http://www.college-portfolio.com

Source: The author, Barbara Ritter, M.A., is a Director of Vocational Education for Bethel School District in Spanaway, Washington. Her accomplishments include serving as director of a consortium of employers and educators that created a highly successful portfolio program. © 1999, Barbara Ritter.

REFERENCES

Chapter 1

Barefoot, B. O. (Ed.). (1993). *Exploring the evidence: Reporting outcomes of freshman seminars* (Monograph No. 11). Columbia, SC: University of South Carolina Press.

Smith, L. N., Lippitt, R., Noel, L., & Sprandel, D. (1981). *Mobilizing the campus for retention.* Iowa City: ACT.

Chapter 2

McClelland, D. C. (1961). The need to achieve [Television episode]. In *Focus on behavior,* No. 8. Washington, DC: American Psychological Association.

McClelland, D. C., & Winter, D. G. (1971). *Motivating economic achievement.* New York: Free Press.

Chapter 3

Willingham, W. W. (1985). *Success in college: The role of personal qualities and academic ability.* New York: College Entrance Examination Board, p. 179.

Chapter 6

Lindgren, H. C. (1969). *The psychology of college success.* New York: Wiley, p. 50.

Walter, T., Smith, D., Hoey, G., & Wilhelm, R. (1987). Predicting the academic success of college athletes. *Research Quarterly for Exercise and Sport, 58* (2), 269–273.

Chapter 7

McKeachie, W. J., Pollie, D., & Speisman, J. (1955). Relieving anxiety in classroom examinations. *Journal of Abnormal and Social Psychology, 50* (1), 93–98.

Chapter 10

Encyclopedic college dictionary. Funk & Wagnalls.

Chapter 11

Appleby, D. C. (1990). *Journal of Staff Program and Organizational Development, 8* (1), 41–46.

Chapter 12

Fondacaro, M. R., Heller, K., & Reilly, M. J. (1984). Development of friendship networks as a prevention strategy in a university megadorm. *Personnel and Guidance Journal, 62* (9), 520–523.

Willingham, W. W. (1985). *Success in college: The role of personal qualities and academic ability.* New York: College Entrance Examination Board, p. 179.

Chapter 13

Siebert, A. (1996). *The survivor personality.* New York: Berkeley/Perigee Books.

Wolin, S., M.D. (1991, January/February). How to survive (practically) anything. *Psychology Today, 25* (1), 36–39.

Chapter 14

Smith, D. E. P., & Semmelroth, C. C. (1987). *The anger habit.* Unpublished manuscript.

Chapter 15

Bromwell, P., & Gensler, H. (1997). *The student athlete's handbook: The complete guide for success.* New York: John Wiley & Sons.

Chapter 16

Johnson, B. (1996). *Everyday heroes.* Marlton, NJ: Townsend Press.

Siebert, A., & Gilpin, B. (1996). *The adult student's guide to survival and success* (3rd ed.). Portland: Practical Psychology Press.

Smith, L. N., & Walter, T. L. (1994). *The adult learner's guide to success in college.* Belmont: Wadsworth.

FEEDBACK REQUEST

Please let us know how you did! How was *Student Success* helpful to you? How did having a success group work out?

Do you have any suggestions on how *Student Success* could be improved? Write to us in care of the following:

Psychology Editor
College Department
Harcourt Brace College Publishers
301 Commerce Street, Suite 3700
Fort Worth, TX 76102

Or leave a message for the psychology editor at this Web site:
http://www.harbrace.com

INDEX

Weekly Schedule

HOUR	Sunday	Monday	Tuesday	Wednesday	Thursday	Friday	Saturday
7–8							
8–9							
9–10							
10–11							
11–12							
12–1							
1–2							
2–3							
3–4							
4–5							
5–6							
6–7							
7–8							
8–9							
9–10							
10–11							
11–12							